Business Economics
Concepts and Cases

GW00692286

Elements of Business Series
Series editor: David Weir
University of Bradford Management Centre

The Elements of Business Series is designed to cover the core topics taught at MBA level with an approach suited to the modular teaching and shorter time frames that apply in the MBA sector. Based on current courses and teaching experience, these texts are tailor-made to the needs of today's MBA student.

Other titles in the series

Business and Society
Edmund Marshall

Management Accounting
Leslie Chadwick

Managing Human Resources
Christopher Molander and Jonathan Winterton

Business and Macroeconomics
Christopher Pass, Bryan Lowes and Andrew Robinson

Financial Management
Leslie Chadwick and Donald Kirby

Managerial Leadership
Peter Wright

Business Economics Concepts and Cases

M. S. Greenwood and M. J. Carter

INTERNATIONAL THOMSON BUSINESS PRESS
I︎T︎P® An International Thomson Publishing Company

London ● Bonn ● Boston ● Johannesburg ● Madrid ● Melbourne ● Mexico City ● New York ● Paris
Singapore ● Tokyo ● Toronto ● Albany, NY ● Belmont, CA ● Cincinnati, OH ● Detroit, MI

Business Economics: Concepts and Cases

Copyright © 1997 M.S. Greenwood and M.J. Carter

First published by International Thomson Business Press

I(T)P® A division of International Thomson Publishing Inc.
The ITP logo is a trademark under licence

British Library Cataloguing-in-Publication Data
A catalogue record for this book is available from the British Library

First edition 1997

Reprinted 1998

Typeset by LaserScript, Mitcham, Surrey

Printed in the UK by T.J. International, Padstow, Cornwall

ISBN 1–86152–048–4

International Thomson Business Press
Berkshire House
168–173 High Holborn
London WC1V 7AA
UK

http://www.itbp.com

To Annie

Contents

Figures

Tables

Introduction
Routes through this book

'It was nothing to me but a lot of unintelligible graphs, which I didn't understand then and I still don't understand'. This was the comment of a young relative, a practising surveyor, who had been educated at one of England's leading polytechnics. Economics was no more than a difficult hurdle to be crossed before she could go on to the really interesting stuff. Perhaps she might have found her present task, with her husband, of building a private practice in times which are extremely difficult for the construction industry, a little easier if her economics course had been more meaningfully presented.

Over 100 universities in the UK are in most cases offering courses in management, either at undergraduate level, MBA level, or both. In most cases they include a compulsory core course in economics. I suspect that many of these courses are seen by the students in much the same light as my young relative describes. The sad thing is that this need not be so.

Economics for management courses have traditionally been one full year in duration and little different from any other first year economics course in other social science degree frameworks. They are usually delivered through lectures supported by one of a handful of very successful textbooks which have been in use for many years both in university and for A level economics courses for at least the brighter candidates. The course usually also requires attendance at tutorial classes, which tend to be didactic and unfocused, degenerating into an interpretation of the week's lecture through what amounts to another mini-lecture. The role of the student tends to be passive. Assessment is usually by sudden death examination using conventional essay questions, possibly supplemented by multiple choice tests, or possibly data response questions.

The content of such courses tends to centre on a corpus of theoretical propositions and models, which purport to explain events in the real world of microeconomy and macroeconomy. Little attempt is made to provide any historical underpinning, or any account of the realities of economic behaviour – unless the course requires a second programme of 'applied' economics to be studied.

A further structural change in universities is gaining momentum. This is the switch to a combination of semesters and modular courses. Two semesters replace the traditional three terms, and courses are structured in half-year 'modules' rather than full-year courses. In many cases this may mean that an economics course originally scheduled for a full year of thirty weeks, is now to be delivered within twelve weeks, and examined after fourteen weeks, along with a couple more foundation modules. This is rather hard on young students, who are still adjusting to all the problems of finding and settling into student accommodation, making friends and undergoing all the tribulations of establishing themselves as independent young adults.

Last year I took over responsibility for the economics foundation course for 250 undergraduates, most of whom were on business and management programmes, together with sixty or so who were studying computers and management, pharmacy and management or maths and management. Less than half had an A level in economics. The course was already published, and could not be changed. It took the form of twelve weeks, covering the essentials of both microeconomic and macroeconomic theory, using a well-known standard introductory text (of 500 pages plus). Despite our best efforts, fear and confusion were the order of the day, and I swore that I would not deliver such an unwieldy and indigestible course again.

When the ordeal was over, my colleague, Martin Carter and I decided to sit down and reinvent the course from the ground up. We asked ourselves two questions: what economics does a management student need to know in order to be able to function well as a manager? How should we deliver such a course in a way which will foster genuine understanding, develop useful skills, and above all be an enjoyable experience? This book has developed out of our efforts to answer these questions. We hope that it will help hard-pressed teachers of business and management students in university, school, and further education college, to reinvent their own courses, with our customers, the students, firmly in mind.

It may be helpful at this point to explain something of the logic behind the book and its relationship to course development. The first, and most difficult decision we had to make was (given the constraint of a twelve-week course), should we concentrate on microeconomics or macroeconomics, or even attempt to do both as in the old course? There is in our view a case for either micro or macro, but not both. We decided that the students would eventually have to operate in a market-based economy, and that they would above all need to understand the behaviour of economic agents in the market-place, both individual consumers and firms. In our university it is possible for the student to go on to elective courses in the second year in either industrial economics, or macroeconomics policy. Our decision, therefore, was to focus on the microeconomics of business but to put in two lectures, and one tutorial as a 'taster', on the basic background of the UK economy over the last twenty years.

The second important decision we took was that the course should be proactive, engaging the students in an active attempt to understand and apply economic concepts, models and theories to real world situations. This resulted in a change in emphasis. The lecture became a means of introducing key concepts and, hopefully, inspiring interest. Tutorials were to be the focal point of the course. We set out to ensure that each week the students were engaged in some activity relating to case material provided by us a week in advance. This helped us to overcome the serious limitations of good teaching practice imposed by the growth of numbers to twenty plus in each class. For at least part of every tutorial the students worked in small syndicates of four or five students. The tutor was thus able to circulate, enabling him to identify students who were in difficulty, and give them help then, or arrange to do so privately later. As an overarching exercise to develop personal skills (of research, teamwork, presentational skills) the syndicates were given a major case study after five weeks or so, on which they were to make a brief presentation in the last tutorial.

The next question was what areas of economics were essential if the students were to develop an ability to think logically as an economist would about matters of business strategy in the modern economy? We decided that these could be reduced to an amount which would be digestible in such a short course in the following areas:

- The basic economic problem of scarcity, choice and allocation.
- The alternatives of market and planned allocation.
- The price mechanism as the basis of a free market system.
- The spectrum of models of the firm in perfect competition, oligopoly and monopoly.
- The Porter schema of structure, conduct and performance as a method of analysing business situations.
- A brief overview of the macroeconomy and its key variables over the last twenty years.

We were determined that our students should understand this limited range of economic theory and be able to apply it to strategic business analysis, rather than simply learn undigested theory by rote as most of their predecessors had done. We hoped by devising suitable tasks to turn the models into something more than 'unintelligible graphs'. Beyond that we also wanted them to lose their distaste for, and fear of, numbers. A Cambridge don was once asked by one of my students what he should be able to *do* when he had finished the Economics Tripos. The don replied by taking down from the shelf a copy of the *Annual Abstract of Statistics*, opening it at random, and remarking that he would expect the student to be able to tell the story in words from a glance at the numbers. In a more limited way this is what we hoped to do. We wanted the student to be able to take a set of unfamiliar data, and at least come up with the right questions which needed investigating, and perhaps one or two hypotheses to test by further enquiry. We wanted the students to develop a set of tools, and skills, which would enable them to approach their later studies, in marketing, financial analysis, production management and business strategy, in a more confident and logical way.

In our view a foundation course is as much about developing a particular mindset, and set of skills as about acquiring quantities of knowledge. If the reader feels some empathy with our objectives, then this book may be a useful starting-point in the process of developing a course suited to the particular needs of groups of student, be they at A level, undergraduate level or MBA level.

If the focus of the course was to be on a sequence of proactive tutorials, then suitable materials were needed on which to hang the activities. The course covered what we felt was feasible in a series of twelve tutorials. In the book we have added cases on areas which we would have liked to cover had more time been available. If the reader is fortunate enough to have a full year of, say, twenty-four tutorials to work in, the full set of seventeen cases should be enough to work with. Within our twelve tutorials we had to restrict ourselves to the following plan.

Week 1 is inevitably a 'get to know you' session, but there is time to have at least a brief discussion of the fundamental problem of economics, the allocating of scarce resources, and the advantages and limitations of the approach of the academic economist in developing theoretical models which may have the power to explain and predict in the uncertain and changing world of economic activity. Tutorial 2 (Week 2) happens before they have really got very far on the theory front, and is used as an opportunity to present them with some simple data, from which they are invited to infer the appropriate questions which need further enquiry. We chose to use data relating to the small firm sector since many of the students will in the future work in this sector. It is also an area where rather wild claims are made by politicians on flimsy statistical evidence which is often misused. By Week 3 they have been exposed to some of the theory relating to individual behaviour in markets, and are beginning to be bombarded with seemingly unintelligible graphs. For this reason we developed an exercise which enabled us to reinvent the demand curve, using data which the students themselves generated. In Week 4 we followed a similar line using simple stylized data to develop the basic cost curves which underpin the conventional static theory of the firm. By Week 5 they have been exposed to the full price mechanism model, and are ready to test its predictive power, and weaknesses, by manipulating the model in response to examples of government interference in the operation of markets. By Week 6 the models of oligopoly and monopoly have been demonstrated, and the tutorial is used to examine, on the basis of some given questions, the case of the coffee industry.

The lectures in weeks 7, 8 and 9 set out the Porter schema of structure conduct and performance. This is really the core of our course, relating as it does very strongly to both industrial economic and business policy electives. We used the case of the recent newspaper price wars as an example of an oligopolist apparently breaking ranks and acting irrationally. The plasterboard industry offered an example of the breakdown of an apparently secure monopoly. Price discrimination in the railway industry offered another interesting example of common business strategy which is best explained through economic analysis. Week 10 gave us one opportunity to have an open discussion on the possible importance for the professional manager of macroeconomics. Week 11 was reserved for the syndicates to finish preparation of their presentation cases for delivery in Week 12. This exercise in self-help team skills, presentational skills and independent application of economic theory and concepts, was based on two of the five cases: ICI/Kermara, Reckitt & Colman/Sara Lee, the ice cream industry, the recorded music industry and the photocopier industry. These cases were all based on Monopolies and Mergers Commission (MMC) reports published in recent years, of which only the Introduction/Summary and Conclusion of the two cases are printed here. The full report is usually available in a university library. The coffee and plasterboard cases were based on summaries of MMC material developed by Chris Pass for use in *Business and Microeconomics* (Pass and Lowes, 1994). The other cases included here were written by Martin Carter and myself.

It is our view that the greatest weakness of our course, due to the time constraints, is the failure to develop more thoroughly modern industrial economics theory. In particular we would have liked to introduce game theory, and the economics of total quality management which are generally ignored by foundation level texts, but which in our view are increasingly important. We have therefore included here discussion of these topics in the theory section, and some cases which we have written but not yet had chance to trial with students. We have also included extra cases which we would have liked to include in the more conventional sections. The Lanzaroti restaurants case is one used by the author over many years to attempt to illustrate the operation of that rare beast, a perfect competition market, or at least one as near to it as we are likely to find. It illustrates how such a market would move down the road of greater concentration, despite efforts by the authorities to keep it in its pristine state. For the price discrimination case we are greatly indebted to Dr Robin Sissions, of Bradford Grammar School, who is a member of the NE Region Rail Users' Consultative Council, and knows more about railways than the previous government ever knew.

Just a word about the practicalities of delivery and assessment. Most introductory texts in economics are designed to be used on a full-year course, and are aimed at students who are either at the start of a full economics degree course, or are taking one or two papers in economics within a more widely based social science course. Such texts are not really suitable for our purposes. The course we have set out here is designed to be used with the companion text *Business and Microeconomics* (see above) by Chris Pass and Bryan Lowes, also of Bradford Management Centre. A slightly simpler text for less confident students is *The Microeconomics of Business* by Nellis and Parker. This however does not include the structure conduct performance schema, which we have used as the core of the course. For further reading students should refer to Griffiths and Wall, *Applied Economics* (1997).

Our practice in tutorials is as follows. Case material is issued to students at least one week prior to use. The one-hour tutorial is divided into a maximum of ten minutes introduction, thirty minutes of syndicate activity, usually centred around issued questions or tasks, and twenty minutes minimum of plenary discussion guided by the tutor. Each student syndicate should be asked to start discussion by responding to one of the questions with a very brief statement. Feedback is provided at the end of each chapter to Activities and Case Study Activities in some but not all cases.

Assessment on our course is by a sudden death two-hour examination. Students are required to respond to a compulsory question on the presentation case, plus two from a selection of two data response and six essay questions. Two pieces of non-assessed coursework are set, for diagnostic purposes only. One is an essay question, and the other a data response. The supermarket case was used for the latter this year. We felt that the problems of equity were too great to permit the formal assessment of the presentation case work, which we specifically wanted to provide an endpiece to the term which would be relaxed and fun.

The authors hope that the lecturers will find ways of using this book to improve the quality of their course in economics for business students' at whatever level. If economics is not enjoyable, and useful, we should not be teaching it. We have suggested below some possible routes through this book which might be used for different types of course.

SUGGESTED ROUTES THROUGH THE BOOK

One-semester foundation course

Student cohort: mostly beginners.
Course structure: 10–12 lectures and 10–12 tutorials.

Chapters 1–3	Lecture 1	Tutorial 1 (Case 1)
Chapters 4–5	Lecture 2	Tutorial 2 (Case 2)
Chapter 6	Lecture 3	Tutorial 3 (Case 3 or 4)
Chapter 7	Lecture 4	Tutorial 4 (Case 5)
Chapter 8	Lecture 5	Tutorial 5 (Case 6)
Chapter 9	Lecture 6	Tutorial 6 (Case 7)
Chapter 10 ⎱	Lecture 7 (Structure)	Tutorial 7 (Case 9)
	Lecture 8 (Conduct)	Tutorial 8 (Case 8)
	Lecture 9 (Performance)	Tutorial 9 (Presentation Case 4)
Chapter 16	Lecture 10 (Review so far)	Tutorial 10 (Review or Presentation)
	Lecture 11 (Introduction to Macroeconomics)	Tutorial 11 (Presentation or Macro)
	Lecture 12 (Review revision)	Tutorial 12 (Revision workshop)

One-year foundation course

Student cohort: mostly beginners.
Course structure: 20 lectures and 10 tutorials.

Chapter 1	Lecture 1 (Introduce course)	Tutorial 1 (Introduce presentation case Chapter 1)
Chapter 2	Lecture 2 (How to tackle case studies)	
Chapter 3	Lecture 3 (What economists do)	Tutorial 2 (Case 1)
Chapter 4	Lecture 4 (Basic problem)	
Chapter 5	Lecture 5 (The market)	Tutorial 3 (Cases 2 and 3)
Chapter 6	Lecture 6 (Market failure)	
Chapter 7	Lecture 7 (Modelling firms)	Tutorial 4 (Cases 5 and 6)
Chapter 8	Lecture 8 (Market structures)	
Chapter 9	Lecture 9 (Oligopoly)	Tutorial 5 (Cases 7 or 8)
Chapter 10	Lecture 10 (Structure)	
Chapter 10	Lecture 11 (Conduct)	Tutorial 6 (Cases 7 or 8)
Chapter 10	Lecture 12 (Performance)	
Chapter 11	Lecture 13 (Beyond theory of the firm)	Tutorial 7 (Cases 10 and 11)
Chapter 12	Lecture 14 (Growth of firms)	
Chapter 13	Lecture 15 (Game theory)	Tutorial 8 (Cases 12 and 13)
Chapter 13	Lecture 16 (Game theory)	
Chapter 14	Lecture 17 (Economics of TQM)	Tutorial 9 (Cases 14 and 15)
Chapter 15	Lecture 18 (Regulation of market power)	
	Lecture 19 (Review Chaps 1–9)	Tutorial 10 (Presentation Case)
	Lecture 20 (Review Chaps 10–15)	

How to tackle case studies
What is a case study?

A case study could be defined in this context as being: *A set of information relating to a business situation, economic context or both, presented in verbal or numerical format, or both, and intended for the use of students to develop or demonstrate analytical, evaluation, decision-making and presentation skills.*

Case material is increasingly used in the assessment and examination process in courses at A level, GNVQ, first degree and MBA levels. In this context it offers an alternative to standard essay-type questions, which test only a limited (if important) range of skills. Case material can be used to test a variety of skills, comprehension, knowledge and understanding of key concepts, analysis through the application of theory, and evaluation of competing perspectives and opinions. It may also be used to test the student's capabilities in oral and written presentation in the report format which is commonly used in business contexts. This contrasts with and complements the essay question which tests the ability to construct a logical and coherent response in continuous prose to a problem put in the form of a question.

A case may fall into one of several broad categories. It may use one or two very short passages from an article or book, or one or two sets of statistical data, presented in tabular or graphical format. Such cases are commonly used in examinations especially at A level as a question to be completed in forty to forty-five minutes. They are intended to enable the student to demonstrate knowledge of a particular section of the syllabus. The questions relating to such cases may be said to elicit either *data response* or *stimulus response*. By data response I mean that they may be answered pretty directly from the material given. In other words they are testing comprehension of the passage. Stimulus response questions use the material given as a starting-point from which the student is intended to infer answers which are based on demonstration of his or her recognition of the parts of the course which bear on the topic, and his or her ability to apply such principles to the material. The questions asked on such case material usually include both types.

Another form of case commonly used in examinations is of fuller length, perhaps a full page of text, or of statistical data. Such cases are presented unseen, i.e. seen for the first time by the student in the examination. They attract the same types of question on a data or stimulus response basis, with the possible addition of a question requiring a response in essay or report format. Cases of this type may take up half of the examination, up to perhaps one and a half hours.

In business examinations, (but not often, as yet, in economics) a longer case may be used as the basis for a whole examination paper of two or three hours duration. This is preseen, i.e. it is issued to the student some time in advance of the examination. It is thus possible for the student to examine every possible application of the theory to this particular case, and to deal with any problems which are inherent in the material.

Cases such as those types described above are commonly used also as teaching vehicles on A level and GNVQ courses, but less commonly and less systematically on university courses. The latter courses are still mostly taught on a traditional pattern of a series of lectures presenting information and theory, backed up by recommended reading and supported by a series of tutorials in which key issues are (supposedly) developed via class discussion, perhaps prompted by either a series of questions posed in advance by the tutor, or on the basis of a brief paper presented by a student. This rather passive model is in our view increasingly inappropriate as a learning experience for students. This is particularly so as tutor groups have grown in size to twenty plus, especially on first year foundation courses. We believe that a strong case can be made for a more proactive approach to teaching. Our external customers, the future employers of the students, require them to have developed certain learning skills which will last a lifetime, rather than have learned specific areas of information which may have a short shelf-life in a fast changing environment.

Students should be enabled to acquire the following life learning skills:

- value curiosity
- plan and organize work/time
- observe objectively
- develop team skills
- develop interpersonal skills
- understand own strengths/weaknesses
- develop self-esteem
- develop communication/listening skills.

If we are to help students develop these skills and characteristics, we need to understand the *process* of learning.

There are basically three learning styles (see Figure P.1). University teaching is still heavily biased towards the first. Every teacher and student has a preferred style, therefore we should attempt to present what we teach in all three styles. We believe that the strongest of the three for permanent learning is the kinaesthetic approach, which we too rarely use in universities. If the student is required to be *active* in his or her learning, he/she is more likely to take *ownership* of what he has learned, grow in self-esteem, and so in confidence. This process may be summed up as in Figure P.2.

Students will hate the first role, and be delighted to move to the second where they may passively accept the tutor's lead. They may be able to move to the third role, where they feel they are working with rather than for the tutor, but will remain dependent on him or her. To move to the fourth role, where students become the instigators and movers in the process and where the tutor becomes the facilitator rather than the director, is a massive and difficult step for many. Once they have been encouraged to take it they will never want to go back.

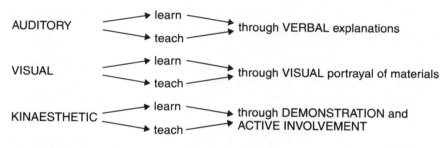

AUDITORY   learn   teach → through VERBAL explanations

VISUAL   learn   teach → through VISUAL portrayal of materials

KINAESTHETIC   learn   teach → through DEMONSTRATION and ACTIVE INVOLVEMENT

Figure P.1 The three learning styles

MOVING TO A QUALITY CLASSROOM ⟶

Teacher style	Do to	Do for	Do with	Enable
Student role	No choice, captive, antagonistic	Captive, passive, dependent	Dependent, accept, follow	independent investigator, actively seeking knowledge
Student reaction	LET ME OUT	I'M OK	IT'S OK	JOY IN LEARNING

DIRECTION IF INCREASING AUTONOMY ⟶

Figure P.2 The kinaesthetic learning process

Source: After Trybus (1992)

This book is the result of our efforts to move cohorts of undergraduate first year students, and foundation course MBA students along the spectrum of increasing autonomy. We would like now to set out briefly the learning strategy which we have sought to adopt in developing this material.

We suggest a five-stage strategy. This presupposes that the case material is being used for teaching purposes and is pre-issued to the students. In examination conditions the process would have to be truncated and actioned very rapidly.

The emphasis of the teaching process is changed. The tutorial becomes the central focus of the course rather than the lecture, which is used to establish the key principles and theoretical concepts which are being taught, in an outline form which is comprehensible to students with no prior knowledge of the subject. (Those with an A level in economics will find some but not all of the lectures merely rehearse known concepts.) These basic principles are to be followed up and consolidated by the student from an appropriate textbook. All this activity precedes a systematic study of the specific case study which is being used to demonstrate the use of the principles, and which will be dealt with in the following tutorial.

The five-stage strategy comprises:

1 Comprehension: read for understanding, using a dictionary of economics to check out any unfamiliar terms. Check out the method used to present statistical data – what are the strengths/limitations of the method used? Research further information which may throw light on the case by searching literature in the library.
2 Relation to theory: which aspects of economic theory may help in the interpretation of the material. Check understanding of these concepts in textbook/lecture notes.
3 Application of theory/analysis: use appropriate models to process data, or interpret the scenario given in the case. Develop a theoretical analysis of the case. Consider the limitations of this analysis in explaining the case.
4 Prediction: what does the theoretical analysis predict will happen next?
5 Evaluation: make judgements about possible responses; by business in decision-making or by government in policy-making. Making judgements in the light of economic theory of the possible consequences of such decisions.

The process which we have set out here is, of course, what an academic economist does for a living. Thus we are seeking to enable our students to become economists, with a serious contribution to make either to government or corporate decision-making, using the rational approach adopted by the profession. The students will find that this is both much more fun, and much more effective, than simple rote learning certain concepts for regurgitation in examinations, to be immediately forgotten when the examination is over.

Where teaching groups are large, i.e. in excess of twelve students, we find it works better if the students work within the tutorial sessions in permanent syndicates of four or five. This encourages them to operate as a self help group outside the tutorial group itself. The tutor would probably be wise to very quickly rehearse the key principles to be used perhaps for ten to fifteen minutes. The syndicates would then spend thirty minutes working on specific aspects of the case. This gives the tutor time to circulate in order to spend more time with individual students who are finding the work difficult. In the final twenty minutes, the syndicates should very briefly feedback their findings to the whole group, with the tutor drawing out general discussion from the points raised.

We also found it helpful to issue at the end of the tutorial, or the following week, some feedback of information which has stemmed out of the process, including occasional model answers to the questions.

In order to cement the syndicates as self help groups, we have also used an overarching major case study on which the syndicates work for several weeks towards a presentation of their findings in the final tutorial session.

Acknowledgements

We would like to pay tribute to the indefatigable efforts of our team of tutors who helped us to trial much of this material: Roy Rimmington, Keith Brunskill, Kalim Saddique and Kath Watson. Chris Pass and Bryan Lowes, for encouraging us to produce this book as a companion to their *Business and Macroeconomics* text. Kath West of Computerwork Unlimited and Sylvia Ashworth for secretarial help. Not least to our long-suffering students who cheerfully encouraged us in our efforts to make the 'dismal science' fun, and relevant to their needs as management students.

We also owe a debt to the economists, past and present, whose work inspired our efforts, particularly those whose books are listed in the Bibliography.

Abbreviations

AFC	average fixed cost
ATC	average total cost
AVC	average variable cost
BBC	British Broadcasting Corporation
BEW	Bird's Eye Walls Limited
BR	British Rail
BT	British Telecommunications plc
CIF	continuous improvement firm
CR	concentration ratio
DGFT	Director General of Fair Trading
EU	European Union
GDP	gross domestic product
LRAC	long-run average cost
MB	marginal benefit
MC	marginal cost
MES	minimum efficient scale
MMC	Monopolies and Mergers Commission
MP/SM	mass production/scientific management
MR	marginal revenue
MSB	marginal benefit to society
MSC	marginal cost to society
MU	marginal utility
NCV	net customer value
NHS	National Health Service
OFT	Office of Fair Trading
PPF	production possibility frontier
RPI	retail price index
RPM	resale price maintenance
SCP	structure, conduct and performance
SRAC	short-run average cost
TC	total cost
TFC	total fixed cost

TVC   total variable cost
VAT   value added tax

Chapter 1

What do economists do?

The human species has evolved as a social animal, living in groups, large or small, which extend beyond immediate kinship boundaries. Such groups require some form of social organization to ensure the provision of food, shelter and other artefacts. In the absence of the instinctive programming of ant or bee communities, such organization has to be socially constructed. The social science of economics has developed over recent centuries as a means by which this socially constructed organization may be understood.

We are not concerned here to trace the history of economic thought. Our objective in this book is to see how the tools and methodologies developed by academic economists may be used by the layperson to understand the economic environment in which he or she is involved as manager or employee. Just as the householder does not need to qualify as a joiner to undertake simple do-it-yourself tasks but does need to know how to measure, use a saw, hammer or screwdriver, so a student of management does not need to become a professional economist in order to make an informed business decision but does need to know how to measure and interpret economic events.

The purpose of this chapter is to impart a basic understanding of the methodology and tool-kit employed by the economist.

The economist regards him or herself as an empirical scientist, that is to say, he or she seeks explanations for observed facts. This process is more difficult for the economist than for the natural scientist because economic facts are more elusive than reactions observed in a laboratory.

Activity 1.1

Ask four friends to write down a definition of unemployment. You are likely to get four different definitions. Consider how total unemployment for the UK would be likely to differ on each of those definitions.

However elusive the facts may be we need rigorous methods by which to analyse, evaluate and interpret these facts. Also, like all scientists we need theories which enable us to model the relationships between observed facts.

Activity 1.2

Suppose you believe that there is a relationship between inflation and unemployment. Consider how, as a rational layperson with a scientific education, you might go about studying that relationship. (If you go on later to study macroeconomics you will see that this is an important topic which provokes much disagreement among economists. You will have just now discovered why this is so!)

If the student is to be able to make sense of economic data and, as our Cambridge don suggested, be able to 'tell the story', then he or she needs a methodology and a tool-kit. This deceptively easy-looking job in fact involves four stages:

1. Telling the story: Collecting, categorizing and collating information (the facts).
2. Interpreting the story: Analyzing the data.
3. Understanding the story by means of 4 and 5 below: Using a scientific method to develop theories.
4. Modelling reality: Using graphs and diagrams to model situations.
5. Using theory and facts: To explain, predict events, and advise on strategies, policies and decisions.

Non-mathematicians will already be worried by the thought that they have embarked on a course which will not make sense because they have no confidence with numerical and mathematical manipulations. In the words of Corporal Jones: 'Don't panic'. We only propose to introduce you gently to a limited range of simple techniques. Those who want more may refer to the more advanced text recommended later in this chapter.

TELLING THE STORY

Collecting, categorizing and collating information

What information do we collect? This problem has two parts. First, how are we to *define* the entity about which we need information? Suppose we are interested in the market for coffee. Are we interested in *all* forms of coffee (beans, ground and instant) or just the most commonly used – instant coffee? Of course it depends on the *purpose* of our investigation. A medical scientist might be concerned to relate the use of *all* forms of coffee to specific medical conditions. An economist is more likely to be interested in the degree of market dominance of certain firms in the mass market for *instant* coffee.

What sources of information exist? In the above case we might decide to collect our own information by asking customers such questions as: 'What brand of instant coffee do you buy? What quantities do you buy per week?' Since we can hardly ask 56 million people, we would need to ask a limited but representative *sample* of manageable size. This might be chosen by random methods, or by some method to achieve a cross-section of the population with the correct proportions of different gender and income groups. (For more detailed discussion of sampling techniques and related problems see the market research chapter of any good marketing textbook.)

Such an exercise is costly and time-consuming. Therefore, for many purposes an economist will go to secondary sources, i.e. collections of data assembled by government or other agencies for their own purposes. This method is much quicker and cheaper, but brings its own problems as you saw in Activity 1.1 where you considered definitions of unemployment. These may differ over time (government official definitions of unemployment have changed more than twenty times since 1982), and between countries. Moreover, they may not reveal the information which you are trying to obtain. Do you think, for example, that 'numbers of persons registered as unemployed, and eligible for benefit', would be the same as 'numbers of persons unemployed but wishing to work'? If not, why not? Economic facts are indeed very elusive!

How are changes in economic facts shown? Telling the story usually involves demonstrating changes in the numbers over time. *This often involves the use of* **time series graphs.** *Such a graph shows time periods on the horizontal axis and numbers describing the entity in which we are interested on the vertical axis.* For example we may be interested in examining changes in unemployment in the last ten years (see Figure 1.1).

We might draw a conclusion from Figure 1.1 that unemployment appears to oscillate in a series of cycles. But might this conclusion be oversimplified? *What if the definition of unemployment changed over this period? What if the size and composition of the workforce changed over this period?* If so, a clearer picture might appear if we did three things.

1 Convert the raw unemployment figure for each year into a percentage of the workforce available in that year. This will eliminate the distorting effects of demographic change.
2 Use one definition – perhaps the original 1982 version, but including categories later excluded from the official figures.
3 Break down the raw data by gender and age groupings.

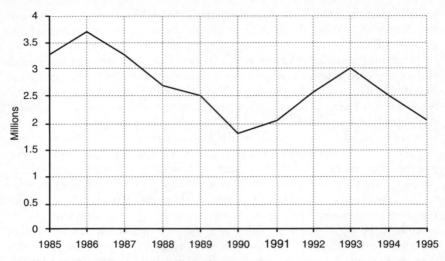

Figure 1.1 Changes in unemployment, 1985–95

Activity 1.3

Using Griffith and Wall's *Applied Economics* (1997) or a similar text, seek out the above versions of unemployment data. Write down briefly the key changes in the labour market which seem to emerge from this data.

Index numbers

Suppose we wish to compare changes in two economic entities over time more clearly than the raw data will permit (see Table 1.1)?

Table 1.1 Price of goods A and B (£ per ton)

	1980	1985	1990	1995
Good A price	80	100	120	150
Good B price	50	60	80	120

We can use an **index number** *which expresses data relative to a given base value.* In our example in Table 1.1 the price of Good A in 1985 (£100) is 1.25 times the price in 1980. If we pretend that the price in 1980 was 100 and call

1984 the *base year* the index has risen to 125 in 1985. The same calculation for Good B shows an index of 120 for 1985. Thus we can conclude that the price of A rose by 25 per cent in the year, while B rose by 20 per cent (see Table 1.2).

Table 1.2 Price of goods A and B relative to the base year (£ per ton)

	1980	1985	1990	1995
Good A price	100	125		
Good B price	100	120		

Activity 1.4

Complete the index in Table 1.2 for 1990 and 1995.

Now suppose Good A is wheat and Good B is barley. We may wish to know what happened to the price of grain over this period including both wheat and barley in one index. We cannot simply add one to the other and divide by 2 because *different quantities* of wheat and barley are included in the general category of 'grain'. To get round this problem we need to *weight* the two commodities according to their relative importance as inputs in the food industry.

Suppose we take the view that barley is more widely used than wheat. We might decide to allocate a weight of 0.6 to barley and 0.4 to wheat. We can then calculate the change in the grain price index over time (the *weighted* average of barley and wheat). In the base year 1980 the grain index is 100 (barley 0.6 × 100) + (wheat 0.4 × 100). By 1985 the index has risen to 122 (0.6 × 120) + (0.4 × 125), a 22 per cent increase.

Activity 1.5

Now calculate the grain index for the year 1990 and 1995.

Because the grain index is a weighted average, it must lie between the indices for the two goods, wheat and barley.

It is obviously much easier to discuss percentage increases in prices of goods over time than to work in raw data. This would also be true of our earlier example of unemployment.

The same principle is used in the calculation of change in the general level of prices (inflation). Thus the retail price index (RPI) is an index of prices of goods and services consumed by households and weighted in each case according to their importance in the budget of the average household. Fourteen categories of goods and services are included. The resulting index shows (or purports to show) the percentage change in the general level of prices year to year. The problem with the RPI is the selection of goods and services to be included and the weighting to be given to each. This is a much more difficult task than our example of a grain price index.

Nominal and real prices and costs

In our earlier example we saw that firms manufacturing food products using grain as the major input faced an increase of 22 per cent in input prices between 1980 and 1985, an average of 4.4 per cent per annum. If the retail prices of their products did not change, they would be worse off (unless they could reduce other costs, e.g. labour by the same amount). However, if the RPI for the period tells us that inflation of the general price level was also running at 4.4 per cent per annum, it is probably the case that they could recoup their increased input and labour costs through higher retail prices.

Real costs *may be calculated by adjusting* **nominal costs** *(measured in £s, or indices based on such data) for changes in the general price level.* For example, suppose the food industry shows the unit labour costs, and the retail price index as shown in Table 1.3.

Table 1.3 Unit labour costs example

	Unit labour costs	RPI	Real unit labour costs
1980	100	100	100
1985	123	125	98.4
1990	165	175	—
1995	177	190	—

Real unit labour costs may be calculated by dividing the unit labour costs in column 1 by the RPI in column 2, and multiply by 100. Thus real unit labour costs in 1985 would be 98.4. The apparent 23 per cent rise in *nominal* terms becomes in *real* terms a *fall* to 98.4.

Activity 1.6

Now calculate the figures for the years 1990 and 1995 in column 3. What has been the percentage per annum fall in real unit labour costs between 1980 and 1995?

Growth rates

Quite often it is useful to have a *unit free* measure of change in an economic variable over time. This might be for example economic growth (of national income), or sales of instant coffee. The *absolute change* in either of these variables would be measured in numbers of £s. But it is much more useful information if we simply change it into a percentage change per annum. To calculate the percentage change take the absolute change, divide by the original number on which the change took place, and multiply by 100. Suppose the national income of the state of Atlantis in 1995 was $35 billion and in 1996 $38 billion, then

$$\frac{38-35}{35} \times 100 = 8.5\%$$

The *growth rate* 1995/6 was therefore 8.5 per cent.

There are many other statistical techniques for the presentation of data which are useful to the professional economist, but which are not essential for the layperson.

INTERPRETING THE STORY

Analysing the data

The mass of economic statistics available may appear overwhelming and meaningless. However making sense of the numbers is not as difficult as it might appear at first sight. Usually we need to discover an answer to one or more of three basic questions.

Can we identify a trend?

We are interested in one particular variable. It might be, for example, 'UK unemployment 1970–1995' or 'The price of crude oil 1970–1994'. Is there any *pattern*, and is there a *trend* in any particular direction over time?

The **time series graph** in Figure 1.2 depicts the progress of inflation in the fictitious state of Atlantis over a twenty-year period. First we can observe that inflation by this measure fluctuates in a cyclical pattern. Periods of rising inflation are followed by periods of falling inflation. Periods of rising inflation appear to be of three to four years duration, followed by periods of falling inflation of between one and seven years duration.

Can we observe a trend over this long period towards generally higher or lower levels of inflation? Yes we can. The dotted line indicates the trend. This is called the *best fit trend line* and is arrived at by ensuring that an equal number of the marked points appear on each side of the line. Although this is a crude short cut it does give us a quick picture of very long-term trends.

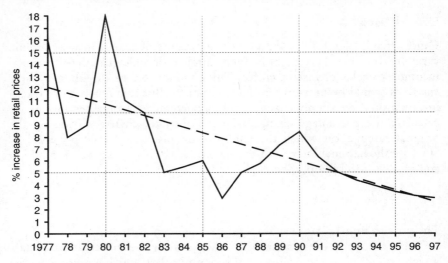

Figure 1.2 An inflation time series graph

If the series began at 1990, or covered the period 1985–90, we would arrive at a distorted view of historical change using this method.

We could add to this graph data for other countries (making sure that it has been collected in a broadly similar way). This would enable us to observe the degree to which the trend to falling inflation is a world-wide trend or confined to Atlantis.

Plotting economic variables in this way against time enables us to describe what has happened in the past. Of course, this process raises all sorts of questions about the causes of observed events.

Can we forecast the future?

It is tempting to think that plotting historical data in this way will allow us to forecast the future. Stock market analysts, of course, do use time series data to forecast share price movements. (These analysts are called 'chartists'.) However they are probably wrong as often as they are right! Simply *extrapolating* – assuming that our variable will follow a similar pattern over time in the future – is very dangerous. Our data in Figure 1.2 tells us nothing about changes in the many variables which might affect inflation – such as money supply, interest rate policy, wages etc. Still less can it tell us what random shocks lie round the corner – such as the oil price quadrupling in 1973/4 – of which the figure of 16 per cent in 1977 is the aftermath, or the further doubling of the oil price in 1978/9 which (partly) caused the 18 per cent figure in 1980. All we can say is that seven years of falling inflation from 1990 to a very low figure of 2 per cent is *likely* to be followed quite soon by a renewed upward trend. But we cannot be certain.

Forecasting the future requires knowledge of the *relationship* between key variables which influence the one in which we are interested.

Relationships between variables

We can relate our observations of the values of two variables by using a scatter diagram. Each point on the diagram represents an observation of two variables in a given year. The pattern which emerges will tell us whether the relationship is:

- positive – if variable a increases, so does b
- negative – if variable a increases, b falls
- no relationship – if increase in a coincides with sometimes a rise, sometimes a fall in b.

Figures 1.3, 1.4 and 1.5 demonstrate what we mean.

In Figure 1.3 the points are enclosed within a very narrow envelope, sloping up from left to right suggesting a very strong connection between increasing car use and the occurrence of road accidents. This might lead us to suggest that increased car ownership causes increased numbers of road accidents. This would be very foolish. You can see why instantly. It would

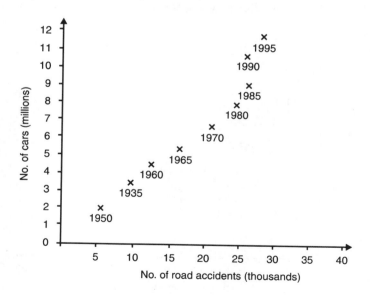

Figure 1.3 Relationship between cars and accidents

make little sense to argue that increased road traffic accidents cause more car ownership. Even a very strong correlation between two sets of data can only suggest possible causal links, it cannot prove them to exist.

In Figure 1.4 we can see that all the points are enclosed within a narrow envelope, sloping downward from left to right. This indicates that as the real (after allowing for inflation) price of cars falls, so car ownership increases. Again the strong relationship suggests the possibility of a causal connection but cannot prove it.

Figure 1.5 we have plotted two variables whose relationship is a very controversial issue among economists: unemployment and inflation. In this data for Atlantis we can observe no relationship between inflation and unemployment.

Summary

Let us summarize where we have got to in our search for simple tools with which to interpret the story by analysing data:

- We can trace changes in one variable over time, and observe trends.
- We can forecast future trends by extrapolating past trends, at the risk of being very wrong!
- We can compare changes over time in one variable between, say, two or more countries, or for the same country in different historical periods.
- We can relate the values of two variables at different points in time in order to observe possible relationships between those variables.

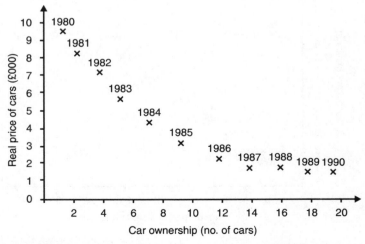

Figure 1.4 Relationship between the price of cars and car ownership

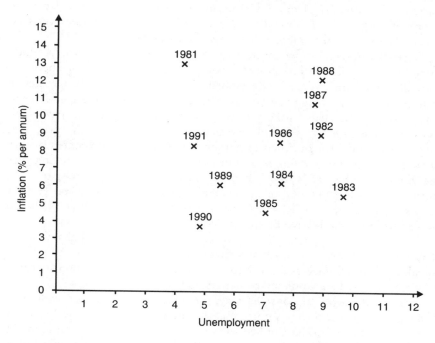

Figure 1.5 Relationship between inflation and unemployment

The economic world is complex with many variables interacting constantly. To consider the interaction of more than two variables requires more sophisticated techniques, involving more complex mathematics than would be appropriate to this book. The techniques discussed so far essentially allow us to *describe* and *interpret* data. To *understand* and *explain* relationships between variables we need *theory*. To develop theory we need a *method*.

UNDERSTANDING THE STORY

Scientific method

Positive versus normative

Economics is often referred to as a social science. In what sense can it be thought of as a scientific discipline?

The essence of the *scientific method* which underpins most natural and social science disciplines is that it is *empirical* and *inductive*. Enquiry proceeds by reasoning from observations of phenomena (whether from the world at large, or from controlled laboratory experiments). It does not seek to fit observed evidence into preconceived explanations.

Repeated observations may lead to the development of a theory which permits explanation of the cause of types of events, or relationships between variables. Sometimes theories developed in this way have strong predictive powers, despite changing conditions. The theory of price explained later in this book, is one such strong theory. Other theories appear to have such powers for a time but later observations may suggest that the proposed relationship has broken down due to a change in the environment within which it occurs. An example is the so-called Phillips curve which was developed in the 1950s and which seemed to suggest a strong inverse relationship between inflation and unemployment. In the 1950s and 1960s it was strongly supported by empirical observation. But since the 1970s the relationship seems to have broken down.

The body of microeconomic theory relating to the behaviour of consumers and firms is constantly being developed and shows no sign of breaking down. It enables us both to *explain* and *predict* with a useful degree of accuracy the behaviour of consumers and firms.

Before we begin to consider ways in which we might use economic theory it is important to recognize that the empirical nature of the discipline means that it can only be applied to positive questions. An example might be: 'How will the income of hill farmers be affected by the BSE crisis?' We can develop a hypothesis as to what might happen using the theory of price (supply and demand) and test it against observations of events in the markets for farm produce.

What the economist cannot do is provide definitive answers to normative questions. These require an expression of opinion as to what should be done. An example might be: 'Hill farmers should (ought) be compensated for the effects of the BSE crisis!' The economist might help to estimate the size of losses attributable to BSE and suggest how compensation would affect agricultural markets. But the decision to offer compensation is for the politician *not* the economist.

Theory and models

Like the natural scientist the economist needs theory to make sense of facts. Economic theory depends very heavily on the use of models. These are simplified constructs which replicate some, but not all, key functions of the real world. They permit data from observations to be processed in the search for explanations and predictions.

Microeconomic models used in this book have two important characteristics:

1 They can only express directly relationships between two variables, e.g. price and quantity, cost and output.
2 They are static models in that all other variables which might influence outcomes have to be assumed to be constant (the *ceteris paribus* assumption – other things remaining the same).

While these limitations are important they do not weaken the predictive powers of the models too much.

Macroeconomic models seek to offer a simplified version of the relationships of the many aggregate variables in the whole economic system. More complex mathematics and the power of computers allows the economist to simulate the interaction of many variables in order to explain and predict events in the whole economic system.

The methodology of economics as a science is summarized in Figure 1.6.

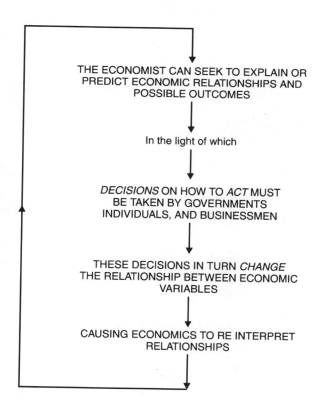

Figure 1.6 Economics as a science

Building models with graphs

Most simple economic models depend on the use of graphs. A graph allows us to examine relationships between two variables. Put in its simplest terms we can identify four types of graph used by economist, which show:

1 Positive relationship: variables which rise and fall together.
2 Negative relationship: variables which move in opposite directions.
3 No relationship: variables which are unrelated to each other.
4 Maximum and Minimums: variables displaying a maximum or minimum.

Positive relationships: Figure 1.7(a) shows a *constant* positive relationship. As the variable on the *x* axis rises so does that on the *y* axis at the same rate. The relationship is *linear*, and slope of the curve is *constant*. In Figure 1.7(b) the slope of the curve becomes steeper as we move out from the axis. In this

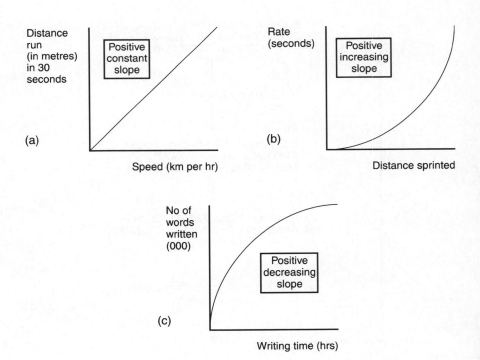

Figure 1.7 Positive relationship graphs

particular case the runner recovers more slowly the further he has sprinted. In Figure 1.7(c) we again have a positive relationship but with a decreasing slope as we move away from the origin. In this case extra hours spent writing produces declining increases in the total number of words written.

Negative relationships: Figure 1.8(a) again shows a linear relationship with constant slope – the more time we spend jogging the correspondingly less time may be spent swimming. Figure 1.8(b) shows a negative relationship with decreasing slope, indicating that the cost per mile for journeys falls, but at a decreasing rate as journey length increases. Figure 1.8(c) has an increasing slope, i.e. there is a trade-off between work and leisure. The curve indicates the various combinations of work and leisure available to us – thus at point *x* we can complete four work tasks and take 6.5 hours of leisure.

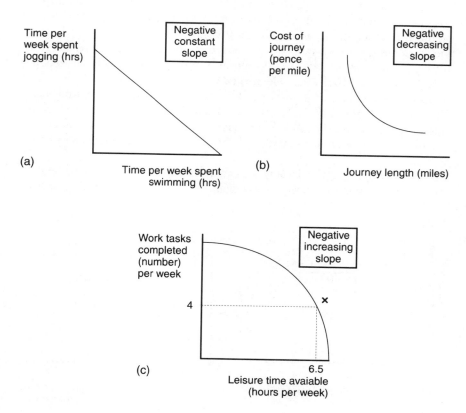

Figure 1.8 Negative relationship graphs

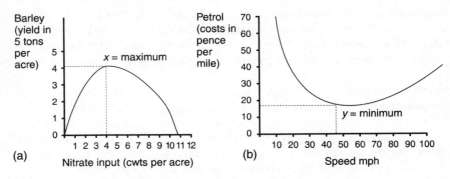

Figure 1.9 Maximum and minimum relationship graphs

Maximum and minimum: In Figure 1.9(a) we can see that increasing inputs of nitrate fertilizer increase barley yields at first, reaching a maximum of 4 tons per acre with an input of 4 cwts of nitrate per acre. Thereafter the use of additional nitrate damages the chemical composition of the soil and causes yields to progressively fall. We can say that the optimum (best) usage of nitrate is therefore 4 cwts, and optimum output (best) of barley 4 tons per acre. In Figure 1.9(b) if we accelerate and increase the speed of a car from rest to approx 42 mph, petrol costs per mile fall (the engine is operating more efficiently in higher gears), but further acceleration starts to increase petrol costs as proportionately more fuel is used to increase speed. The fuel cost of our motoring is minimized at 42 mph. We have optimized our use of fuel.

No relationship: Figure 1.10(a) we can see that the propensity of hens to lay eggs is completely unaffected by changes in the price of poultry feed (it

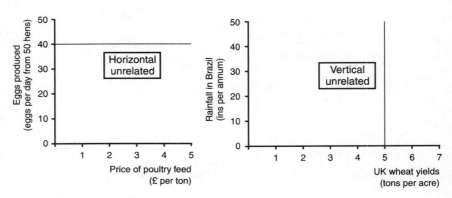

Figure 1.10 No relationship graphs

might be related to amounts of feed, but that is a different question). In Figure 1.10(b) it is fairly obvious that wheat yields in the UK are unaffected by changes in rainfall in Brazil (it would be affected by changes in UK rainfall, but that is a different question).

Activity 1.7

Since we are likely to meet examples of these different graphical expressions of relationships later in the book, it would be a good idea now to invent your own example of each type.

Figure 1.11(a) illustrates the calculation of a positive slope – that is where both x and y go up together. When x goes up from 2 to 5, y goes up from 4 to 6. Thus a change in x of 3 brings about a change in y from 4 to 6. Therefore the change in x, (Δx) = 3, and the change in y (Δy) = 2.

$$\frac{\Delta y}{\Delta x} = \frac{2}{3}$$

In Figure 1.11(b) we have a negative slope (when x goes up, y goes down), when x goes up from 2 to 6, Δx = 4, while y goes down from 6 to 3, Δy = 3, therefore

$$\frac{\Delta y}{\Delta x} = \frac{-3}{4} = \text{the slope}$$

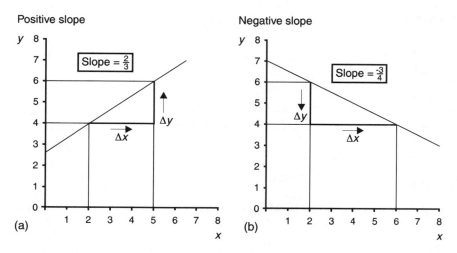

Figure 1.11 Example of positive and negative slope

The slope of a positive relationship is a positive number, while the slope of a negative relationship is a negative number.

The theory question of slope

Definition: slope

The slope of a relationship is the change in the value of y (the vertical axis on the graph) divided by the value of x (the horizontal axis).

The Greek letter Δ is used to represent 'change in', thus Δy means 'change in the value of y' and Δx means change in value of x. Thus the slope of the relationship between y and x is

$$\frac{\Delta y}{\Delta x}$$

If a *large* change in y is associated with a *small* change in x, the slope is *large* and the curve on the graph is *steep*. Conversely if a *small* change in y is associated with a *large* change in x, the slope is *small* and the curve is *flat*.

Calculating slope: In the case of *straight lines* the slope is the same wherever you calculate it, that is the slope of a straight line is constant. Two examples are shown in Figure 1.12 to illustrate this.

In the case of a *curved line*, the slope is not constant, but will be different at each point on the line. Two calculations may be used: as at a point on the line and across an arc of the line. To calculate the slope at point a in Figure 1.12(a),

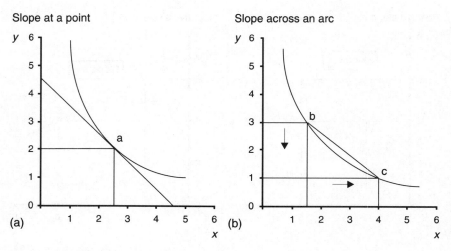

Figure 1.12 Example of curved line slope

draw a line across the graph which just touches point a and no other. At a the slope will be the same as at all points on this line. Thus when x changes from 0 to 5, it is associated with a change in y from 4.5 to 0 therefore

$$\frac{\Delta y}{\Delta x} = \frac{-4.5}{5} = \text{slope at point a}$$

In Figure 1.12(b) we want to calculate the slope across the arc b to c on the curve. To do so we draw a line between points b and c, and then calculate the slope of that straight line.

In moving from b to c, x goes up by 2.5 (then $\Delta x = 2.5$), while y goes down by 2 (thus $\Delta y = 2$).

The slope between b and c is therefore

$$\frac{\Delta y}{\Delta x} = \frac{-2}{2.5}$$

That is -2 divided by 2.5, which is the same as

$$\frac{-4}{5}$$

Summary

Let us summarize what we have learned about graphs as used in economics.

- *Time series graphs* plot one or more economic variables on the y axis against time on the x axis. Used to establish trends (past) and forecasts (future).
- *Scatter diagrams* plot relationships between two variables, which may be positive, negative, or non existent.
- Graphs are used to construct simplified *models* of relationships between two variables (e.g. price of a product and quantity demanded). Such models require all other variables which may be influential to be held to be constant (the *ceteris paribus* assumption).
- The *slope* of the curves on such a diagrammatic model are important in representing the strength of the relationships illustrated.

USING THE TOOLS OF ECONOMICS

We hope that you have persevered with our attempts to explain the economist's tool-kit. If you have, much of what follows later in the book will be more accessible.

In each chapter of this book we have tried to set out one group of related concepts, and to provide you with case material on which to use both the basic tool-kit and the concepts set out in that chapter. We have kept in mind your interest in economics – which is to have available a particular cast of mind and set of ideas to enable you *to make better business management decisions* in the future.

At this point we just want to point out one or two examples of what we mean. A marketing manager would be unable to offer good advice on pricing policy without an understanding of the theory of supply, demand and price. A business strategy consultant will be better able to advise on an acquisition with the help of a structure, conduct and performance analysis of the industry sector. A new entrant to a business sector would need to understand Game Theory if he or she is to predict the possible response of firms already in that business.

Now you have some idea what it is that economists try to do, and how they do it, the time has come for you to try your hand. In Case Study 1 we present you with a selection of data on a particular topic 'The Small Firm Sector'. From this we would like you to try to tell the story and understand the story.

SUMMARY

This chapter has introduced the following ideas:

- **Microeconomics** deals with the behaviour of individuals, households and firms within a market-place.
- **Macroeconomics** deals with the behaviour of whole economic systems.
- The economist distinguishes between *positive* and *normative* questions.
- The economist collects, interprets and analyses *economic data*.
- Economic analysis is based on the use of *theory* and *models*.
- Economists simplify a complex world by making assumptions about the degree to which we act *rationally* and have the *knowledge* to do so.
- The real economy is *dynamic* whereas microeconomic models are inevitably *static*.
- Economists proceed by three stages of analysis:
  1 observations and problem formulation
  2 explanation by developing (or using) a theory
  3 testing the theory on data from the real world.

CASE STUDY 1: THE SMALL FIRM SECTOR

Objectives

1 To defuse fear of economics.
2 To illustrate some of the techniques used to present economic data and their limitations.
3 To practise the interpretation of such data.

Methods

1 To consider the role of the small firm in the UK economy (using data derived from Griffiths and Wall, 1997: 68–70).
2 In doing so to generate some general statements and questions about the role of small firms.
3 To consider alternative and more striking ways in which the key data might be presented.

Background

In the 1980s there was a revival of interest among both economists and politicians in the UK small business sector. Small firms were seen as the acorns from which great oak trees of companies would emerge to revive the UK's moribund manufacturing sector. They were also seen by some as the best hope for reduction of the now apparently permanent high levels of unemployment. These beliefs may well turn out to be more myth than fact.

UK small business statistics

There are two major official statistical series which map trends in the number of small businesses. These are VAT registration and deregistration data and self-employment data; the latter being obtained primarily from the quarterly Labour Force Survey. Value Added Tax (VAT) data cover all businesses registered for VAT and thus are free from sampling error but the most important limitation of this data, is that it excludes those firms which trade below the VAT threshold and those which trade mainly in exempt or zero-rated goods and services. Self-employment data, is a very rich source of information on individuals, but is based on a sample survey and according to Bannock and Daly (1994, in Griffiths and Wall, 1997) may include many people who are arguably not involved in enterprise. Despite these qualifications, these two sources of data enable us to chart the very large increase in the number of UK small firms during the last decade.

VAT registrations and deregistrations

The number of VAT-registered firms increased by 420,000 (33 per cent) over the period 1980 to 1990 (Bannock and Daly, 1994). From examination of the net change in the stock of VAT registered firms, it is evident that the increase was not a steady rise over the period but rather that the rate of increase accelerated rapidly from 1985 to 1989, before falling back in 1990 due to a drop in the number of registrations rather than to a rise in deregistrations. Regional estimates show that the number of VAT registered businesses rose substantially in every region between 1980 and 1990, ranging from an increase of 19 per cent in the North West to 46 per cent in the South East.

The VAT data distinguish between sole proprietorships, partnerships and incorporated businesses. Since the end of 1979, for the UK, the rate of increase has been greatest among sole proprietorships, at nearly 40 per cent, and least among partnerships, at 24 per cent. The number of companies increased by 33 per cent. However, it is principally in the late 1980s that the numbers of sole proprietorships have increased rapidly; in the early 1980s there were substantially faster increases in the number of companies. Sole proprietorships have the highest rates of turbulence (total registrations plus deregistrations as a proportion of the number of businesses).

Self-employment

The growth in self-employment was one of the most significant changes to the labour market during the 1980s. The total number of self-employed in the UK in June 1990 was 3,547,000, an increase of 65 per cent over the period since 1980. The proportion of the workforce in self-employment increased from 8 per cent in 1980 to 12.5 per cent in 1990. Female self-employment increased much faster than male self-employment during the decade to a peak of 858,000 in 1990, more than double the figure for 1980. However, in 1990, women still accounted for only 24 per cent of all self-employment (*Employment Gazette*, October 1994, in Griffiths and Wall, 1997).

There have been increases in the number of self-employed in all regions over the period.

Estimated numbers of firms in the UK

There is no central register of firms in the UK. When an individual receives income from a business they must register with the tax authorities but these details are not collected on an enterprise basis. Furthermore, many self-employed people work in partnerships which are not taken into account in the self-employment data from the Labour Force Survey. When a firm reaches a certain level of turnover it must register for VAT, but estimates suggest that almost 1 million firms are too small to be included in the VAT statistics (Bannock and Daly, 1991, in Griffiths and Wall, 1997).

Graham Bannock and Partners Ltd used VAT and self-employment data together with other sources of information on the small firm sector to arrive at statistical estimates of the number of firms in the UK. These estimates are presented in Figure 1.13 which shows the dramatic rise in the small firms in the late 1980s and subsequent fall in numbers as the UK economy went into recession in the 1990s.

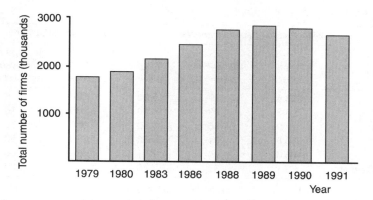

Figure 1.13 Total number of firms in the UK, 1979–91

Data source: Small Business Statistics, Table 4.1: 80, Bannock and Daly (1994), in Griffiths and Wall, 1997.

Survival and failure rates

The survival/failure rates for small businesses generally are difficult to gauge accurately but commonly are indicated by reference to VAT registrations and deregistrations: Although some 10–11 per cent of all VAT firms deregister each year, of those formed in any year, 12 per cent will fail in their first year, 26 per cent within two years and 36 per cent within 3 years (Stanworth and Gray, 1991, p. 11 in Griffiths and Wall, 1997). It is apparent that the vulnerability of businesses to failure is greatest in their earlier years.

It would be helpful at this point to read chapter 4 in Griffiths and Wall *Applied Economics*.

Table 1.4 Number of small firms* relative to population: selected countries

Rank	Small-firm population (million)	No. of small firms per 1,000 of population (UK = 100)
1 The Netherlands	1.2	370
2 France	3.1	250
3 Japan	5.4	202
4 USA	8.0	157
5 West Germany	1.9	133
6 Canada	0.6	109
7 UK	1.3	100

Note: * The definition of small firms for each country was decided upon after consultation with the relevant government departments of those countries.
Source: Bannock, 1980

Table 1.5 Small firms* in manufacturing

	Manufacturing establishments		Manufacturing employment		
	Total (000s)	*Small-firm share (%)*	*Total (million)*	*No. of estab. per 100,000 employed*	*Average no. of employees per establishment*
Italy	628.5	99	5.30	11,850	8
Japan	744.3	99	10.89	6,830	15
Canada	32.0	95	1.70	1,880	53
USA	350.8	94	18.52	1,890	53
UK	108.0	94	7.11	1,520	66
West Germany	93.1	93	7.48	1,240	80

Note: * Small firms are defined as those having less than 200 employees.
Source: Adapted from *Financial Times*, 3 May 1983, in Griffiths and Wall, 1997

Table 1.6 Shares of enterprises and employment: UK and EUR12

	Micro (0–9)	*Small/medium (100–499)*	*Large (500+)*
Enterprises:			
UK	90.1	9.7	0.2
EUR12	91.3	8.6	0.1
Employment:			
UK	23.2	46.8	30.0
EUR12	26.9	45.0	28.1

Source: *Enterprises in the European Community*, European Commission, 1990 in Griffiths and Wall, 1997

Table 1.7 Number of businesses, employment and turnover share by size band (end of 1989)

Employment size band	*Number of businesses (thousands)*	*Share of total (per cent)*		
		Businesses	*Employment*	*Turnover*
1–2	2,025	67.8	12.3	4.2
3–5	596	19.9	10.0	4.7
6–10	181	6.1	6.3	4.1
11–19	92	3.1	6.0	4.3
20–49	57	1.9	7.7	6.0
50–99	18	0.6	5.8	3.7
100–199	9	0.3	7.2	13.6
200–499	6	0.2	10.6	17.9
500–999	2	0.1	6.7	11.2
1,000+	1	0.0	27.5	30.4
Total	2,988	100.0	100.0	100.0

Source: Daly and McCann, 1992 in Griffiths and Wall, 1997

Table 1.8 Employment and output by size of firm, 1958, 1968 and 1989

Size of firm	1958		1968		1989	
	Total employment (%)	Total net output (%)	Total employment (%)	Total net output (%)	Total employment (%)	Total net output (%)
1–24	5.8 ⎫	5.2 ⎫	5.9 ⎫	5.2 ⎫	⎫	⎫
25–99	9.9 ⎬ 15.7	8.4 ⎬ 13.6	7.6 ⎬ 13.5	6.3 ⎬ 11.5	⎬ 24.6	⎬ 18.9
100–199	8.0	6.9	5.6	4.7	7.0	5.6

Sources: Business Monitor, Report on the Census of Production, PA 1002, Summary Table, 1991 and earlier dates, in Griffiths and Wall, 1997

Activity 1.8

1 What general questions come to mind about the *origins* and *validity* of these sets of data?
2 Think carefully about each table. In each case what *statements of fact* can you develop which tell the kernel of the story?
3 What possible *explanations* can you offer for these statements?
4 What question(s) does each table suggest which are *positive* and capable of further investigation by an economist?
5 For ONE of your questions, jot down a systematic method by which you might investigate the question further.

Feedback to Case Study 1

General questions arising from the data

1 How do we define a 'small firm'?
2 Do all countries do so in the same way?
3 How do we collect the data?
4 How accurate is the data given here?

UK small business data update

Two sources available:

1 *VAT registrations and deregistrations* – (excludes 1 million firms which are too small to register)

   1980–90   Increased by 33 per cent (increase greatest 1985–90), mainly among sole proprietor firms.

2   *Self-employment* (source Labour Force Survey) (excludes 'black economy')

   1980–90   Increased 65 per cent in total, and from 8 per cent to 12.5 per cent of total employment.

   Of VAT registered firms, 74 per cent fail within 3 years.

Specific statements/questions derived from given data

Table 1.4 statements:

- UK, Canada and West Germany have much *lower* concentrations of small firms in the economy.
- Whereas Japan has 2 × UK, France 2.5 × UK.
- Netherlands is a special case – why? Small agribusiness.

Table 1.4 questions:

- Is this a useful measure of small firm concentration?
- Why are small firms much more important in Japan and France?

Table 1.5 statements:

- In six leading economies 93–99 per cent of manufacturing firms are small.
- Average size in number of employees is 50–80, except in Japan and Italy.
- Italy and Japan have 11 × and 6 × respectively number of firms per 100,000 employees.
- Small firms appear to be dominant in Japan and Italy (manufacturing).

Table 1.5 question:

- Why are manufacturing firms so much smaller in Italy and Japan?

Table 1.6 statements:

- In the UK, 0.2 per cent of firms are 'large' (500+ employees) but employ 30 per cent of the workforce.
- The UK appears to be close to EUR 12 average on this measure.

Table 1.6 questions:

- Is EUR 12 average meaningful?
- What extremes does it conceal?

Table 1.7 statements:

- Almost 3 million firms with less than 20 employees only provide 28.6 per cent of total employment and 13 per cent of turnover (0.0000095 per cent each).

- Whereas 3,000 firms with 500+ employees provide 34.2 per cent of total employment and 41.6 per cent of turnover (0.14 per cent each)
- and 1,000 firms with 1,000 + employees provide 27.5 per cent of total employment and 30.4 per cent of turnover (0.3 per cent each).

Table 1.7 questions:

- How many small (less than 200 employees) firms would be needed to replace *one* firm with over 1,000 employees (in turnover and employment)?
- If small firms in UK are insignificant, why should they be encouraged?
- Is it realistic to suggest that a policy to aid small firm growth can compensate for employment lost through deindustrialization?

Table 1.8 statements:

- Contribution of small firms declined from 1958–68
- but *rose* sharply 1968–89.

Table 1.8 questions:

- Is this a consequence of deindustrialisation (and what is this anyway)?
- Is this evidence sufficient to justify a small firms policy?

Chapter 2

The basic problem: scarcity, choice and allocation

SCARCITY AND CHOICE

Here is the fundamental proposition of economics: however abundant resources (materials, skills, land, etc.) might appear to be, human wants are always likely to exceed our capacity to provide.

Even if you won first prize in the National Lottery, and set out to decide how to use your £5 million, you would always be able to find good causes to support however good you are at spending money. The earth's natural and human resources are *always* scarce in relation to human wants. We do therefore spend all our time making choices between desired goods and services, because our resources, individual or communal, are *never* sufficient to carry out all our desired economic transactions.

Thus the first interesting question faced by the economist is, how do we make choices? The answer is quite simple. We make these choices between alternative ways of allocating (using) scarce resources on the basis of *opportunity cost*.

Definition: opportunity cost

The cost of carrying out one choice (say buying a new car) is at that moment, the opportunity forgone (say buying a new kitchen).

Activity 2.1

What might be the opportunity cost to a TV broadcasting company of making next year an extra major dramatic series based on a classical author such as Dickens or Thackeray?

BASIC TOOL-KIT

Let us remind ourselves of the basic tools which the economists use (covered in detail in Chapter 1). We need to use models (based on theories) in order to analyse and give meaning to data.

Definition: model and data

A model is framework, often in graphical format, which is based on assumptions which simplify the complexities of the real world. It helps us to think about problems in an organized way.

Data is information collected by many agencies for a variety of reasons. It is the only link the economist has with reality.

By feeding data into models we can begin to make sense of reality, generating explanations and predictions.

Two kinds of data presentation may be of interest to an economist. First, changes in a variable over time are plotted on a graph, with magnitudes of the variable on the vertical axis and time periods on the horizontal axis (see Figure 2.1).

Next we are attempting to explore the relationship between two variables. Each point on the diagram represents the magnitude of one variable (sales volume) given the other variable's magnitude (price) at that point in time. From Figure 2.2 we can establish that there is a pattern. If we

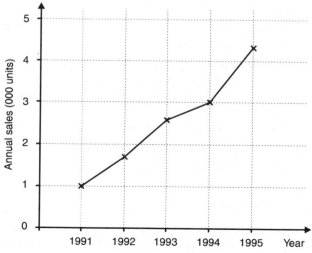

Figure 2.1 Time series data

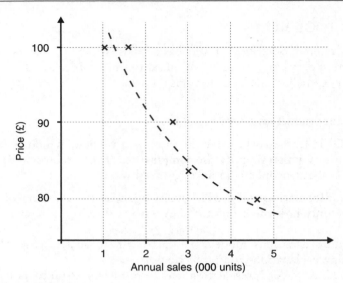

Figure 2.2 A scatter diagram

draw a line through the points which have an equal number of points on either side, and most of the points are quite close to the line, then a negative relationship appears to exist between the variables.

However the existence of this relationship does not prove a causal connection. We cannot say that if price falls it causes volume to increase. We can only say that this seems to be likely, given the historical data and other things being equal.

You might already have noticed that there are a number of thoughts which arise from this proposition:

- There must be some physical limit to the *total* amount of goods and services that a community can generate at any time.
- There are various combinations of goods and services which may be produced within that limit.
- There probably are a great many ways in which the total amount of goods and services produced might be shared by the population, some more or less equitable than others.

ALLOCATIVE MECHANISMS

If individuals and society as a whole are constantly faced with an endless range of choices to be made, by what means do they make those choices? This is obviously a question of central concern to an economist, just as it is to you as an individual and as a manager trying to make your budget spin out over all the things which must be done.

Basically three mechanisms are available:

1 *Central planning*: where government, for example, makes all allocative decisions between alternatives which might be summed up as 'guns' or 'butter'. Such decisions will be based on strategic considerations as to what the people ought to want, stemming from the subjective views of those who happen to be in government. (We will see later that this also takes place inside firms.)

2 *Markets*: where individuals and firms make decisions on what to produce and consume, on the basis of what they feel they want to consume, and on their guess as to what their firm needs to produce in order to satisfy the perceived needs of the public. (The question is *how* are these decisions made, we will address this later).

3 *Some combinations of the above*: where some decisions are left to individuals and firms, while others are made by government for us. (The question then is *which* should government make?)

Where government makes all the decisions, a *planned economy* exists. Planned in the sense that government must attempt to accommodate its choices within the overall resource constraint. Where individuals and firms make the decisions, there must exist some mechanism through which decisions may be made. We refer to this mechanism as the market. For markets to exist either barter must take place (which is very limiting) or money must exist to measure value, and enable transactions to take place. Where some combination of the two methods operates (which is the case in almost all economic systems) we refer to this as a *mixed economy*. In a mixed economy decisions have to be made as to which goods and services will be left to market forces to generate, and which should be provided by government and financed by a levy (taxation) on all citizens.

We in the UK are currently moving away from government provision in many fields towards market-based systems. This is the problem which faces the British Broadcasting Corporation (BBC) and the National Health Service (NHS). We have summarized the argument so far in Figure 2.3.

THE PRODUCTION POSSIBILITY MODEL

We saw that the basic economic problem is the allocation to different uses of inherently scarce resources to meet human wants. Resources consist of three categories, land (including all natural resources extracted from the land or sea), labour and capital (surplus income used to develop plant, machines and technology). These are combined in appropriate quantities to carry out specific tasks by entrepreneurs who see an opportunity to satisfy a want. The entrepreneurs may be private individuals, or state organizations.

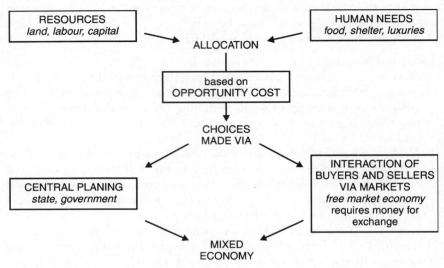

Figure 2.3 The economic problem

There must be some limit to the amount of goods and services which may be produced. This will be determined by the current state of technology, and the amount of resources available. If the resources are combined and used in the best possible way, then production will be maximized. In overall terms this will ensure the availability of the maximum amount of goods and services to satisfy wants.

We can see that a number of other questions arise, such as: how do we arrive at the most efficient way of using resources, how do the decisions get made about what to produce and in what quantities, and how are they to be shared out fairly? We will tackle these questions later. At this point we want to discover whether we can model the process of resource allocation in such a way as to derive explanations and predictions about the economic dilemma on an initially limited scale. To do so we will construct a simple model, the production possibility frontier model.

THE PRODUCTION POSSIBILITY FRONTIER

We have seen that to construct models it is necessary to simplify – a simple diagrammatic model can only deal with two variables at once (see Figure 2.4). So let us make some assumptions:

- Let food represent all essential goods and services which are necessary for life.

- Let films represent all consumer luxuries, which are desirable but not essential to life.
- Let us put some numbers on each variable, quantities of units.
- Plot food units on the vertical axis, and films units on the horizontal axis.
- With the available resources the economy is able to produce various quantities of food, plus films, on the basis of more food less films and vice versa.

If all resources are devoted to food, twenty-five units can be produced, if all resources are devoted to films, twenty-eight may be produced. If we join these points on the diagram, we have a range of possible combinations of food and films which may be produced given present resource and technology constraints. That is to say at any point on the line AE the economy is operating efficiently.

Thus at point B some resources are used for films rather than food, and twenty-two units of food may be produced, plus nine units of films. The trade-off is three less units of food to gain nine of films. The slope of the curve describes the trade-off, or opportunity cost. What about point G? Here ten units of food are being produced and eighteen of films. At G the economy is inefficient because more could be produced of one good without sacrificing any of the other. There are unemployed resources and if the economy were better organized, it could move say to point C or D, or any point in between C and D.

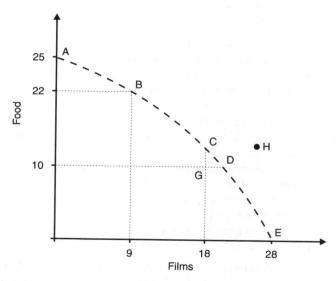

Figure 2.4 A production possibility frontier

What about point H? This point lies beyond our line A to E. We can produce any combination of food and films on or below that line, but none at any point beyond the line.

Activity 2.2

Can you write down below:

1 Three reasons why an economy might be operating at point G.
2 Three ways in which the line AE (the production possibility frontier) may be pushed outwards until it includes point H?

As usual our model has generated more questions than answers. For example:

- How do we get to AE?
- How do we push the frontier out to include H?
- Who decides what proportion of food and films are produced in our national output?
- How do we share the produce out equitably?

Can you spot the question which cannot be tackled by positive economics? If not, go back a few pages and make sure you know the differene between positive and normative statements or questions.

We have developed our first model. Can we derive any general propositions from it?

- Society should seek to produce at AE the frontier, i.e. produce as efficiently as possible, since people would like to consume as much of both types of produce as possible.
- It is wasteful of scarce economic resources to produce at any point below AE, that is, everybody loses.
- Society must find some way of choosing the point on the production possibility frontier which describes the desired proportions in which films and food be produced.
- If society wishes to consume more than is permitted by AE, then it must find some way of increasing resources (population growth, find fresh deposits of natural resources, borrow capital from abroad, or improve technology and ensure that it is efficiently deployed).
- The combination of products chosen by society will be determined either by the market or the government or some combination of the two.

Right now we can develop this idea a little further together with the help of Vilfredo Pareto, a famous Italian scholar working in the early twentieth century. It has been implicit in all that we have said so far that the test of any economic system is whether it permits all its citizens to maximize their satisfaction (which Pareto called 'welfare'). For this highly desirable state of affairs to exist three conditions must be fulfilled:

1 Distribution of goods between consumers must be optimized.
2 Allocations of inputs into productive users must be optimized.
3 The output of goods must be optimized (at the production possibility frontier which we have just examined).

It is unlikely that these conditions can be perfectly fulfilled in practice, for reasons which will emerge as the course develops. However, if the conditions could be fulfilled we could arrive at the **Pareto optimal welfare condition.**

Definition: Pareto optimal welfare condition

An allocation of resources is Pareto efficient for a given set of consumer tastes, resources and technology, if it is impossible to move to another allocation which would make some people better off and nobody worse off.

To summarize:

- A move from point G in Figure 2.4 to any point between C and D is *Pareto improving*.
- All points on AE are *Pareto optimal*.
- No points inside AE are Pareto optimal.

We are left with two big questions at the end of this section:

- By what mechanisms does the economic system strive to attain Pareto optimality? A positive question.
- Even if we achieve Pareto welfare, how are the goods and services to be shared? A normative question if we are thinking of fairness, but a positive one if we are simply interested in how it happens.

We suggested that there are basically two ways in which allocative decisions may be made, by planning (such as by the government) or by markets. Our next task is to build an understanding of how markets work, and how they might fail. We are unlikely to achieve Pareto welfare maximization if markets fail, and then governments must act.

SUMMARY

The principal ideas which we have introduced in this chapter are that:

- *scarcity* arises from the limited availability of resources and the unlimited nature of human wants
- society must therefore make *choices* between alternatives
- the true cost of something is the *value of the rejected opportunity* – called the **opportunity cost**
- there are two basic mechanisms for making allocative decisions: *planning* and *markets*
- a definition of **efficiency** is when society's output is *on the production possibility frontier* and when *no individual can become better off without making someone else worse off* – known as **Pareto Optimal**.

Activities feedback

Activity 2.1 answer

Whatever number of game shows, soap episodes, or documentaries could have been made for the same cost as the drama series.

Activity 2.2 answers

1 Any three of the following: unemployment, low labour productivity, unused land, lack of demand, bad management of resources.
2 Reverse any of the above; develop new technology.

Chapter 3

Modelling the market

INTRODUCTION

Whether we like it or not, we all spend much of our time playing the market game. Buying a London Underground ticket, filling up the car with fuel, buying a newspaper or a can of Coke involves us in a market-place just as much as if we were to go to a street market to buy vegetables. The economist is interested in a number of questions:

- What do markets do?
- How do they work?
- Do they ever fail?
- If they do fail, can society intervene to make them work better?
- If so, how should we do so?

Later we shall be looking at some of these issues in specific contexts, but at this stage we need to understand the mechanics of markets as economists have modelled them.

Definition: market

An exchange mechanism that brings together buyers and sellers of a product, factor of production (land, labour or capital), or financial security. The market may or may not have a specific geographical location.

More specifically:

'A group of products which consumers view as being substitutes for one another' (Pass, Lowes and Davies, 1988).

The efficient operation of a market depends on successful transmission of information among buyers and sellers. From the buyers' point of view, the important information relates to the merits of products and services in relation to their function, and for sellers the opportunity to utilize their resources advantageously. You will notice that I have been rather vague as to what form these merits and opportunities might take, and the manner in which they might be transmitted. The basis of the economist's view on these matters is as follows:

- **Price** acts as the signal, which can contain the information required for the consumer to make the comparisons needed to measure opportunity cost and make rational decisions.
- **Profit** provides the motive and the signal for owners of factors of production in deciding to what use those factors might be put.

Activity 3.1

1 You are thinking of buying a new hand held Dictaphone, you discover that these may be bought from a selection of six models, from different manufacturers, at prices ranging from £22 to £140.

Do you make your choice solely on price? If not, what other factors do you take into consideration? List them.

2 You are planning to use the Dictaphone to rough out the first draft of a book which you have in mind.

Do you make your decision about the nature and content of the book on the basis solely of the profit (in the form of royalties) which you might make from it? If not, what other factors do you take into account? List them.

A little earlier we decided that the economist must really start from the assumption that people act rationally in their own self-interest. We have introduced a further possibility, that it is possible for price to contain all the information necessary for rational decisions to be made. I think Activity 3.1 will have convinced you that this is not so and that actions are rarely entirely based on information which price can convey. However, in the interests of constructing a simplified working model of economic decision making, we must continue to sustain these assumptions, for the time being at least. We have also suggested that if markets could work, then welfare (satisfaction) would be maximized for all. As we develop the model you will see how this might be so. Before you dismiss this possibility on the grounds that we have just established that price cannot provide all the information we need, and that profit alone cannot be the only motive at work for suppliers, consider the alternative possibility – that markets might in fact be the best way of solving the resource allocation problem even if they are inherently messy.

Messy markets

The market is frightening, even terrifying. It's not pretty. It's surely irrational. Yet over the long haul, the unfettered market works for the most rational of reasons. It produces more experiments, more tries, more wins, more losses, more information processed (market signals) faster than any alternative.

(Tom Peters, 1992: 485)

As you read the next rather rarefied section, it is important to bear in mind Tom Peters's wise words. If the unfettered market works faster and better than the alternatives of state dictate and planning, or even manipulated market-places, then use of the market should be considered a possibility, even for activities which we have grown used to thinking of as only appropriately delivered through state activity or intervention.

The argument in the rest of this chapter is very condensed. Remember, we are building a simplified model of reality, not painting a detailed portrait.

THE LAW OF DEMAND

The **law of demand** is that the quantity of a good demanded (per period of time) will *rise* as price *falls* (*other things being equal*). There are two reasons for this:

- *Income effect*: the fall in the price of a product will increase the consumer's real income, affecting his decision making to a degree dependent on the proportion of his income spent on this product.
- *Substitution effect*: the price fall means that the good is now cheaper relative to others. This good will now be substituted for some other. The extent to which substitution occurs will depend on the availability and similarity of possible substitutes.

Activity 3.2

Now try to restate the above arguments for a situation where the price of goods has risen.

If we now assume that all other influences on demand for a product in the market other than price do not change, we can develop the relationship between price and demand in diagrammatic form. In this model price is always conventionally plotted on the vertical axis of a graph and quantity demanded on the horizontal axis (see Figure 3.1). Thus spending £150 buying a widget would seriously reduce real income, and a cheaper

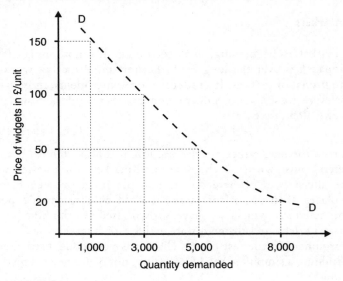

Figure 3.1 The demand curve

substitute would be sought. Total sales are therefore only 1,000 units. At lower prices, (£100, £50 and £20) progressively larger quantities would be bought because it would make sense for consumers to substitute widgets for some other product.

We can therefore conclude that demand for goods will rise as price falls, and fall as price rises. The curve DD is the demand curve. It normally slopes downwards from left to right.

The model which we have just developed needs just a little more explanation. Each individual consumer would have a demand schedule showing how much he or she would purchase at a range of prices. If we sum all the individual schedules together, we will have a market demand curve. This is what we have drawn in Figure 3.1.

All this may seem to be a statement of the obvious, so let's see whether we can develop the model a little further:

- Movements along the demand curve indicate relationships between quantity demanded and price.
- The shape of the curve (steep or shallow) indicates the degree of responsiveness of quantity demanded to change in quantity demanded to a big change in price. If it is very shallow there will be a very big change in quantity demanded in response to a small change in price. This phenomenon is known as price elasticity of demand. You may be

interested in reading more about this in the Technical appendix at the end of this chapter.

- We can say at this stage that a change in price will cause a change in quantity demanded, represented by a shift along the demand curve.
- But we do not yet know why the curve sits where it does.

We can make our model more powerful if we consider what factors (other than price) might influence the state of demand for a good. The additional factors influencing demand may be summarized as follows:

- Taste: perceptions of the desirability/usefulness of the goods.
- Substitutes: number and availability of substitutes (e.g. if the price of a competing substitute such as tea/coffee rises, demand for the good rises. If the price of a complementary good rises, cigarettes/matches, demand for the goods falls.)
- Income: if income rises, demand for the goods will rise.

Thus we can summarize:

- Demand for a good depends on its own price (P), on the price of substitutes (Ps), on consumers; income (I) and on consumers' tastes (T).
  Demand = f(P,Ps,I,T)

where 'f' is 'function of'.

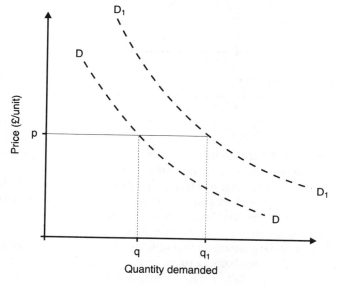

Figure 3.2 A shift in the demand curve

- Changes in price cause shifts in the level of demand along the demand curve. Changes in determinants of demand other than price will cause shifts of the whole curve from left to right or right to left.

This process is illustrated in Figure 3.2. If the real income of all potential purchasers of widgets rises, then it is likely that more widgets will be bought at any price. Thus, at price p, q_1 widgets will be bought rather than q.

Activity 3.3

On Figure 3.3, draw what happens to the demand curve in the following circumstances:

a) a cheaper substitute product comes on to the market.
b) the widget manufacturing company launches a massive advertising campaign.

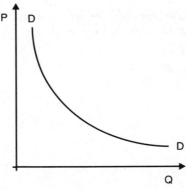

Figure 3.3 Activity diagram

THE LAW OF SUPPLY

If we want to model the behaviour of markets it is not enough to deal only with the consumer, we need to look at the behaviour of suppliers of goods.

The **law of supply** is that it is likely that producers of goods will prefer to supply more at high prices and less at low prices (all other factors being equal). New suppliers are likely to enter the market if price rises, old suppliers are likely to leave the market if price falls.

Just like consumers, suppliers will individually respond to changes in price. Any supplier will want to supply more if price is high and less if price is low. If we sum together the likely responses of all suppliers of a product, we can produce a supply curve (Figure 3.4) to add to our diagram of the market.

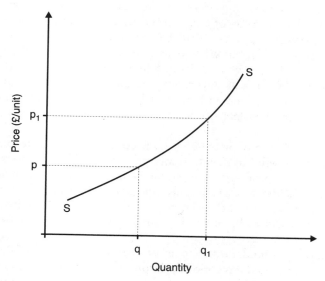

Figure 3.4 The supply curve

As with demand, changes in price will cause movement along the curve. At price p, quantity q will be produced, where if price rises to p_1, quantity supplied will rise to q_1. But there are other determinants of supply which may shift the curve to left or right, less or more respectively being produced at any given price. These might be:

- Costs of production – these may be changed by changes in input prices, technology, reorganization, government taxes/subsidies.
- Profits available on substitute or alternative products – e.g. effect of satellite TV on supply of terrestrial channels.
- Random shocks – e.g. drought effects on supply of grain.

We can conclude that the supply curve is likely to slope upwards from left to right, and its slope will reflect elasticity of supply in response to changes in price.

We are now ready to complete the construction of our simple model of the market by putting the demand curve and supply curve on to the same graph. The completed diagram is called the price (or market) mechanism.

THE MARKET MECHANISM

If we now plot the demand and supply curves on the same diagram, we can determine the output and price towards which the market will tend to move given the current conditions in the market. That is we will assume that none of the other determinants of demand and supply, other than price, changes. You will instantly see a problem here. Market conditions are inherently dynamic and unstable, but we have assumed static conditions in the market place. This is obviously unrealistic, but necessary if we are to build our simplified model. It will nevertheless retain quite strong predictive and explanatory powers. Even with our restrictive assumptions, we can simulate quite a number of effects of changes in other variables. First the simple model.

In Figure 3.5, at any price above £5 producers will want to supply more than consumers will buy, while at any price below £5 consumers will want to buy more than producers will put on the market. We can now draw a very important conclusion: there is only one output and one price which will satisfy both producers and consumers – in this case 3,000 units at £5 each. The market is said to be in equilibrium at point E where the demand and supply curves intersect.

This model is fundamental to most economic theory. It is a powerful explanatory and predictive model, despite the limitations imposed by our initial assumptions which cause it to be a static not a dynamic model. It is very important that you grasp this model at an early stage. If you want to

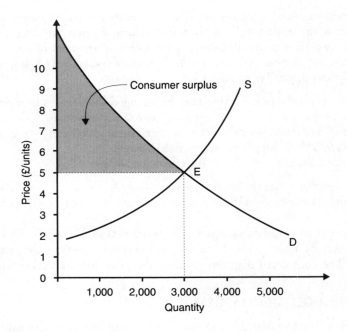

Figure 3.5 Market equilibrium

understand the mechanics of the model in more detail, you will find that we return to this later. Before we move on to an Activity which invites you to manipulate the model to examine its predictive powers, here are a couple of important reminders:

- Be careful not to confuse shifts along the demand and supply curves (due to changes in price) with shifts of the curves (due to changes in factors other than price).
- Changes in price change quantities demanded or supplied along the curve. Changes in other factors change the conditions of demand or supply by moving the curve.

ACTIVITY 3.4

Here are three demand and supply diagrams, representing three different markets. Each market is affected by an event described under the diagram. Try to use the diagram to make predictions of what would happen in each case:

1 Labour Market (Figure 3.6)

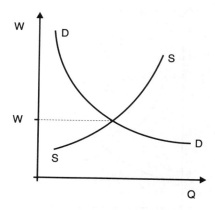

Figure 3.6 Labour market: demand and supply curves

The government imposes a minimum wage which is above the current equilibrium wage, W.

2 Domestic fuel (Figure 3.7)

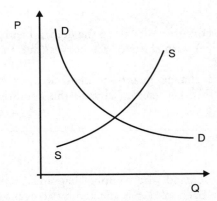

Figure 3.7 Domestic fuel: demand and supply curves

The government imposes an increase in VAT.

3 Coffee (Figure 3.8)

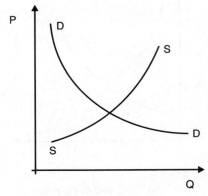

Figure 3.8 Coffee: demand and supply curves

The coffee crop fails?

MARKETS AND CONSUMER WELFARE

The demand curve does not only convey positive information about quantities bought at various prices. It also contains important normative information. By indicating the *willingness to pay* of society for given quantities it implicitly indicates the consumers' valuation of the product in terms of opportunity cost. Thus in Figure 3.5, to the left of point E when less than 3,000 are produced, the willingness to pay of consumers is greater than the willingness to supply of producers.

In this case an increase in output is Pareto improving since it leaves no one worse off:

- Consumers are better off as they can consume more at a lower price.
- Producers are better off because they can be paid more than they require to increase production.
- Only at E is this no longer the case, so E is a Pareto optimum. (Refer back to Chapter 2 to remind yourself about this idea.)
- A shift away from E would make someone in the economy worse off. If fewer than 3,000 units are produced, some consumers would go without and the rest would pay a higher price. If more than 3,000 units are produced, the price would fall below £50 and producers would no longer cover their costs.

At the equilibrium E *consumer surplus* is available to all buyers, that is, all buyers before the last one bringing us to point E would have been willing to pay more than the actual price of £50. Thus the shaded area on Figure 3.5 represents the total consumer surplus generated by the market. This is at its maximum at point E and so the equilibrium is efficient in terms of consumption.

SUMMARY

The important ideas about markets that we have studied in this section are:

- The **law of demand** – consumers wish to buy more at a low price and less at a high price. This is represented by the demand curve which slopes downward.
- The law of supply – the quantity which producers offer for sale will rise if the price rises. This is represented by the supply curve which slopes upward.
- The market mechanism is the process by which the price adjusts until the wishes of consumers are just matched by the offers of suppliers. This is where the demand curve crosses the supply curve. It is the market equilibrium price.
- The market equilibrium is an efficient allocation because a move away

from it would result in either reduced consumer surplus, or in lost surplus for producers.

TECHNICAL APPENDIX: ELASTICITIES

Price elasticity of demand

Definition

Price elasticity of demand measures the responsiveness of quantity demanded of a good to a change in price. It is calculated by the following formula:

$$\text{price elasticity of demand} = \frac{\% \text{ change in quantity demanded}}{\% \text{ change in price}}$$

Key classifications of elasticity

- If the change in demand is more than proportionate in its response to a price change demand is said to be price elastic.
- If the change in demand is less than proportionate in its response to a price change demand is said to be price inelastic.
- If the change in demand is of equal proportion in its response to a price change demand is said to be unit elastic.

The value of price elasticity is determined by availability and price of close substitutes. If there are no, or few, substitutes then the demand will be inelastic, or vice versa.

The use of price elasticity

Why is price elasticity important? It turns out that a knowledge of price elasticity immediately tells us how revenue receipts are affected by a change in price. We can see this as follows:

- Total revenue = price × quantity demanded.
- Because the demand curve slopes downward, price and quantity demanded move in opposite directions. So an increase in price, which tends to increase revenue, is accompanied by a reduction in quantity, which tends to decrease revenue. The net effect of a price change on total revenue therefore depends on whether the change in quantity is proportionally larger or smaller than the change in price.
- Consider the effect of a 10 per cent price increase:
  - If demand is price elastic, quantity demanded falls by more than 10 per cent, so that total revenue decreases.

- When demand is price inelastic, quantity demanded falls by less than 10 per cent so that total revenue increases.
- If demand is unit elastic, quantity demanded falls by exactly 10 per cent and total revenue is unchanged.
• The effects would, of course, be reversed for a price reduction. The revenue effects of reducing price would be as follows:
  - If demand is price elastic a price reduction increases revenue.
  - If demand is price inelastic, a price reduction decreases revenue.
  - If demand is price unit elastic, a price reduction leaves revenue unchanged.

Graphs

Elasticity will show up on our representation of the demand curve in the slope of the curve (see Figure 3.9). (Beware the distorting effect that a change of scale in the diagram might introduce.)

For reasons which may be demonstrated mathematically, elasticity will be different at different points on the demand curve.

Example: should there be advertising on the BBC?

A suggested alternative to the licence fee for funding the BBC is to require the corporation to sell airtime for advertising. A key question in this debate is whether or not the increased number of advertising slots would increase the total revenue available to the broadcasting industry.

If we assume that there is no unmet demand at current airtime prices, the only way to sell additional slots would be to reduce the price to advertisers. You can now see that putting advertising on the BBC would increase total advertising revenue for the broadcasting industry if the demand for advertising slots is price elastic, but would reduce it if demand is price inelastic.

Estimates of advertising price elasticities are quite variable, but several authoritative studies suggest that the demand for TV advertising is price inelastic. It has also been suggested that the demand for radio advertising may be price elastic. It was partly because of these estimates that the 1986 Committee on Financing the BBC (the Peacock Committee) recommended that BBC TV should not be required to sell advertising, but that advertising should be considered as an option for Radio 1 and Radio 2.

Although elasticities are potentially useful in the way suggested by the BBC example, there can be severe practical difficulties in measuring them, as there is often insufficient data at a sufficient range of prices. Demand studies lead to statistical estimates, which often have quite wide confidence intervals.

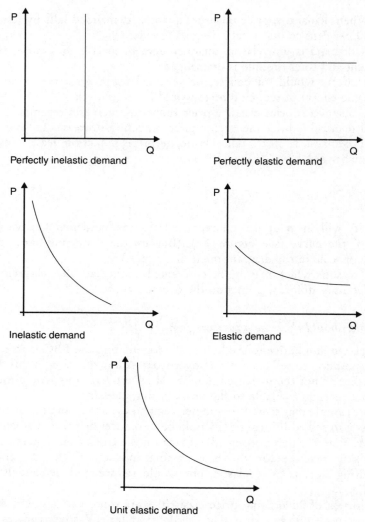

Figure 3.9 Elastic/inelastic demand curves

Income elasticity of demand

Definition

Income elasticity of demand measures responsiveness of quantity demanded to a change in income. It is measured by the following formula:

$$\text{income elasticity of demand} = \frac{\text{\% change in quantity demanded}}{\text{\% change in disposable income}}$$

If response of demand to a change in income is more than proportionate, demand is said to be income elastic. If response of demand to a change in income is less than proportionate, demand is said to be income inelastic. Staple products (e.g. bread) tend to have an income elasticity of demand of less than one (inelastic), whilst luxury products are likely to have income elasticities of greater than one (elastic) e.g. electrical goods. It is clear that increases in income are likely to cause increases in demand for most (but not all) products.

Cross elasticity of demand

In many markets there are a number of similar versions of the product available, e.g. cars. The demand curve for cars (as a generic market) is likely to be relatively inelastic both on price and income, since few direct substitutes exist. However, *within* that market a number of products are available from several manufacturers aimed at the same market niche. The demand for each product is therefore likely to be much more elastic than that for cars in general.

We can use elasticities to examine the impact on both market demand, and the demand for individual products of changes in the price of substitutes, e.g. railway travel for cars as a whole, or Vauxhall Astra for Ford Escort. This relationship is called cross elasticity of demand, and is measured by the following demand, and is measured by the following formula:

$$\text{cross elasticity of demand} = \frac{\text{\% change in quantity demanded of good A}}{\text{\% change in the price of product B}}$$

If a small change in the price of good B results in a large increase in demand for good A, indicating a high cross elasticity value, then A and B may be regarded as close substitutes. Thus where products are substitutes, cross elasticity value will be positive. If two products are complementary to each other, e.g. tennis rackets and tennis balls, then an increase in the price of one will lead to a fall in the demand for both, i.e. the cross elasticity value will be negative.

CASE STUDY 2: THE OASIS CONCERT

Newcomers to economics will have found the development of a theory of the market in this chapter rather abstract. You may feel that it says nothing about *your* behaviour as a consumer. The exercise which follows is intended to make that missing connection. You are asked to make a simple decision – what is the highest price you would pay to attend a concert given by the popular band Oasis. If you can collect this information from a reasonable number of other students, we can develop a realistic picture of this particular market. Your entrepreneurial interests might also be activated – you may see the possibility of profit for yourself if you could arrange such a concert, that is if you became an entrepreneur in the business of promoting concerts. We also hope you will develop a better feel for the possibilities and weaknesses of conventional economic models.

A consumer demand exercise

Objectives

1 To use real world data to construct a demand curve.
2 To consider the implications of the demand curve derived.
3 To give students an opportunity to manipulate economic data and to see how a model is developed.

Methods

1 It is suggested that students work in pairs on the material provided.
2 Make sure graph paper is available.
3 Data to be generated from the student questionnaire.

How much are you prepared to pay for a pop concert? The questionnaire in Figure 3.10 is intended to collect data which we will use to study the economics of consumer demand. Please indicate your answer to the questions. Obtain as many responses as possible from friends by copying this sheet for their use.

Case study feedback

Introduction

Firms usually have some discretion over the price they charge consumers, unless they are in a perfectly competitive market (see later in the course). So what price should they charge, and how should they decide? This exercise uses the demand curve model with your data, collected in the survey, to find the price that maximizes the income from a pop concert. We will explore the principles and practicalities of the model.

OASIS CONCERT THIS SATURDAY!!

Suppose that the band from Manchester is playing (in your town) this Saturday, starting at 9.00 pm. Would you want to go? What is the HIGHEST PRICE you would be prepared to pay and still be willing to go?

If you would not be interested in going, even if tickets were free, then please put a cross in the box below in answer 1.

If you would be interested, then please put a circle round ONE ONLY of the prices in the list below in answer 2. If you would only go if the concert is free, then circle zero. Note that we want to know the maximum price which you would consider paying. Do not say what you think the actual ticket price might be, nor what you think the market will stand. We will examine those issues in class. We just want to know the highest price at which you would still go to the concert.

1   I *would not* go to the Oasis concert even if it were free. (Please put a cross in the box.) ☐

2   I *would* be interested in the Oasis concert. The maximum price which I would pay is circled below.

£99	£89	£79	£69	£59	£49	£39	£29	£19	£9
£98	£88	£78	£68	£58	£48	£38	£28	£18	£8
£97	£87	£77	£67	£57	£47	£37	£27	£17	£7
£96	£86	£76	£66	£56	£46	£36	£26	£16	£6
£95	£85	£75	£65	£55	£45	£35	£25	£15	£5
£94	£84	£74	£64	£54	£44	£34	£24	£14	£4
£93	£83	£73	£63	£53	£43	£33	£23	£13	£3
£92	£82	£72	£62	£52	£42	£32	£22	£12	£2
£91	£81	£71	£61	£51	£41	£31	£21	£11	£1
£90	£80	£70	£60	£50	£40	£30	£20	£10	£0

Figure 3.10 Oasis concert questionnaire

Questionnaire results

(Insert your own data in place of the examples given below.)

- Questionnaires counted: 203
- Would not go to the Oasis concert: 19
- Maximum willingness to pay of remainder distributed as follows:

£0	£2	£3	£4	£5	£6	£7	£8	£9	£10	£11	£12	£13	£15	£16
8	2	3	1	10	4	2	7	5	27	3	12	1	28	2

£17	£18	£19	£20	£22	£25	£26	£28	£30	£35	£37	£40	£50	£69	£99+
1	3	1	23	2	22	2	3	5	1	1	2	1	1*	2

* In fact, 13 questionnaires indicated a willingness to pay £69. Careful handwriting analysis indicated that all these were submitted by the same individual!

Tasks

1 Calculate the quantity of tickets sold at each price (demand schedule) and the revenue for each quantity sold (revenue schedule in Table 3.1 below). We will do this for prices of £30 and below, as demand and revenue at low above this price.
   a) At any given price, all those whose willingness to pay is above that price will buy tickets.
   b) The dominant consumers of pop concerts are the 16–24 age group.
   c) The questionnaire sample is representative of Bradford's 16–24 age group. (Pretty unlikely!)
   d) Bradford's 16–24 year old population is about 53,000.

Table 3.1 Revenue schedule

Price	£30	£28	£26	£25	£22	£20	£19	£18	£17	£16	£15	£13
Number of sample with wtp > P (1)												
Quantity Demanded (1) ÷ 203 × 53,000												
Revenue = Quantity × Price												
Price	£12	£11	£10	£9	£8	£7	£6	£5	£4	£3	£2	£0
Number of sample with wtp > P (1)												
Quantity Demanded (1) ÷ 203 × 53,000												
Revenue = Quantity × Price												

2 Plot demand curve. (Price on the vertical axis, quantity demanded on the horizontal axis) Cf. fig. 3.1.
3 Plot revenue curve. (Revenue on the vertical axis, quantity demanded on the horizontal axis).
4 The revenue curve is rather jagged (see discussion below). Draw an approximately smoothed version of the revenue curve on your graph. Roughly what price maximizes revenue? What is the revenue? How many tickets are sold?

Feedback   Compare your results with Table 3.2, and Figures 3.11 and 3.12.

Table 3.2 Demand and revenue schedules

Price	£30	£28	£26	£25	£22	£20	£19	£18	£17	£16	£15	£13
Number of sample with wtp > P (1)	13	16	17	39	41	64	65	68	69	71	99	100
Quantity Demanded (1) ÷ 203 × 53,000	3.4K	4.2K	4.4K	10.2K	10.7K	16.7K	17.0K	17.8K	18.0K	18.5K	25.8K	26.1K
Revenue = Quantity × Price	102K	117K	115K	254K	235K	334K	322K	320K	306K	297K	388K	339K

Price	£12	£11	£10	£9	£8	£7	£6	£5	£4	£3	£2	£0
Number of sample with wtp > P (1)	112	115	142	147	154	156	160	170	171	174	176	184
Quantity Demanded (1) ÷ 203 × 53,000	29.2K	30.0K	37.1K	38.4K	40.2K	40.7K	41.8K	44.4K	44.6K	45.4K	46.0K	48.0K
Revenue = Quantity × Price	351K	330K	371K	345K	322K	285K	251K	222K	179K	136K	92K	46K

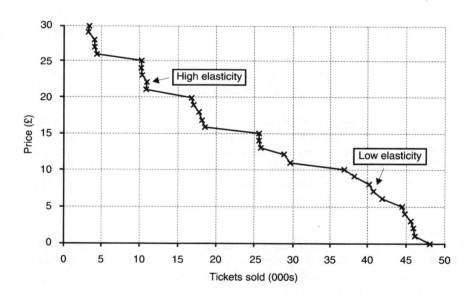

Figure 3.11 Demand curve

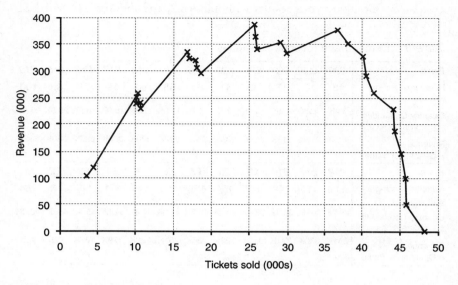

Figure 3.12 Revenue curve

Discussion points

Demand curve

1 Why does the demand curve slope down in this case?
2 What would happen to the demand curve if there were to be a Blur concert the following night?
3 What would happen to the demand curve if the government gave a start-of-year book grant of £30 per student?
4 Suppose the organizers choose a price of £10 per ticket. What is the consumer surplus for a student with a willingness-to-pay of £25?
5 How would you go about estimating the total consumer surplus if the price were, say £10?

Revenue curve

1 Why does the revenue curve have the general shape that it does? That is, why does it initially increase as quantity increases, and then turn round and decrease as quantity increases further? (If you are stuck, look in Pass and Lowes, 1994).
2 Why do you think the revenue curve is jagged? Is this telling us something about the market, or just about the survey? What might you do to overcome this problem?

3 Is maximizing revenue the same as maximizing profit?

Sample, questionnaire procedure and assumptions   Do you think the results are representative of the potential market? The results and assumptions imply that 70 per cent of Bradford's 16–24 age group would want tickets at £10, no less than 37,000 people! Is this realistic? What might be done to make the survey more accurate?

Linking revenue and elasticity

Price elasticity of demand measures the price sensitivity of the quantity demanded (the slope of the demand curve), expressed in terms of proportions. That is:

$$\text{Price elasticity of demand} = \frac{(\% \text{ change in quantity demanded})}{(\% \text{ change in price})}$$

- If demand is price elastic (>1), then a 1 per cent reduction in price leads to a more than 1 per cent increase in quantity sold.
- If demand is price inelastic (<1), then a 1 per cent reduction in price leads to a less than 1 per cent increase in quantity sold.
- If demand is unit elastic ($=1$), in price, then a 1 per cent reduction in price leads to exactly a 1 per cent increase in quantity sold.

We can link revenue and price elasticity as follows.

- If demand is price elastic, a price reduction will reduce revenue, since the gain from selling more exceeds the loss from reducing price.
- If demand is price inelastic, a price reduction will reduce revenue, since the gain from selling more is less than the loss from reducing price.
- If demand is unit elastic, a price reduction will leave revenue unchanged, since the gain from selling more exactly balances the loss from reducing price.

Now, by comparing your demand and revenue curves, you can see which part of the demand curve is elastic (corresponding to the upward sloping part of the smoothed revenue curve), which part is inelastic (where the revenue curve is downward sloping) and where it is unit elastic (where the revenue curve is level). Try checking this by calculating approximate elasticities from your demand curve. Pick a price (P), note the corresponding demand (Q). Then mark at short range along the curve either side of P and Q, and note the corresponding AP and AQ. You may need to draw a smoothed version. The elasticity is then found by calculating. It only need be rough!

Discussion points feedback

Demand curve

1   The downward slope is essentially due to the distribution of tastes among potential consumers, who consequently have different willingness to pay. (Pass and Lowes's, 1994, discussion of indifference curve analysis in box 2.1 is not really relevant here, as we are looking at the demand for a single event. The indifference curve assumes you trade-off between variable quantities of goods.)
2   Demand would move left, as Blur fans divert their income towards their preferred group.
3   Demand would move right. Even if the grant is in the form of a voucher, it raises the students' disposable income, and more will go to the concert.
4   £15.
5   Area under the whole demand curve, above the £10 price line (cf. Figure 3.5).

Revenue curve

1   See discussion of elasticity above.
2   The saw-tooth pattern is partly sampling 'noise' which could be reduced given a larger sample. But, there is also a systematic problem asking people to pick prices, as the tend to focus on 'pricing points' like £10, £20 and £25, which causes bunching in the demand curve and peaks in the revenue curve. Averaging each cluster would smooth out the curves.
3   They are the same only if variable costs are zero. This is approximately true of a pop concert as, for a given venue, the costs do not change much with the number of tickets sold: most of the costs are fixed. See later lectures on profit maximizing and chapter 5 of Pass and Lowes.

Sample, questionnaire procedure and assumptions   The main distortion may be that people gave the price they would pay if they were to go. They perhaps did not indicate the true likelihood that they would actually go. The willingness to pay question is probably quite good for estimating the shape of the demand curve. A separate question on the likelihood of attending, or a completely separate questionnaire to a more representative sample of the population, might give a better indication of the position of the curve. Of course, people would come from much further afield than Bradford, so one should construct a geographically distributed sample.

Chapter 4

Market failure

COMPETITION AND PARETO OPTIMALITY

The argument as we have developed it so far argues that social efficiency (Pareto optimality) will be achieved where people behave rationally under perfectly competitive conditions. People may be said to behave rationally where no activity is undertaken whose marginal benefit (MB) is less than its marginal cost (MC). Consumers will optimize consumption and firms productions where MB = MC. The consumer will achieve private efficiency where his or her marginal utility (satisfaction) (MU) equals price (MU = P). The producer will do so where marginal cost equals price (P = MC).

If there are no costs to society beyond those identifiable as being incurred by producers and no benefits to society, other than those enjoyed by the consumer, then the marginal cost to the firm is the same as the marginal cost to society (MC = MSC) and the marginal utility of consumption to the individual consumer is the same as the marginal benefit to society (MU = MSC) then social efficiency (Pareto optimality) has been achieved.

Should this balance of social cost and benefit be disrupted by shifts of demand or supply, price adjustments will occur until general equilibrium is restored in all markets where MSC = MSB (marginal benefit to society). This would represent a restoration of general Pareto optimality. This may be defined in a socially efficient level of production, consumption and exchange in all markets.

COMPETITION MAY NOT WORK

We seem to be suggesting that allocation efficiency may be achieved both in specific market sectors and in the economy as a whole by simply creating perfectly competitive conditions in all markets. The implication would appear to be that there is no role in such an economy for collective action through the activities of the state. However, even in societies whose political system is most committed to a market solution to the problem of allocation of scarce resources, the proportion of national income disposed of by the state usually exceeds 25 per cent. In the case of the UK, despite the best efforts of a government in office for eighteen years with a firm commitment to the market, government expenditure still persists at 40 per cent of GDP (gross domestic product), while much legislative effort is devoted to manipulating private sector markets.

We have to ask ourselves why this is so. In what way may markets fail to deliver Pareto optimality?

The reasons for market failure and state intervention may be summarized as follows:

1 Delays in market response to changes in conditions.
2 Imperfect markets. Market power.
3 Externalities.
4 Public and merit good provision.
5 Equity of distribution.

We will consider some of these possibilities here and leave others for consideration in a later chapter.

Some of the assumptions on which we have constructed the argument for the use of markets as the most socially efficient allocative mechanism are quite clearly flawed. In a complex modern economy it is unrealistic to assume that consumers can have perfect knowledge of market conditions. Nor can producers have perfect knowledge of the markets for factors of production which they may need to use. A change in market conditions cannot produce an instant response by producers and the owners of factors of production to the new price signals in the markets. Our model of the market is static, whereas in reality markets are dynamic. Responses to change will always occur after a time-lag. The target of social efficiency in allocation is always just out of reach.

CONSUMERS VERSUS PRODUCERS

Moreover the interests of consumers and producers are in *conflict*. The consumer seeks to make choices which will maximize utility (satisfaction) gained from a variety of products and services. He or she wishes to buy the most suitable products at the lowest possible price. In contrast the producer seeks to maximize profits, the difference between the total revenues he or she earns and the total costs he or she incurs. (In practice the producer may settle for less than maximum profit if he or she is prepared to substitute more leisure for less financial return.)

What the producer does not want is to be forced by open competition to earn only just enough to stay in business rather than take the best job obtainable as an employee. What the producer really wants to do is to appropriate some portion of consumer surplus to him or herself as extra profit by producing less at higher prices than would prevail in a competitive market. Consider the example in Activity 4.1.

Activity 4.1: The three chippies

Suppose in a large village of 10,000 people there are three fish and chip shops in the high street. Between them they can just supply the demand in the village for fish and chips. There is no other fish and chip shop within five miles.

Each proprietor opens at all meal times seven days a week. So long as they all produce meals of identical quality, it will be impossible for one shop to raise prices without losing all its business to the others. Any attempt to win business from the others by price reductions causes the shop to run into losses and eventually close. They are all forced into a position where they make just a bare living.

An ambitious new owner inherits one of the shops. He wishes to make a better living for his family. Which of the following strategies might he adopt and why?

1 Commit arson and burn down the neighbouring shops.
2 Borrow money to buy the other businesses and close them down, then expand his own premises.
3 Make an agreement with the other shop owners to raise all their prices by 20 per cent.
4 Add alternative fast foods to his menu.
5 Convert the upstairs flat to a restaurant.
6 Offer a delivery service.
7 Offer a greatly improved product at a higher price.

Any of the above (apart from 1 which is likely to land him in prison) represents a possible strategy. Each may be justified by economic arguments. All will to some extent cause this particular market to become imperfect. Some may cause a deadweight loss of welfare to all consumers of fish and chips in this market. Others may not. In later chapters we will discuss some of these types of behaviour in more detail.

All we need to recognise now is that the inherent tension between the motives of consumers and producers is likely to lead to an imperfect market.

Another problem with markets as allocators lies in the possibility that some necessary goods and some which are desirable for all may simply not be generated by market forces. Economists refer to these as public and merit goods. Examples would be on the first case defence capability and law and order enforcement, both of which may realistically only be provided effectively by social co-operation. Examples of merit goods include education and health services, which would be provided by markets for some (those who could afford them and are willing to sacrifice consumption to have them), but which would not be available on an equal basis for all.

DIRECT INTERVENTION IN MARKETS

In the rest of this chapter we propose to limit ourselves to two cases where there are arguments in favour of intervention by the state in certain types of market situation. As we shall see, such interventions may cause distortions in both the target and related market. Whether the effects of the resulting distortions outweigh the gains in general social welfare is a normative issue which may be debated by economists but not definitely answered. The two types of market failure which we shall consider here are: a) the case of externalities; b) the problem of equity. Before we do so, let us summarize the argument so far.

Summary

In the real world, markets are unlikely to fail to achieve social efficiency. This is because perfectly competitive conditions, if they ever occur, are not likely to persist. Markets only respond to any disequilibrium after a time-lag, if at all. Markets are unable, or unlikely, to supply certain public and merit goods. Furthermore, markets may be unable to produce what society perceives as an equitable (fair) distribution of goods and incomes, and cannot take account of externalities.

EXTERNALITIES AND EQUITY

The problem of externalities

The market can only produce a socially efficient allocation of resources if the actions of one consumer have no adverse effects on another consumer, and the actions of producers have no adverse effects on society as a whole.

In reality the actions of producers and consumers do have side-effects. These may be beneficial, but more often represent a cost to society additional to those borne by the producer or consumer. Externalities may be summarized as follows:

- **External benefits**, *occur when the benefits of consumption or production are experienced by persons* other *than consumer or producer*. Examples might be: the keen newspaper reader who collects the used papers on behalf of a communal fund to replace a worn out public swimming pool; or a property developer who develops a site which was previously an unsightly wasteland and so improves the amenity of the neighbourhood for all residents.

- **External Costs,** *occur where a cost is borne by persons other than the consumer or producer.* Examples might be: where the atmosphere in a restaurant is spoilt for the majority of diners by a minority who insist on smoking cigarettes; or where a farmer neglects a silage clamp with the result that silage effluent kills all the fish in a prime stretch of river.

The private benefit gained by the newspaper reader, plus the benefit to the community, from the waste-paper collection, results in a social benefit. While the profits made by the farmer due to neglect of silage dump repairs plus the cost to the community from the pollution of the river, results in a social cost.

The problem of equity

We have seen earlier that an economy which enjoys the conditions of perfect competition through all markets is capable of delivery through competitive equilibrium in all markets, one particular Pareto efficient output. That is, the economy will produce at one point on the production possibility boundary, described as point A in Figure 4.1. How is this outcome determined?

The product possibility frontier, BC in Figure 4.1, represents the Pareto optimum combinations of food and public goods which this economy is

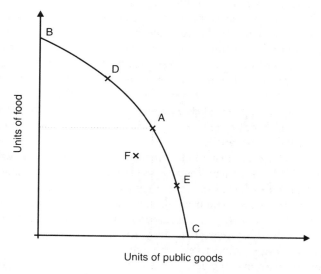

Units of public goods

Figure 4.1 Pareto optimality

capable of producing given present resources, skills and productivity rates currently available. Point A represents a possible combination, determined by competitive equilibrium in a market with a given initial distribution of ability, income and wealth. Other combinations, such as D or E might be perceived as being more equitable. To achieve a new equilibrium intervention would be required. This might, itself, by distortion of the free market, lead to a new output, at say F, which is *not* Pareto efficient.

Varying innate ability, ambition and financial wealth will, through the market for factors of production, generate widely differing levels of income. This will also determine the pattern of consumer demand.

Thus different distributions of ability and wealth will lead to different Pareto efficient combinations of outputs. The economist (being only able to answer positive questions) cannot say which is the most desirable. Only the politicians can make this normative judgement.

It looks as if a government of right-wing ideology could argue that no intervention is required by government to steer the economy toward efficiency. The forms of competition will (if unobstructed) ensure allocative efficiency and a Pareto optimum outcome. If due to widely differing levels of income earning potential among the population, the outcome is seen by a substantial number of people as grossly unfair, the government can induce a shift to a more equitable outcome through redistribution of income by taxation and benefits.

A government of a more left of centre ideology might see such actions as necessary but not sufficient to achieve an equitable outcome. They would consider the obstacles to achieving allocative efficiency through a competitive free market economy as just too great for the idea to be plausible. They might therefore wish to intervene more directly to correct failure in specific markets. In practice most governments incline to this view, whatever their position on the desirability of a free market economy.

Specific intervention in the market process by government destroys the delicate mechanism of competition. *We have seen that competitive equilibrium is Pareto efficient since the actions of producers in setting marginal cost equal to price, and consumers setting marginal benefits equal to price, will ensure that the marginal cost of producing good will just equal the marginal benefit to consumers.*

If society's marginal cost of producing a good does *not* equal society's marginal benefit from consuming the good, a *distortion* will occur. Even the solution suggested earlier of seeking greater equity of distribution of income by redistributive tax and benefits will in reality cause *distortions*. If taxes are raised the marginal benefits of commodities which are taxed will no longer be equated with their marginal cost. At the resulting equilibrium the economy is no longer allocatively efficient.

The government may decide that the disadvantages of the inefficiency cost resulting from redistributive taxes are less than the advantages of greater equity of the distribution of income and wealth. *The theory of the second best suggests that, since the first best solution is unacceptably inequitable, the distortions that result from intervention must be accepted. But they can be minimized if intervention is spread over a number of markets rather than loaded on to one, or few markets.*

This argument leads to the probability of a proliferation of interventions in many markets. For a fuller exposition of these arguments you may wish at this point to read the introducing chapter on *welfare economics* in any standard introductory economics text (e.g. Begg, Fischer and Dornbusch, 1991; or Sloman, 1991).

At this stage we want you to begin to see how the simple theoretical tools covered in our earlier chapters might identify the consequences of the distortionary effects of government attempts to correct market failure by direct intervention by price and other controls, or direct subsidies or indirect taxes on consumption.

CASE STUDY 3: INTERVENING IN MARKETS

Exercise

Objectives

1 To establish by syndicate and group discussion the power of the simple supply and demand (S&D) model as a predictor of the consequences of intervention in markets.
2 To consider the possible reasons for such interventions.
3 And whether intervention will serve its purpose.

Methods

1 Syndicates to use an S&D diagram to consider (20 minutes) *one* of the following cases and present back their findings:

   a) The EU (European Union) establishes an *intervention price* for wheat which is above the world price for wheat, in order to protect the livelihood of inefficient European farmers.
   b) The EU establishes a minimum wage for all member countries to be set in UK at £4.15 per hour, in order to prevent the exploitation of unskilled labour.
   c) The UK government seeks to alleviate poverty by establishing a minimum price for butter which is 25 per cent below going market price.

Further questions

1 What other undesirable consequences might result in an externality (cost not borne by the supplier) to society?
2 a) What might be the effect on other wages in the economy of a minimum wage at this level?
  b) What macroeconomic consequences might occur?

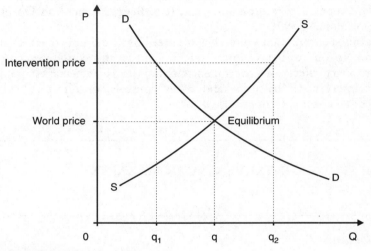

Figure 4.2 Exercise feedback graph (a)

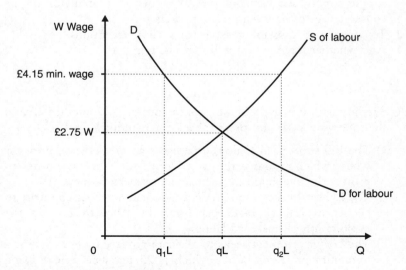

Figure 4.3 Exercise feedback graph (b)

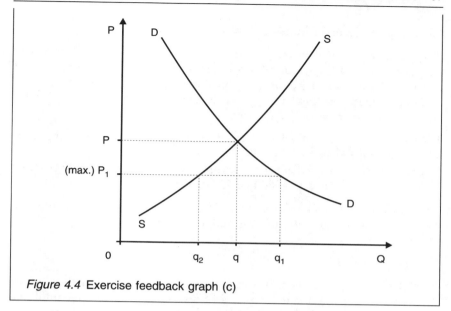

Figure 4.4 Exercise feedback graph (c)

Exercise feedback

1a) See Figure 4.2. The result of the EU intervention price is a surplus supply of $Oq_2 - Oq_1$. Because supply has been increased from Oq in equilibrium, to Oq_2 while demand has fallen from Oq to Oq_1. The surplus must be sold, destroyed, or given away to the Third World as aid.

1b) See Figure 4.3. OW is going market rate for low grade labour, resulting in total employment of Oq_1. At minimum $OqL_2 - OqL_1$, worker's are unemployed of which: $OqL - OqL_1$ = increase in recorded unemployment; $OqL_2 - OqL_1$ = increase in number willing to work, but unemployed.

1c) See Figure 4.4. Op is current market price for butter and Oq is demand for butter at this equilibrium price. Op_1 is new maximum price. Demand increases to Oq_1 but supply falls to Oq_2, therefore a shortage occurs.

   Either government must RATION butter to ensure fair allocation *or* with rationing some butter will be sold on a black market at inflated prices, while some willing customers will get no butter.

CASE STUDY 4: RENT CONTROLS

The essay on rent controls which follows refers in general terms to the effects of rent controls. The notes which follow describe the UK housing situation.

Changing patterns of housing

The UK private rented accommodation sector has shrunk considerably over past decades. In 1914, around 90 per cent of UK households rented their accommodation. By 1980 only 13 per cent of the housing stock was privately rented and this had declined further to 8 per cent by 1987. This decline was accompanied by the rise of two other major sectors:

1 Owner occupation, which accounted for 55 per cent of the housing stock in 1980 and 65 per cent by 1987.
2 Local authority rented accommodation, which accounted for 35 per cent of the housing stock in 1980 and 27 per cent by 1987.

The number of privately rented houses and flats declined from 6 million in 1951 to 4.3 million in 1961 and 1.6 million by 1986.

UK rent controls

In 1915 the UK government introduced wartime controls over the rents of dwellings to constrain rent increases. These controls persisted until the 1960s. Three Rent Acts in 1965, 1974 and 1977 gave residential tenants in privately rented property lifetime security of tenure, gave the tenants the right to a *fair rent* which was assessed by a Rent Officer and extended those rights to tenants of furnished rented accommodation as well as unfurnished accommodation.

The 1980 Housing Act reduced the scope of the Rent Acts, allowing landlords to let new properties on *assured tenancies* of up to twenty-one years and *shorthold* tenancies of up to five years at a market rent negotiated with the tenant. The 1986 Housing Act extended the assured tenancy scheme and subsequent legislation removed rent controls on any new lettings of private housing.

Rent controls

'Landlords are taking advantage of the current housing shortage to raise rents.'

This is a fairly moderate version of a popular protest against rising rents. It is not uncommon to read in some sections of the Press that landlords are 'exploiting' the situation by charging exorbitant rents or by 'rack renting' the hapless tenant. Apparently the typical landlord is an unprincipled person who readily avails himself of the urgency of other people's needs to line his pockets.

Now, as those who listen fairly regularly to 'brains trust' programmes must have realised, one can gain a reputation for shrewdness in a very short time merely by asking colleagues to explain the meaning of the words they use. Like most useful gambits it can be overdone. In this instances, however, we are justified in asking that the term 'current housing shortage' be elucidated, for we are not likely to make sense of the behaviour of landlords unless we know more precisely the nature of the situation to which they are reacting.

We might, of course, interpret a housing shortage in the light of some ideal standards, for example, every family of four should have, at least, three bedrooms and two living rooms with a total of not less than 11,500 cubic feet of space. Such a norm sounds humane and reasonable. It might be prescribed by a conscientious social worker in the belief that it is not too far ahead of existing standards in most parts of the country, but it is obviously a very fleeting norm. A hundred years ago it would have sounded wildly extravagant. A hundred years hence, if population continues to expand, it may again sound wildly extravagant. But today, there can be wide differences of opinion, both as to what is desirable and as to what can be afforded.

The economist, however, can be very complacent about all this. He need not stick his neck out on so controversial an issue. Without saying a word about ideal or undesirable standards he can go now to talk about a shortage of anything in perfectly unambiguous sense. To the economist there is a shortage simply if, at the existing price, the maximum amount that people want to buy – in this case, the use of house-room, exceeds the maximum price that sellers are willing to put on the market at that price.

It must be admitted, in passing, that it is not always easy to measure the actual excess of the quantity demanded over that being supplied. For one thing, the goods in question may not belong to a homogeneous class. Houses, for instance, may be classified into broad or fine divisions according to the problem in hand. If we want to illustrate the working of broad principles, as we do here, there is an advantage in supposing that all houses are equally desirable so far as the public is concerned. We can, at a later stage, consider what modifications of our conclusions are necessary, if any, when we remove this simplification.

There are, again, difficulties about gathering data, as well as difficulties of interpreting the facts once we have them. If, for example, we observe that the prices of all types of housing are rising and we also have information that no additional housing has been provided, we might conclude that the rise in price will lead to a diminution of the excess demand. For as prices rise, people will not be able to afford as much housing. However, from the fact that house prices rise, we cannot be certain that the excess demand is being choked off. For it is possible that, just at the same time as some people are seeking to buy less housing at the higher price, other groups want to buy more housing, either because of increased incomes, or, possibly, because of increased migration into the area. And these additions to the total demand for housing may more than offset the reduction in demand of the first group. Thus, even though there has been a rise in price, excess demand is greater than before. With these new demand conditions – those arising from migration had higher incomes – the required equilibrium price may be much higher than before.

For all that, however, the economist's concept of a shortage – the excess demand associated with a given price – presents no difficulty, and it is with concepts, and not their measurement, that we are concerned now.

The tendency, in the absence of government or other controls, for the price to rise when there is an excess demand at that price is a response which is taken as axiomatic by economists. It is a response which may appear to the reader as intuitively reasonable. If, however, he is loath to rely merely on intuition (for which reluctance I have nothing but praise), he can infer as much from observing the trading that is done on the floor of any stock or commodity exchange. Though the response of prices may be more tardy and erratic in less organised markets, for instance the market for second-hand cameras, the proposition is no less valid.

It may be emphasised that there is nothing automatic about this price behaviour. Prices do not rise of themselves unwilled by man. They are deliberately raised either on the initiative of some of the sellers or of some of the buyers according to the custom of the market. It may thus be the literal truth that landlords raise their rents when, at the prevailing price of house-room, there is just not enough to go round. To that extent a fallacy does not inhere in the quoted statement per se. Nonetheless it does attract to an implied 'ought' in that statement. That is to say, there is an implication in the statement that landlords are misbehaving or breaking the rules in some sense. And it is in this implication that a misunderstand, if not a fallacy, can be detected.

Let us be quite clear on this point before considering the consequences of attempting to restrain the landlords' behaviour in times of a housing shortage. The reader is not being asked to acquit the landlord of greed or even of 'undue' greed. He is being invited to believe that in business affairs greed is the rule and not the exception; indeed that it is the mainspring of the market mechanism as it exists in the free enterprise systems of the West. At least as far back as Adam Smith, economists have been making the assumption that each man pursues his own interest only. No doubt there are circumstances in business when it is not politic to appear too grasping. In large organisations, moreover, frequent alterations to price lists can be highly inconvenient. But for all that, we shall not go far wrong in our interpretation of business activities if we continue to suppose that a man will sell dearer if he believes he can thereby increase his present and future profits. 'Exploiting the market' – or – that which sounds less offensive but comes to the same thing – 'charging what the traffic will bear' – is accepted by economists as normal business practice. However, if we cannot condemn the reaction of landlords to a housing shortage without at the same time condemning the system of private enterprise, we might yet take the view that in this particular instance a rise in the price would be unusually damaging and, therefore, that measures to inhibit the free play of the market mechanism are justified. We shall devote the remainder of this essay to an examination of this view.

Though the material consequences of rent controls are not difficult to trace, the passions which are aroused by this inflammatory topic make it troublesome to discuss in mixed political groups, large or small. Invariably, unless the chairman is very determined, the features of the various rent restriction acts come under attack by some and are defended no less vehemently by others. Experience in conducting such a discussion suggests that before allowing temperatures to rise, the participants agree to abstract from any legal or political issues associated with the rent acts, and to regard the housing shortage as a commodity in short supply to which, in the first instance, at least, general economic principles will apply.

Let us then forget about the differences between types of houses and imagine a rise in rents steep enough to wipe out all excess demand, in the economist's use of that term. In the 'short run' – say, during the following year – we can ignore the building of additional houses, for they will be too small a proportion of the existing stock of houses to make much impact on rents. Rents during this period will therefore be above 'normal', that is, above the existing costs of providing new house-room – and this rise in the price of house-room relative to the price of all other things acts to serve notice on the community that house-room has become scarcer and that people must economise on its use. At the higher prices, as people do economise in its use – as they agree to occupy fewer rooms and to seek no longer (at the higher prices) to occupy a larger house or flat – the shortage (in the economist's sense) will disappear.

In the longer run, we attend to the effect on rents as the proportion of new houses coming onto the market grows. As we should expect, additional houses bring down the high price attained in the short run to the level of the normal price (which just covers costs of providing house-room), profits disappear, and there is no further incentive to increase the resulting stock of houses. We may then talk of the market for house-room as being 'in equilibrium', there being no tendency for the stock of accommodation or the price of house-room to change.

A centrally planned economy faced with a housing shortage would not be criticised if it exacted economy in the use of scarce housing, and also initiated a building programme to meet the current deficiency. In these respects, therefore, there is little fault to find with the repercussions of the market mechanism. Of course, if prices are not permitted to rise, we cannot expect people to further ration their consumption of house-room and the shortage will continue. Moreover, if prices do not rise, profits are not made, and businesses are not attracted into building houses. If houses are to be built, the government must then step in and build them.

But, cries some impatient reader, this ivory-tower business is all very well in its way, yet what of the hardship suffered by the poor when rents are allowed to rise without limit? Let me assure that reader that a tender conscience is no necessary handicap to the economist. Not only can we admit that a rise in price of house-room bears harder on the poor than the rich, as of course does a rise in the price of anything that is consumed by both groups, but we can contemplate doing something to alleviate this hardship. The real issue then becomes one of the best methods of achieving this desideratum. And since it was regard to equity that prompted us to think of rent controls as a means of helping the needy, we must consider, also on grounds of equity, the following points which may be raised against rent controls.

First, it is a blunt and indiscriminating weapon. There are poor landlords and there are rich tenants; at any rate, there are many landlords (and landladies) who are poorer than their tenants. In such cases – and they are far from few since, before the First World War at least, small house property was a favourite medium for the investment of small savings – rent controls may constitute a transfer of real income from the poor to the rich.

Second, even if we supposed all landlords to be better off than their tenants, rent controls – which may be regarded as a compulsory subsidy from the landlord to the tenant equal to the difference between the controlled price and the estimated market price – discriminate against the owners of a particular class of property in an arbitrary manner. The discrimination is arbitrary in two ways. One, controls are applied to housing but not in general to other goods and services. Two, the controls are not symmetric. If the government also fixed minimum rents, when rents would otherwise fall, landlords would feel less free to grumble. As it is, landlords are freely permitted to lose money in times of too much housing but are not suffered to make any during a shortage.

Nor is it satisfactory to argue that such procedure be accepted as part of the inevitable hazards of private enterprise along with unforeseeable changes in consumer's tastes, in technical innovations, or in the political situation. The last three are risks which the businessman tacitly accepts. He has not yet accepted government intervention of this particular sort since, according to the prevailing political philosophy of the West at least, the business of the government is to alleviate hardship or misfortune that results from the operation of natural or economic forces; to promote equity, not to create inequities.

(Mishan, n.d. 1969)

How markets work

Price *rises* when excess D occurs and *falls* when surplus supply exists. But markets are *made* by economic agents, they do not happen automatically. One cannot condemn behaviour of landlords in raising rents, or selling off rented houses without condemning private enterprise.

But markets may be said to *fail* on social benefit/cost grounds and so intervention by government may be *justifiable*. In this case the *stock* of houses cannot respond in the short run to excess D and rents may therefore be temporarily above normal, i.e. the cost of supplying new houses – the *supply is fixed in the short run*. The longer run agents respond to higher rents by building new properties to rent.

THE MARKET RETURNS TO EQUILIBRIUM at *normal* rent. Increased rent (price) *signals* need for rented houses, *AND* potential for profit.

If this mechanism is blocked, government must supply houses, i.e. we are forced into a command economy:

- controlled rents
- government supplies houses to make up shortfall, on grounds of equity.

Arguments against rent control

1 Some landlords are poorer than tenants – i.e. control transfers income from poor to rich.
2 Even if all landlords are richer, controls involve a subsidy (market price – controlled rent), from landlord to tenant in an arbitrary way.
3 Landlords can lose money in times of surplus housing, but not make money in times of shortage – inequity is therefore promoted by controlled rents.
4 The burden of transferring income from rich to poor should be borne by the tax system as a whole, not be a penal charge on landlords.

5 Council properties funded by local tax and let below market price fulfil that function.
6 The failure to adjust rent control parameters to the change in money values forces down the real value of rents.
7 Problem with a semi-controlled market is that mobility is promoted for those who can pay, but prevented by council property – which forces you to stay put.
8 Controlled rent sector landlords are unable to recoup even the cost of repairs, therefore a large part of housing stock deteriorates.

Can we now *explain* and *predict* housing market using the S&D model? Consider Figures 4.5 and 4.6.

Solutions

Subsidize landlord

Landlord receives direct subsidy perhaps via tax concessions, supply increased (at all rents possible) – SS curve shifts to SS_1 (see Figure 4.7). Oq_1 demand can be met at rent r_1, at new equilibrium. Increase of $Oq_1 - Oq$.

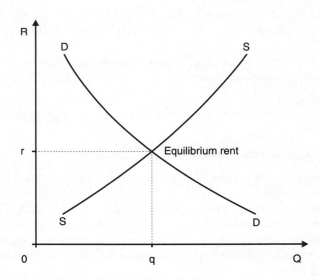

Figure 4.5 Supply and demand: equilibrium rent

Ration housing

Quantity of unsatisfied tenants in Figure 4.6 is q_2/q_1 who must join waiting lists and quality on a points basis – as in council housing.

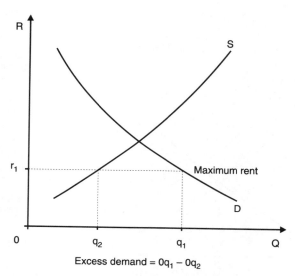

Figure 4.6 Supply and demand: maximum rent

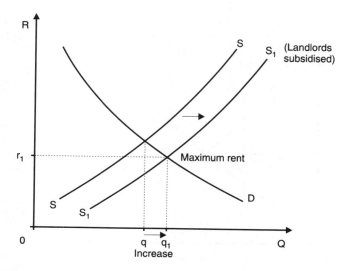

Figure 4.7 Subsidize landlords

Reduce demand for rented property

Reduce demand for rented property at all prices by making substitutes cheaper – (lower interest rates on mortgages, 100 per cent mortgages etc.). The maximum rent of r, is now the equilibrium rent (see Figure 4.8).

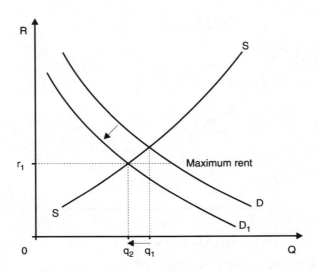

Figure 4.8 Reduce demand for rented property

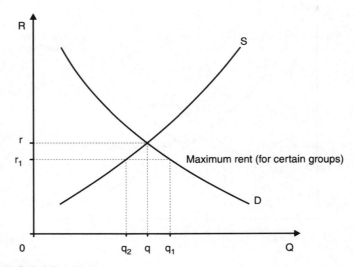

Figure 4.9 Subsidize tenants

Subsidize tenants

Market is left to clear at Or (Figure 4.9) but certain favoured groups, e.g. disabled and single parents, are subsidized directly by housing benefit and pay only Or_1. Supply of rented housing is at Oq – the equilibrium in current conditions of S&D, but weaker citizens are protected. *However,* many new claimants arise. Landlords are getting market clearing rent. This leads to change in the conditions of both S&D.

New conditions

Follow the situation in the last section, price remains at r (Figure 4.10). Supply of rented property increases to Oq_3 from Oq. Demand shifts to Oq_3 and the market is still clear at r.

What is the problem?

The government has spent £x billion on housing benefits to encourage private sector landlords who make profit at market clearing rent of Or. Therefore, some taxpayers have had income shifted to other taxpayers by government. *Both* certain groups of tenants *and* landlords benefit.

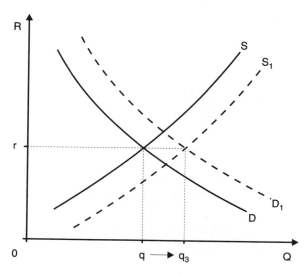

Figure 4.10 New conditions

Case study feedback

Problems of definition

These arise for 1) housing, and 2) housing shortage.

Avoid value judgements

Avoid making such judgements, e.g. 'exploitive landlords' or 'rents ought to be lower'.

Simplifying the problem

Use *assumptions* to build a simplified model. Modify as assumptions are removed. Be aware of changes in quantity demanded due to change in price, as against changes in the other conditions of demand (D) – price of substitutes, income and taste – which cause a shift of the D curve.

Assume economic agents pursue own interests – correctly. Houses are homogenous.

Chapter 5

Modelling the behaviour of firms

INTRODUCTION

The consumer in the market-place, who places demands on scarce resources in order to satisfy some want or need, may be an individual, household, firm, public sector organization, charitable organization or government agency. Whichever it may be, the aim is to maximize satisfaction. The supplier of goods and services to these demanders, may be a private firm or a publicly owned organization. Our aim is to generate a general theory of supply which will enable us to explain and predict the behaviour of such suppliers. Thus for initial simplicity's sake, we will start from this definition of a supplier, which for the sake of linguistic brevity we will call simply a 'firm'.

Definition: a firm

A firm is an organization, owned by private individuals, shareholders or the state which transforms inputs of resources into goods and services which are intended for consumption.

PROFIT MAXIMIZATION

To simplify the analysis we assume that the motive for the firm is

- *Private sector*: to maximize profit (or minimize loss)
- *Public sector*: to break even year on year.

The decisions which firms have to make are about using information on costs and revenues at different levels of production in order to decide on output and price. Therefore we need to be able to analyse the determination of costs and revenues. But first let us define some key terms.

Definitions

Revenue: amount earned by selling products over a given period.

Costs: expenses incurred in producing and distributing the outputs for sale.

Normal profits: the earnings which are just sufficient to make it possible to retain in that business the original capital invested, and the proprietor's input of time.

Supernormal profits: residual earnings of the firm after all other costs have been met, including normal profit.

Earnings: residual profits less tax, which are partly paid as dividends to shareholders, and partly retained in the business for development.

For the moment we will have to accept an initial rather unrealistic assumption about the behaviour of businesses – that they seek to maximize profit. If we do accept this assumption, then it follows logically that the firm must choose the best level of outputs, and demand conditions. The firm must therefore seek to minimize costs of production – it must seek to be efficient.

One way of putting it is that the firm must seek that output which produces the maximum difference between total revenue and total cost. There will be some output at which total revenue is exactly the same as total costs – which is the firm's break-even point. Above that output profits will be earned, below that output losses will be incurred (see Figure 5.1).

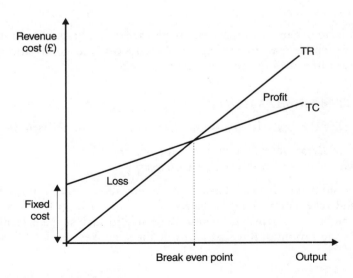

Figure 5.1 Break-even output

Total revenue will rise in a straight line from the origin if any number of increased outputs can be sold without reducing price. But even if sales do not have to be made at lower prices as output rises, costs may suddenly rise as output approaches plant capacity and night shifts and overtime have to be worked. Thus, as we can see in Figure 5.2 there is a specific output at which profit is maximized.

MARGINAL COST AND MARGINAL REVENUE ANALYSIS

In the analysis which follows, we are going to look at the output decision of a firm whose goal is to maximize profit. The model which we will study deals with a firm producing physical products, such as motor cars or television sets, for sale on the open market. For reasons which become clear later, the position is different for intangible products like television broadcasts, but this model is a step along the way.

We can develop the argument in a more detailed way by introducing another very important new concept, the *margin*. We can illustrate this concept diagrammatically, and we will build the analysis up in three stages. The first stage will explain marginal cost, the second stage will look at marginal revenue and the final stage will demonstrate how profit is maximized when marginal cost equals marginal revenue.

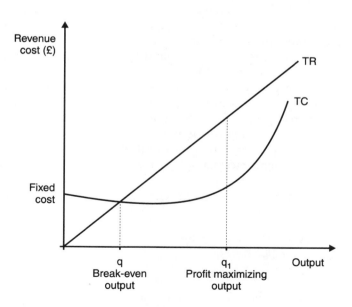

Figure 5.2 Point of maximised profit output

Definition: the concept of the margin

The marginal unit (of consumption or production) is the last one to be consumed or produced.
The marginal cost of output is the extra cost incurred by producing one additional unit of output.
The marginal revenue is the extra revenue generated by selling one additional unit of output.

We can make an important deduction from this:

1   If marginal cost (MC) is less than marginal revenue (MR), the revenue generated by producing one additional unit is greater than the cost incurred, and so producing one more unit will increase profit.
2   If MC is greater than MR, the revenue generated by producing one additional unit is less than the cost incurred, and so producing one more unit will decrease the profit.
3   Therefore, profit is maximized when MC = MR.

Marginal cost

Figure 5.3 shows the relationship between the three important cost concepts: total cost, average cost and marginal cost. We will explain the shapes of these graphs in a moment.
    The total cost line (TC) shows the whole cost of production to the firm as it varies the number of units of output Q. The average cost line (AC) shows the average cost per unit (and so it is found by dividing the total cost by the number of units: AC = TC ÷ Q).
    The marginal cost line (MC) is the additional cost of one extra unit of production: that is, at any value of Q, MC is equal to the change in TC if output changes to Q + 1 (this is the slope of the TC line).
    Let us explain the shape of the lines in Figure 5.3. Their shapes each reflect a different aspect of how costs are affected by the level of output; in fact each graph presents essentially the same information but in a different way.
    Starting from the left of the graph (Q = 0), as output increases, the three graphs do the following

1   The TC curve becomes less steep.
2   The AC curve falls.
3   The MC curve falls.

These changes reflect how as output increases:

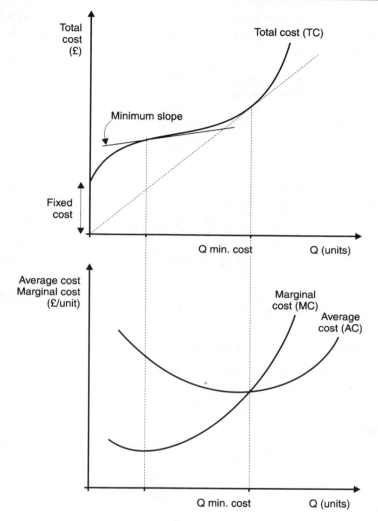

Figure 5.3 Total cost, average cost and marginal cost

- increasing returns are gained in the use of variable inputs. For example, labour can be used more efficiently on a production line as output increases and people specialize in different aspects of the work. This brings down both MC and AC, making the increase in TC less steep.
- Fixed costs (which cannot be avoided whether or not production occurs, e.g. rent, lease on machines) are spread over more units of output, which brings down AC.

Eventually, as output increases further and the firm's output capacity is approached, the firm is faced by increasing marginal costs. This is because for most firms, the availability of some input to production becomes a constraint. This may be labour, if overtime payments are needed, but also could be a shortage of space for production, or rising transport costs if production becomes spread out, or rising management costs if the organisation becomes too large. The result is that:

1 The MC curve turns upward.
2 The TC curve starts to get more steep.
3 The AC curve turns upward.

Thus, decreasing returns, which always set in eventually, cause the MC and the AC curve to be U-shaped.

You might notice that in Figure 5.3, the level of output $Q_{mincost}$, is technically the most efficient, because this is where the average cost per unit of output is at its minimum. Increasing output beyond $Q_{mincost}$ increases the average cost per unit. You might also notice that the MC curve crosses the AC curve exactly at $Q_{mincost}$, where average cost is lowest. This is no coincidence, for it is a mathematical property of the average and the margin, but the explanation need not concern us here.

Activity 5.1: a cricketer's season

Here are the scores of a batsman who started and finished the season well, but did badly mid-season:

Table 5.1 Batsman's runs

Week	Score	Total runs	Average
Wk 1	60	60	60.0
Wk 2	35	95	47.5
Wk 3	25	120	40.0
Wk 4	15	135	33.7
Wk 5	10	145	29.0
Wk 6	20	165	27.5
Wk 7	22	187	26.8
Wk 8	35	222	27.7
Wk 9	42	264	29.3
Wk 10	64	328	32.8
Wk 11	73	401	36.5
Wk 12	86	487	40.5

Plot the figures for *score* and *average* on the graph in Figure 5.4. The weekly score is equivalent to marginal cost, and the average score is equivalent to average cost. Check your graph against the answer in the Activity feedback section.

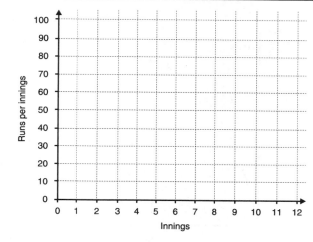

Figure 5.4 Graph for cricketers' scores

Marginal revenue

Figure 5.5 shows the relationship between total revenue, average revenue and marginal revenue.

- The total revenue line (TR) shows how the total income of the firm varies with the number of units sold Q. Revenue is simply the price multiplied by the quantity sold ($P \times Q$).
- The average revenue line (AR) shows the average income per unit of sales. But notice that the average income per unit sold, is simply the demand curve for the product concerned.
- The marginal revenue line (MR) is the additional income received from selling one extra unit of production. That is, at any value of Q, MR is equal to the change in TR if output increases to $Q + 1$ (this is the slope of the TR line).

We can explain the shapes of the lines in Figure 5.5 as follows. We established earlier that the demand curve (also the average revenue curve) slopes downward, that is to say, the price for each unit sold falls as output increases. Now, this implies that the TR curve does not rise in a straight line, but gets less steep as output increases. This is because the extra revenue obtained from selling an extra unit is partly offset by the reduction in price needed to achieve the extra sale, which affects all units sold. Thus the net increase in revenue of each extra unit sold is less than the price of that unit, and continues to be still less with each extra sale. Eventually, the revenue lost from cutting the price on all units can exceed the revenue gained from extra units sold. Then revenue will begin to fall even though more units are sold, as shown beyond Q_{maxrev}.

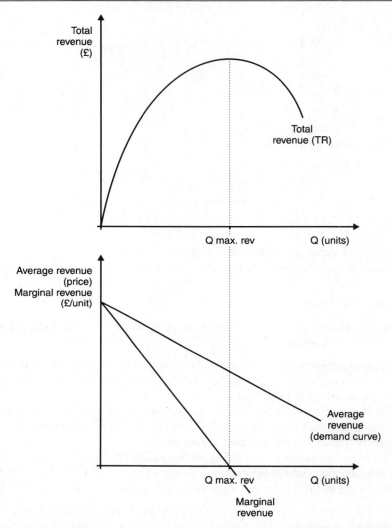

Figure 5.5 Total revenue, average revenue (demand) and marginal revenue

The MR curve falls more steeply than the AR (demand) curve. This is because, as just described, the extra revenue from selling one more unit must be less than the price obtained per unit, since the price of all units sold has to be reduced to sell the extra unit. MR becomes zero at Q_{maxrev}, since this is the point at which an extra unit sold ceases to add a positive marginal revenue. Beyond Q_{maxrev} marginal revenue of sales is negative, which is to say that total revenue falls as quantity sold increases.

PROFIT MAXIMIZING OUTPUT

We can now look at profit maximizing output again. Recall the statement in which we introduced marginal cost and marginal revenue: *If marginal cost is less than marginal revenue, it is worth while to produce another unit. If MC is greater than MR, it is not worth while producing an extra unit.* Therefore: *Profit is maximized when MC = MR.*

Figure 5.6 shows the TR and TC curves, and the MC and MR curves. The output at which MC and MR intersect is the output at which the firm will

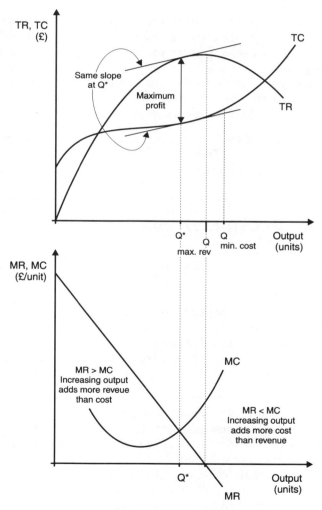

Figure 5.6 Profit maximizing output

maximize its profits. In the real world a firm probably does not operate by pursuing exactly this level of output. It may not know when it has reached this level until it is too late. But a firm trying to maximize profit will behave approximately this way. Remember we are still constructing a simplified model which will help us to understand the real world.

SUMMARY

In this chapter we studied the behaviour of a private firm, trying to maximize profit. We used a graphical model based on the following concepts:

- **Marginal cost** – the extra cost of producing one additional unit.
- **Marginal revenue** – the extra income from selling one additional unit.
- Profit increases if output is increased when marginal revenue is greater than marginal cost.
- Profit decreases if output is increased when marginal revenue is smaller than marginal cost.
- Profit is greatest where marginal cost and marginal revenue are equal.

We compared graphs of total revenue and total cost with graphs of marginal revenue and marginal cost. They provide two alternative representations of the firm's best choice of output.

CASE STUDY 5: COSTS EXERCISES

Exercise 1

Objectives

1 To give students an opportunity to understand models of *market structures* by manipulating simple data.
2 To begin the process of developing an understanding of the uses of microeconomic models as a means of interpreting business decisions.

Methods

1 Students to work individually or in pairs.
2 Use given data to construct a set of cost curves for a firm (average fixed cost (AFC), average variable cost (AVC), Average total cost (ATC), marginal cost (MC)).
3 Tutor to establish via group discussion the importance of the relationship between ATC and MC.
4 And to show that MC is the supply curve.

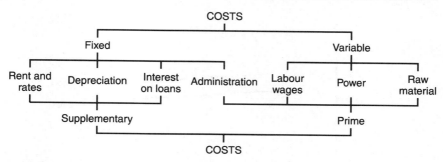

Figure 5.7 Structure chart

Question 1: would a businessman agree with this?

Table 5.2 The cost schedule of a firm (1)

Output Units	Fixed cost £	Variable cost £	Total cost £	Average cost £	Marginal cost £
100	100	700	800	8.00	—
101	100	706	806	7.98	6
102	100	709	809	7.93	3
103	100	710	810	7.86	1

ATC	100 = 8.00	AVC	100 = 7.00	AFC	100 = 1.00
	101 = 7.99		101 = 6.99		101 = 0.99
	102 = 7.93		102 = 6.95		102 = 0.98
	103 = 7.86		103 = 6.89		103 = 0.97

Table 5.3 The cost schedule of a firm (2)

Output Units	Total cost £	Average cost £	Marginal cost £
20	270	13.5	—
30	320	10.7	5
40	400	10.0	8
50	500	10.0	10
60	630	10.5	13
70	790	11.3	16

In the example in Figure 5.8 (see also Table 5.2) **fixed costs** are £100, whatever output is produced. Thus as output increases they are spread over increasing numbers of units produced. The *average fixed cost* will therefore

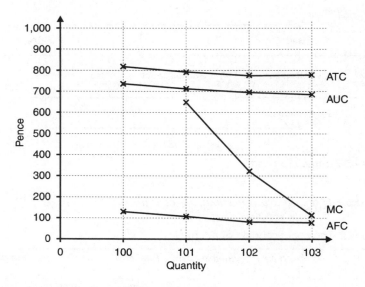

Figure 5.8 Feedback graph relating to Table 5.2

fall as output rises. **Variable costs** increase as output rises, but not proportionately, because all factors of production are being used more efficiently, generating increasing returns to sale.

Because both average fixed costs and average variable costs are falling, naturally average total costs (per unit of output) are falling also. At this stage the **marginal cost** of (adding one more unit of output) falls dramatically as production becomes more efficient.

In the case of Figure 5.9 (see also Table 5.3) ATC are falling at first as combinations of factors are used more efficiently. After a certain point the fall in ATC induced by spreading fixed costs over increased output, is more than offset by the increasing inefficiency caused by adding more variable factors than can work effectively on the existing fixed size of plant.

At outputs below twenty units, the marginal cost is probably falling as the fixed plant is used more efficiently by increasing numbers of variable factors. As inefficiency begins to appear (perhaps just below twenty units), MC begins to rise. However it is still below ATC until an output of fifty units is reached. Up to that point it is worth adding an extra unit of output. Only when the cost of adding one more unit of output (MC), starts to exceed the ATC, does plant become inefficient.

We can conclude that at output of fifty units, where MC = ATC, the plant is being run with optimum efficiency.

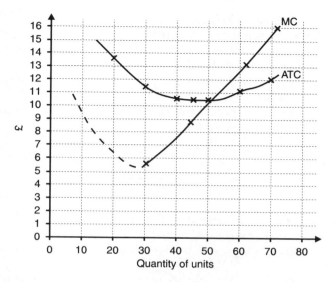

Figure 5.9 Feedback graph relating to Table 5.3

Question 2

Can we therefore conclude further that firms will always seek to produce this optimum output, where MC = AC?

The answer is no they would not necessarily do so. It will depend on the nature of the market in which they are operating. We have no information in this case about the *conditions of demand* for the firm's products. In that case we do not know what the firm's *average revenue* (total revenue ÷ output) might be at different levels of output. Nor can we calculate what the **marginal revenue** (revenue from the last unit sold) of the firm might be.

THEORY OF THE FIRM: SUMMARY

- We assumed that firms will always seek to maximize profits.
- We identified short-run situations where some factors are fixed.
- Therefore in the short run firm's efficiency will increase with output as fixed costs are spread over more outputs, and variable factors are used more efficiently.
- As inefficient use of variable factors sets in and outweighs the effect of the spread of fixed costs, average costs rise.
- Marginal costs fall at first, as output rises, but began to rise as inefficiency sets in.

- The point where AC = MC represents the most efficient use of the plant, and the lowest cost per unit of output.
- In the long run all factors are variable, but economics of scale and eventually diseconomies of scale still occur.
- Thus in the long run, the firm still operates as its most efficient output where AC = MC.
- However, this is not necessarily the output level chosen since this is affected by demand conditions.

Exercise 2

Objectives

- To practise using the economists' cost classifications:
  - by cost type; *fixed costs, variable costs*
  - by method of representation: *total costs, average costs, marginal cost.*
- To see how a firm's costs change with changes in its level of activity: the generalized patterns called cost curves.
- To think about how costs are influenced by the scale on which the firm chooses to operate.

Methods

- We use a made up example: a knitwear manufacturer producing sweaters.
- Sweater production involves several stages, such as knitting, making up, labelling and packing, which must be shared among the production team.
- We will assume that the firm's equipment is *fixed*, comprising two knitting machines plus ancillary equipment like tables etc.
- The firm's resulting *fixed costs* are rents on buildings and equipment. These are *unavoidable*, whether it produces or not.
- The firm's *variable costs* are its labour costs, by varying the number of workers.
- Table 5.4 gives details of fixed costs, material costs, how production varies with the number of workers and the wage rate. We can use this information to calculate the missing cost quantities.

1   Fill in the blank spaces in Table 5.4 for

    total labour cost, total material cost, total variable cost, total cost, average fixed cost, average variable cost, average total cost.

2   Complete the calculations of *marginal cost* in Table 5.5.

Table 5.4 Production and cost data

Fixed costs: £50 per day
Wage: £25 per day
Materials: £2 per day

Labour (number of workers)	Maximum output (sweaters per day)	Total fixed cost (£/day)	Total labour cost (£/day)	Total material cost (£/day)	Total variable cost (£/day)	Total cost (£/day)	Average fixed cost (£/sweater)	Average variable cost (£/sweater)	Average total cost (£/sweater)
0	0	50	0	0	0	50	N/A	N/A	N/A
1	4	50	25	8	33	83	12.50	8.25	20.75
2	10	50							
3	13	50							
4	15	50	100	30	130	180	3.33	8.67	12.00
5	16	50	125	32	157	207	3.125	9.81	12.94

Source: adapted from Parkin and King 1992

Table 5.5 Marginal costs

Output (sweaters per day)	Total cost (£/day)	Calculation: $\Delta TC/\Delta Q$	MC (£/sweater)
0	50		
		$(83 - 50) \div 4$	8.25
4	83		
10	120		
13	151		
15	180		
		$(207 - 180) \div (16 - 15)$	27
16	207		

3 Plot the following graphs:
   a) on one set of axes:
        Horizontal axis: output (sweaters/day)
        Vertical axis: cost (£/day)
            total fixed cost (TFC)
            total variable cost (TVC)
            total cost (TC)
   b) on another set of axes:
        Horizontal axis: output (sweaters/day)
        Vertical axis: average cost (£/sweater)
            average fixed cost (AFC)
            average variable cost (AVC)
            average total cost (ATC).

   I suggest you do this in pairs, one plotting (a) and the other (b).
4 Plot the values of *marginal cost* on graph (b).
   NOTE: The horizontal position of each point for marginal cost should be at the *average* of the outputs used to calculate it. For example, the first point should be plotted at 2 sweaters/day, the average of 0 and 4.

Further questions

Once you have completed the graphs, join up with another pair. I suggest you first compare graphs to see if you both have the same answers! Now consider the following:

1 Can you explain the following features of the shape of the average cost curves:

   a) The downward slope of the AFC curve?
   b) The initial downward slope of the AVC and ATC curves?
   c) The upturn of the AVC and ATC curves?

(b and c reflect what are technically labelled *increasing returns to the labour input* and *diminishing returns to the labour input*. You should consider what *causes* these effects).

2 What do you notice about the points at which the MC curve crosses the AVC and ATC curves? Can you see an intuitive reason for this observation?

3 The costs you have been working with reflect the firm's position when some of its resources are *fixed*; that is its production facility and equipment which we've said incur an unavoidable daily cost. These fixed facilities limit the economic output of the firm as the ATC curve slopes upward ever more steeply. But this is only a constraint in the *short run*. In the long run *everything is variable*, and the firm could change its capacity by taking on more machinery, or by changing its machinery so that it could achieve a higher output with the same quantity of labour, or by automating some currently manual operations. This change in capacity is also known as a change in *scale*. Draw a sketch showing how the firm's ATC curve might change if it can increase the number of knitting machines, or automate some of the other production stages. You might draw a *family* of average cost curves showing how they are affected by the scale, or capacity, of the firm.

Feedback to Exercise 2

Table 5.6 Completed version of Table 5.4

Labour (number of workers)	Output (sweater per day)	TFC (£/day)	TLC (£/day)	TMC (£/day)	TVC (£/day)	TC (£/day)	AFC (£/unit)	AVC (£/unit)	ATC (£/unit)
0	0	50	0	0	0	25	N/A	N/A	N/A
1	4	50	25	8	33	83	12.50	8.25	20.75
2	10	50	50	20	70	120	5.00	7.00	12.00
3	13	50	75	26	101	151	3.85	7.77	11.62
4	15	50	100	30	130	180	3.33	8.67	12.00
5	16	50	125	32	157	207	3.125	9.81	12.94

Table 5.7 Complete table 5.5

Output (sweaters per day)	Total cost (£/day)	Calculation: ΔTC/ΔQ	MC (£/sweater)
0	50		
		(83 − 50)/4	8.25
4	83		
		(120−83)/(10−4)	6.17
10	120		
		(151−120)/(13−10)	10.33
13	151		
		(180−151)/(15−13)	14.50
15	180		
		(207−180)/(16 −15)	27.00
16	207		

Discussion points

1 (a): Fixed cost spread over more output.
  (b) and (c): Usual arguments for *increasing returns* followed by *diminishing returns*
  – e.g. L = 1, that worker has to do all tasks;
  – L = 2 allows each to specialize (perhaps one knits full-time while the other does other tasks plus some knitting on the second machine - division of labour);
  – L = 3 allows both knitting machines to be in use while a third worker carries out other tasks;
  — L = 4 the additional worker allows a little more division of labour, perhaps specialization within one task, such as making up: one sews on right arm, another the left. But the extra output from increasing division of labour diminishes as the gains from increasing specialization get less.
  – Stress the **law of diminishing returns** as a counterpart of the **law of demand**. At least in the *short run* output cannot be expanded indefinitely without coming up against diminishing returns to some inputs. So, for a given capacity (capital equipment), as output increases, two things happen: revenues grow less rapidly or decline and costs eventually rise. So there is an economic limit to the output of any given size plant (see below).
  – Simple representation of a firm as AC curve and an MC curve.
2 MC crosses both AVC and ATC at their *lowest point*. Reason: if MC < AC, an additional unit must *reduce* the average; if MC > AC, an additional unit *increases* average; if MC = AC, an additional unit leaves average unchanged, so MC = AC at point where AC is *level*.

3 **Economies of scale** – incresaing scale shifts AC curve as follows:
   a) to the *right*: in buying more knitting machines the knitwear company should be able to produce a larger quantity with equal costs;
   b) *downward*: increasing output can give increased opportunities for specialization and automation.

One can draw a family of AC curves at different scales. The envelope around these curves is called the **long-run average cost curve (LRAC)** – see Figure 5.10.

Once all opportunities for specialization and automation are realized, the firm has achieved *lowest possible cost*. The scale at which this occurs is called the **minimum efficient scale** (MES).

The replication argument implies an extended flat portion of LRAC.

Eventually, **diseconomies of scale** are likely to set in, due to some resource constraint or to managerial inefficiency as the firm becomes larger. Then the LRAC will begin to rise.

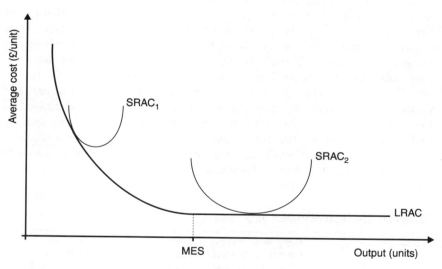

Figure 5.10 Long-run average cost curve

Chapter 6

The spectrum of market structures

Before we study the behaviour of firms further, it will be helpful to consider the structure of markets. The classifications used are somewhat arbitrary, and may be varied for different purposes. What is important here is to recognize that these structures comprise a *spectrum*, ranging between two important *limiting cases* (see Table 6.1). The limiting cases are perfect competition and monopoly. Pure examples of these are unlikely to exist in the real world, and most markets lie somewhere between these two extremes. Nevertheless, for the time being our analysis will focus on the two limiting cases. Their (relative) simplicity means that they offer insights into the outcomes in real markets, while avoiding the considerable analytical complexities that arise when studying the intermediate market structures. The main point that we should notice is that market structure will determine conduct and performance of firms. By conduct we mean the strategies and actions of firms in deciding on prices, scale of output, product characteristics, etc. By performance we mean the way firms behave in terms of cost reduction, innovation and product development. Later, we will consider performance in the wider sense in terms of performance of markets.

Table 6.1 Spectrum of market structures

Perfect competition	Many seller and many buyers for each product. (Therefore, products are in effect undifferentiated). Easy entry and exit	⇓
Monopolistic competition	Few sellers and many buyers for each product type, but many near-substitute products (i.e. products are differentiated). Easy entry and exit.	⇓
Oligopoly	Few sellers, many buyers. Could be a single product, or a few or even many products. Multiple products would be differentiated. Barriers to entry	Fewer suppliers ⇓
Duopoly	As oligopoly, but only two sellers	
Monopoly	A sole supplier to many buyers. Barriers to entry	⇓

MODELS OF MARKET STRUCTURE

We now need to examine in simplified form the models developed by economists in order to explain the behaviour of firms in different market situations. We will endeavour to keep the complexities of the argument to the minimum needed to see the possibilities and weaknesses of the market mechanism as a means of allocating scarce resources. This will lead us later on to consideration of circumstances in which markets may fail in some way. If they do fail, then it may be that there is a role for society, through the mechanism of the state, to minimize that failure, perhaps by regulation, or even to install some system which does not rely on the market.

In Figure 5.6 we developed the following proposition: *Profit is maximized at the output where total revenue from sales exceeds total costs of production by the greatest amount, which is the same output where marginal cost is equal to marginal revenue, i.e. MC = MR.* But so far we have not fully explained the relationship between a firm's marginal revenue (the additional revenue from one extra unit of sales) and price and demand in the market place. We shall see that these relationships differ according to market structure, and it is for this reason that the conduct and performance of firms depends on the structure of the market.

The perfect competition model

The market structure of perfect competition has the following characteristics:

- There are many small firms in all industries.
- Firms are profit maximizers.
- There are no barriers to entry or exit, and firms can readily switch resources between uses.
- For any given product there are many perfect substitutes, so that consumers choose which to buy solely on the basis of price.
- Consumers have perfect knowledge of prices and suppliers in the market on which to base decisions.

Although we did not stress it at the time, the supply and demand analysis of market which we discussed in Chapter 3 was implicitly a model of perfectly competitive markets. In that section, we confined attention to analysis of the market as a whole, but here we are going to look a little more deeply at what happens at the level of the firm as well as at the level of the whole market.

Let us consider the behaviour of demand, both at the level of the market and at the level of the firm. We decided earlier that the demand curve for any product is likely to slope downwards from left to right. Take, for example, beer. The demand curve for the whole brewing industry will slope downward from left to right, since there is always the possibility for substitution (of, say, lager or lemonade). The demand curve for each brewery will slope similarly, but less steeply. Why? Because there is the possibility of substituting say Tetley's for Bass or John Smiths. That is, there are several possible close substitutes for the product of any brewery.

There is a limited number of large breweries, each with a level of brand loyalty. What if beer were homogenous, like milk? Suppose that there were thousands of small breweries, none of which could establish brand loyalty because the product was always very similar whichever brewery made it, and one of the firms were big enough to spend money creating a false loyalty through advertising? What shape would the demand curve be then? For the whole industry it would still be the same shape as before, downward sloping. But if any individual brewery tried to sell at a price above the market price, it would sell nothing, since consumers can buy perfect substitutes at the market price. Thus, at any price higher than the market price, the firm's demand falls to zero, so the firm's demand curve is horizontal (see the left-hand side of Figure 6.1). In a competitive market, the firm can only charge the price dictated by market supply and demand.

A term used to capture this idea is that in perfectly competitive markets, firms are *price takers*. They are individually too small to influence the market price, and any attempt to sell above the market price will result in zero sales. It is the implications of this for the marginal revenue of the firm that we must show in our model in order to predict and explain the behaviour of firms in a perfectly competitive market.

Marginal revenue is the additional revenue received from selling one extra unit. Now, if a small firm, facing a horizontal demand curve, increases its sales there is no effect on market price from the increase in sales. Therefore, the firm gains additional revenue equal to the price multiplied by the number of additional units sold. The marginal revenue of each extra unit is

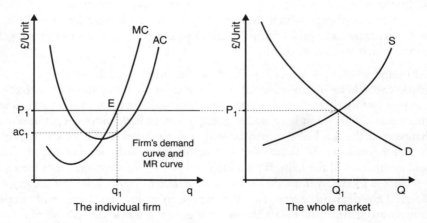

Figure 6.1 Perfect competition model

simply equal to the price, i.e. in a competitive market, MR = P. Now, recall that profit is maximised when MR = MC. Therefore, the profit maximising level of output for a firm in a competitive market is that at which price is equal to marginal cost. This is at point E in Figure 6.1.

We can now demonstrate how the process of dynamic adjustment of perfectly competitive markets leads to the idealized efficiency properties of this market structure. Consider the firm shown in Figure 6.1. Its profit maximizing level of output is q_1, which it sells at market price P_1, but for which the average cost is ac_1. It therefore makes a supernormal profit, since the selling price exceeds the average cost. Under the assumptions of perfect competition, new firms can freely enter the market, and the supernormal profits currently being earned will tempt new firms to enter. This will shift the market supply curve to the right (see Figure 6.2), and the market price will fall. New entry, and hence falling prices, will continue until supernormal profits have been eliminated, that is until price falls to P_2 in Figure 6.2, which is equal to ac_2, the minimum point of the individual firm's average cost curve. We can also conclude that the firms in this market are the lowest cost producers, since any firm which could produce at cost lower than the market price would be able to enter and earn supernormal profits for at least a limited period.

Now, the outcome of this process is both allocatively efficient (or efficient in consumption) and technically efficient (or efficient in production). It is allocatively efficient because there is no redistribution of resources which can make someone better off without making someone else worse off. The willingness to pay for the last unit (the price) just equals the opportunity cost of the last unit (MC) and any alteration in output would reduce the surplus enjoyed by at least some consumers or producers. It is technically efficient because the firms which remain in the market are the

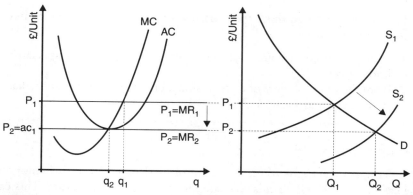

Figure 6.2 Adjustment in perfect competition

lowest cost producers and, what is more, they produce at the lowest point of their average cost curve.

Now let us summarize what we have discovered.

The miracle of competitive markets

If a market is perfectly competitive:

- *It is* **technically efficient** *(efficient in production).* The profit motive encourages firms to find the lowest cost method of production, and to enter markets until only normal (zero) profits are earned. Then, all firms operate at their most efficient output, minimizing average cost per unit, and maximizing their use of resources. We are on the **production possibility frontier** because we are at the lowest average cost.
- *It is* **allocatively efficient** *(efficient in consumption).* Consumers have maximum choice, at the lowest possible price. The profit maximizing motive induces price-taking firms to select that output on the **production possibility frontier** where P = MC, that is willingness to pay for the last unit equals the opportunity cost of the last unit.

If *all* markets in the economic system are *perfect* the whole economy is *allocatively and technically efficient.* The **Pareto condition of welfare** is fulfilled, no one can be made better off without someone being made worse off. This is what Adam Smith meant by the invisible hand of the market. *Idealized markets are truly miraculous.*

Is this in fact a likely scenario? Are there any circumstances in which markets might fail? We shall consider imperfect markets shortly. We looked at other reasons for market failure in Chapter 4, but first reinforce your understanding of the argument so far by doing Activity 6.1.

Activity 6.1

How closely do you think the market for video recording tape comes to a perfect market:

1) from the point of view of the householder (with no specialist knowledge)
2) from the point of view of a professional broadcaster, (with specialist knowledge and more stringent requirements).

The monopoly model

At the opposite extreme of the spectrum of market structures is monopoly, the case when a single firm is sole supplier to a particular market. This can only arise if the firm's position is protected by barriers preventing other firms from entering the market. We can represent monopoly neatly in our diagrammatic model, as shown in Figure 6.3. The firm is now the only one in the industry and its demand curve is therefore the same as the industry demand curve, downward sloping from left to right, at a slope determined by the extent to which substitutes exist from other industry sectors (e.g. if the monopolist is a railway company, then car travel is a substitute for rail travel).

The demand curve indicates how the price, which is also the average revenue, falls as output increases since higher outputs may only be sold at lower prices. For the reasons we discussed earlier the marginal revenue of each extra unit sold is less than the price at which it is sold. This is because the extra revenue obtained from selling the extra unit is partly offset by the reduction in price needed to achieve the extra sale and which affects all units sold.

The firm seeks to maximize profit, which will be achieved at the output where MC = MR, which is point E in Figure 6.3. At that output, Q_m, the demand situation dictates that price will be P_m. As you can see, this price is significantly above the average cost of production at that level of output, ac_m, so that the firm makes a substantial monopoly profit.

What can we say about the efficiency of this monopoly outcome? First of all, we should note that the price at which product is sold is considerably higher than the marginal cost of the product, and so this is allocatively inefficient (i.e. inefficient in consumption). There are unsatisfied consumers

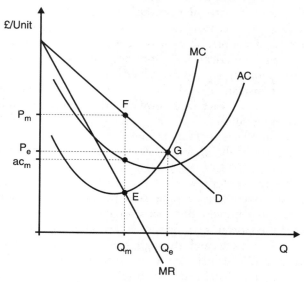

Figure 6.3 Monopoly model

whose willingness to pay is less than P_m but greater than MC, whose demand is represented by the segment FG of the demand curve. Efficiency would require that the monopolist undersupplies the market, and there is a loss of welfare for consumers equal to the area of the triangle EFG (the dead-weight loss of monopoly).

Furthermore, supply may be technically inefficient (i.e. inefficient in production) for two reasons: because there is no potential entry into the market, there is no strong incentive for the monopolist to find the lowest cost method of production; and it may even tolerate some wasteful production methods. It would only be by coincidence if the monopolist happened to produce at the minimum of its AC curve. You can see that ac_m in Figure 6.3 is not the lowest average cost. This condition is only brought about in competitive markets by the entry process we studied in Figure 6.2.

MARKET STRUCTURE IN PRACTICE

We pointed out at the start of this section that perfect competition and monopoly are two limiting cases at either end of a spectrum of market structures. Most real markets have a structure which is at some point on the spectrum between these extremes.

In fact, it might be expected that, if either extreme existed in reality, they may well not persist indefinitely. Consider, for example, our assumptions on which the perfect competition model was based. A fundamental assumption was that the products are undifferentiated, that is there are many suppliers of any particular product or product form. But if firms can differentiate their product from others in the market they begin to appeal to different groups of people. They may achieve this by product innovation (adding new characteristics), by improving quality or by altering public perception and product loyalty (by advertising). This would affect product demand so that instead of each firm in an industry facing a horizontal demand curve, they will each face a downward sloping demand curve. It will remain relatively shallow, since the other products are still quite close substitutes but in effect, so long as they can convince the public that the product differs from all others in the market, the firm has a degree of monopoly power.

Likewise a pure monopoly is unlikely to remain unchallenged, for one reason because government competition policy is designed to challenge excessive monopoly power. But increasingly, the barriers to entry which might protect the power of monopolies are breaking down through the globalization of markets and through technical change. For example, a company such as BT (British Telecommunications plc), which would have once been thought to have been a natural monopoly because the costs of installing a competing telephone network were prohibitively high, now has competition from the networks being installed by cable TV companies, and from cellular radio networks, as well as a government imposed requirement to provide *common carrier* access to competitors on its own network.

In many industries, the size of the *minimum efficient scale* of supply (that is, the output at the minimum of the long run average cost curve) is a significant proportion of the size of the market. Therefore a fairly small number of minimum efficient scale firms can often supply the whole market. Many markets are thus naturally oligopolies. Detailed economic models of oligopolistic markets are beyond the scope of the present treatment, and are dealt with in detail in Chapters 7–14, but we might note one or two points of importance:

- If the firms in an oligopoly can collude together, they have the potential to exercise a considerable degree of monopoly power. They will, of course, be liable under government competition policy for severely anti-competitive behaviour, but this may not prevent the firms from finding some means of collaborating to their mutual benefit. Collusion of this sort is often tacit rather than explicit.
- If any collusion, either tacit or explicit, is to occur, it is more likely to be sustainable if there are fewer firms in the market. Therefore, existing firms have an incentive to prevent the entry of new firms into the market, and may do so by erecting barriers to entry. These can take many forms, but an obvious example is the promotion of customer loyalty to a particular brand by intensive advertising.
- Collusion is far from being the only possible outcome in oligopoly. It is also possible for firms to engage in *cut-throat competition*. They may be locked in a struggle for dominance, or even survival, in a market where each firm thinks it has more to lose by not fighting than by fighting.

SUMMARY

This chapter has examined the economic outcomes in two extreme market structures. We discovered the following:

- In perfect competition, individual firms are price takers and face horizontal demand curves.
- Therefore in perfect competition, firms choose the level of output where price (or willingness to pay) is equal to marginal cost, corresponding to efficiency in consumption (allocative efficiency).
- The process of dynamic competition in competitive markets means that only the lowest cost producers remain in the market, and that they produce at minimum average cost. So competitive markets are also efficient in production (technically efficient).
- In a monopoly market structure, the firm can get a higher price and greater profit by restricting output. Therefore, monopoly is inefficient in

consumption. Without competitive cost incentives it may also be inefficient in production.

- The structure of most markets lies between these extremes, and so there is usually scope for firms to exploit some monopoly power.

SUMMARY OF CONCLUSIONS: CHAPTERS 1–6

Now let us draw together our key conclusions so far:

- Resources are always scarce in relation to insatiable human wants.
- Some means must be found to decide how they should be allocated between different uses.
- Such a mechanism must be able to decide
  a) what to produce
  b) how to produce it
  c) who to produce it for.
- Alternative mechanisms are
  a) central planning
  b) markets
  c) some combinations of a) and b).
- At their best markets can get close to responding to peoples' needs and wants with allocative and technical efficiency.
- We can state a precise condition of **allocative efficiency** (efficiency in consumption), which is when the consumers' willingness to pay for the last unit produced (the market price) equals the marginal cost (opportunity cost) of production.
- **Technical efficiency** (efficiency in production) means using the lowest cost method of production available. For any given output this means costs are given by the average cost curve of the lowest cost technology. The most productively efficient level of output is at the minimum of the average cost curve.
- Perfectly competitive markets populated by profit maximizing firms lead to the ideal outcome of allocative and technical efficiency.
- Markets are prone to imperfections, such as monopoly power, when profit maximization may be an obstacle to the efficient application of resources.

TECHNICAL APPENDIX: THE PROFIT MAXIMIZING FIRM IN MONOPOLISTIC COMPETITION

This model describes the market structure in numerous real world markets, for example printing.

Assumptions

- Many firms.
- These firms can act independently without worrying about competitor's actions.
- Freedom of entry into the market.
- Only one firm in any location.

It is therefore similar to *perfect competition* except in one important respect. Its products are to a degree *differentiated* from those of its rivals. It therefore faces a *downward sloping demand curve*.

Conclusions

The firm will (as in the other market structures) maximize profit where MC = MR. The demand curve (AR curve) will be more elastic than in a monopoly, since substitutes are available, if inconveniently. The firm will make supernormal profits equal to the shaded area in Figure 6.4 *in the short run*.

In the long run supernormal profits will attract *new entrants* into the market. This will reduce demand for the original firm's product, causing the D (AR) curve to shift to the left. This process will continue as more new entrants appear. Eventually equilibrium will be established when all firms are earning only normal profits as in Figure 6.5.

It should be noted that output is lower and price higher than would be the case if the market were perfectly competitive.

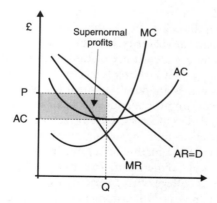

Figure 6.4 Monopolistic competition in the short run

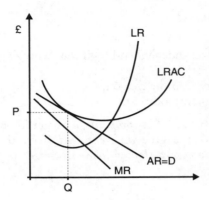

Figure 6.5 Monopolistic competition in the long run

CASE STUDY 6: THE LANZAROTI RESTAURANTS – AN EXAMPLE OF PERFECT COMPETITION

Lanzaroti is one of the Canary Islands, and is a very popular all the year round resort. The principal resort on the island is Puerto del Carmen, a former fishing village now greatly expanded in size. The government of the island has set out regulations to maintain a distinctive atmosphere, seeking to avoid the development of large numbers of high-rise hotels. Most of the accommodation is self-catering villas and apartments, and very few buildings of more than two storeys have been permitted. There are only a couple of hotels in Puerto del Carmen. As a result most holidaymakers eat out. In the old town and along the coastal strip (about a mile long), there are many small shop units, of which the majority have been developed as small restaurants and cafés. They offer a wide variety of European and Asian cuisines. All are of small size (thirty to fifty covers). Local by-laws do not permit advertising. Most of these businesses are family owned. It is possible to walk around all the restaurants inspecting the menus and facilities within a day.

As a result of all these factors these restaurants are all price takers. It is possible to attract customers in varying numbers at the going market price (about 1,000 pesetas for a main course) but few or none at any other price. For example, a local council initiative to establish a training restaurant attached to the local college with a very high standard of cuisine and service was a failure within a year. No customers materialized because the price was over 150 per cent of the going price.

How would you use the theoretical models we have developed to explain or predict the behaviour of restaurant firms in this market-place?

Questions

1 How would our model explain the existing circumstances?
2 How would it explain the circumstances if one restaurant which was able to staff its operations entirely with family rather than hire labour?
3 How might the proprietor of one restaurant differentiate his or her product and gain a temporary advantage by doing so? What would our model have to say?
4 Suppose a local supermarket chain were to buy up twenty strategically placed restaurants how might it affect the market? What would our model have to say?
5 Suppose a competing supermarket firm bought up twenty restaurants, how would this affect the market?
6 Suppose the island government decided in order to pursue a programme of infrastructure development, it needed a new source of revenue, and took over compulsorily both restaurant groups? What prediction would our model offer?

When you have attempted all these questions, check your answers against the suggested approaches in the feedback section.

Case study feedback

1 The circumstances described in the case study are as near as possible to perfect competition. All the firms have identical cost structures. Since consumers have perfect knowledge of the market, all firms face an identical demand and marginal revenue curve which is horizontal. Any firm which seeks to win market share by cutting prices will make losses and close down. Since all its customers will go elsewhere, any firm which raises prices will also either close, or return to the price which operates across the whole market.

All firms in the market will make only normal profit – the opportunity cost of alternative uses of the capital and proprietors' labour. This situation is represented in the conventional diagram in Figure 6.6.

A firm in any market structure will maximize profits where output is such that MR = MC. In perfect competition the MR is the same as price, (since the D curve is horizontal). *Therefore the profit maximizing output for the Lanzaroti restaurant is that at which price = marginal cost, that is output oq.*

2 In this case the firm in question is obviously paying family members lower wages than those using hired labour. It will therefore have *lower* average and marginal costs than the others. For a time it will make supernormal profits. But (assuming there is no legal minimum wage in operation) the other restaurants are likely to lower their wages.

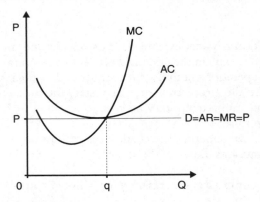

Figure 6.6 Normal profits model

The market will quickly return to an equilibrium position where all make only normal profit, but since all forms have lower costs, prices will also be lower in all restaurants.

3 There are many ways in which one restauranteur may differentiate his or her product. For example, by offering live music, or flambeaud steaks to attract customers. But whatever he or she does others will follow, and any temporary advantage gained will be lost as the market returns to the original equilibrium.

4 Diversification by a strong supermarket company into the restaurant business on this scale would create a situation of monopolistic competition (see the Technical appendix to this chapter). Financial and marketing economies of scale would enable this strong player to reduce costs in the medium term, enabling the company to develop a brand image promoting customer loyalty even at higher prices. Supernormal profits would be earned. Meanwhile, smaller and weaker restaurants would exit the market. Market concentration has begun.

5 The entry of another strong player would continue the process of concentration described above. The two strong groups would begin to dominate the market. Weaker firms would continue to exit. The demand curve for the two big groups would be downward sloping rather than horizontal. At this point both are earning supernormal profits. What happens next depends on the strategic decisions taken by the two groups.

Scenario A: If both seek to win market share from each other by instigating a price war (as in our newspaper industry case), both will in the long run find that supernormal profits have been competed away (see Figure 6.5). Meanwhile small restaurants will continue to exit the industry unless they can cultivate a niche market.

Scenario B: If the two groups decide to collude on price, while competing only on non-price characteristics, they can preserve their supernormal profits. This will enable them to acquire more small restaurants, thus building up market share. The *concentration ratio* will rise. From the customer's point of view a monopoly situation has developed. It will be made worse by the high cost of competing through advertising. There will be less choice and higher price than in a competition market, but possibly a product of more consistent quality.

6 In this case a public sector organization would have a large market share. It would be likely to display x inefficiency, causing higher costs than the industry average, while offering a highly priced but inferior product. There would be scope for entry by aggressive and efficient private sector companies with lower costs, lower prices, and better quality products. The public sector organization would probably become a loss-maker and have to be sold back to the private sector.

CASE STUDY 7: PRICE DISCRIMINATION IN THE RAILWAY INDUSTRY – AN EXAMPLE OF MONOPOLISTIC BEHAVIOUR

Exercise

Objectives

1 To develop economic explanations of the apparently illogical pricing practices of British Rail (BR).
2 To give students an opportunity (in syndicates) to develop interpretative, evaluative and presentational skills.
3 To understand the usefulness of economic theory in business decision-making.

Methods

1 Students to prepare in advance by rereading Pass and Lowes (1994) Chapter 2, and Griffiths and Wall (1997) pp. 192–7.
2 And studying the data provided in BR pricing strategies.
3 Syndicates to be given fifteen minutes to consider their findings (based, hopefully, on informal preparation before the tutorial).
4 Syndicates to present back to group.

Pricing of rail fares: A brief guide

Before 1968, train fares in Britain were based on a uniform rate per mile. All Second Class fares had their First Class equivalents and First Class accommodation was provided on virtually all passenger trains. Only the fringes of the branch line network offered one-class accommodation, usually on trains consisting of just one vehicle. Within a standard, simple fare structure of Ordinary Singles and Ordinary Returns (long-distance Returns would offer a small discount, but Ordinary Returns for local journeys were normally twice the single), there were, of necessity, some discounted tickets. British Rail, like the old railway companies before them, have always sought to fill spare seats off-peak by offering Cheap Day Returns. In London and the South-East and in major provincial conurbations (e.g. Glasgow and Manchester), Cheap Day Returns were valid only after 09.30 Mondays–Fridays (but unrestricted at weekends) and return travel from London in the evening peak (16.30–1800) was also banned. For long-distance travel, Weekend Returns (First and Second Class) were set at attractive prices determined by the market. These fares were crucial to the marketing impact and commercial success of the very first *Inter-City* branded trains – those from Euston to Birmingham, Manchester and Liverpool which began running in 1966 when electrification of those lines was completed.

1968 was a watershed year for Britain's railways. The Government-fostered notion (now largely abandoned by Government but still commanding significant public support) that the railways are a public service, rather than, strictly speaking, a commercial undertaking, was replaced by what we would now call the 'business-led' approach. The introduction in 1968 of *Selective Pricing* freed British Rail from Government intervention in pricing (although Government stepped in from time to time in the 1970s in an effort to control high inflation). Selective pricing also meant the end of mileage-based fares. At a time of frequent fare increases, the opportunity was always taken to raise more revenue from lines which were lucky enough to have benefited from investment in new signalling or trains. Premium increases could be as much as between two and three times the rate of inflation.

In pure business terms, selective pricing has been an unqualified success. As Government subsidy for the railways has fallen progressively, *headline* fares – i.e. the full-priced, unrestricted tickets – have increased sharply in real terms. In the 1970s, soaring inflation (and damaging labour disputes) made life hard for the railways. The three horrendous fare increases of 1975 – 15% in January, 12.5% in March and another 15% in September – all but killed leisure travel and desperate measures were taken to attract bottoms to seats. *Ladies' Day* tickets fell foul of emerging sex equality legislation.

The commuter market, however, especially in London, has always been captive. It is not immune from depredation, but reductions in the number of passengers travelling into London (for instance the fall from 488,000 in 1988 to 377,000 in 1994 – it has just started to rise again) owes much more to more general economic factors than to rail fare rises or pricing policy.

Is it blue or is it white?

The biggest change in the national long-distance fares structure came in the late 1970s when British Rail decided to withdraw Weekend Returns. There was consternation at the time, but the replacement of the Weekend Return by the Saver removed a long-standing irritant. Previously, no long-distance ticket existed (other than the strato-spherically-priced Ordinary Return) which permitted return travel the *following* day (outside a Friday–Monday of the same weekend). This circumstance meant that a passenger travelling from, say, Leeds–London, travelling out on a Monday and returning Tuesday (or any day before Saturday) had no access to a discounted ticket and was bound to pay the equivalent of the current Open Return (£96 at today's prices!). The Saver, on the other hand, was and is valid for one month. The outward journey must be made on the date shown, but the passenger may return any day within one month, subject (in the case of the lower-priced SuperSaver) to a ban on Friday travel (as with the outward journey) and (in the case of journeys via or from London) to evening peak restrictions Mondays–Fridays. The reason for the original inflexibility was, of course, the desire to charge business travellers (presumed to be on expense accounts) the highest fares possible. For the rest of mortality, various 'period' returns had been offered with varying nomenclature and conditions: the 17-day return, for example, priced 15–20% above the Weekend Return, but well below the unimaginably expensive full return fare, won some passengers for rail, but you had to stay at your destination at least until the first Saturday following your outward journey. One major cause for lamentation was that no First Class discounted long-distance fares were offered under the new Saver structure – managers had evidence that, outside the prosperous South-East, demand was insufficient and that business travellers were trading down to lower-priced tickets when they (or their companies) would have otherwise paid the full whack.

The ascendancy of marketing experts was apparent in the curious strategy which BR developed for hiding the fact that train fares were high. *Low* Saver and *High* Saver, to distinguish between the off-peak (i.e. non-Friday) and premium-rated fare intended to ensnare the weekend traveller, was thought to be too simple and revealing. These tickets became known as the *Blue* (for some reason, thought to signify 'cheaper') and *White* Saver. To justify this absurd nomenclature, charts were produced with permitted dates and trains shaded in. Eventually, SuperSaver and Saver replaced the colour-coded terminology (the colours were never applied to the tickets themselves, by the way).

The Saver fare was pioneered by Ron Cotton, a BR manager based in Liverpool who later achieved fame as the man appointed to oversee closure of the Settle–Carlisle line. In the teeth of a determined campaign to shut the line, Mr Cotton applied his marketing flair and increased loadings on an enhanced service fivefold, enabling the Government to grant, grudgingly, the 1989 reprieve. Because the Saver and SuperSaver ticket's allow a month's stay (including a break-of-journey option on the return within the ticket's validity), passengers have a degree of flexibility which has proved attractive. Restrictions apply to journeys to/from and via London on Mondays–Fridays, but for all other UK journeys, Saver and SuperSaver travellers may use any *trains*; and the only restrictions as to *days* relate to SuperSaver travel on all Fridays, to Saturday travel in July and August and to travel on other named peak days around public holidays.

One important exception is that within the former *Network SouthEast* area, long-stay journeys wholly within that area are still charged at the full Ordinary Return fares, except that a Network Awaybreak, heavily restricted and invalid on peak-hour trains, is available with a mere 5-day validity. Thus, a journey from, say, Oxford–Brighton involving a longer stay is punitively expensive. There is some disquiet as to how much business the railways turn away as a result. Occasionally, some even question the wider effects of charging such high fares – the effects on road congestion, for instance – but there is no national transport policy worthy of the name. Until there is, railway managers will always be expected to charge as much as the market will bear. For the same reason, long-distance Day Returns (for journeys over 50 miles) were subsequently withdrawn (except for journeys wholly within the former *Network SouthEast* area) and those passengers forced to use SuperSavers (or, of course, Savers on Fridays). This withdrawal simplified the fare structure, but increased by as much as a third the cost of long-distance day return travel. Since then, the various Regional Railways companies have adopted a policy of offering long-distance day return fares for selected journeys above 50 miles (typically distances of around 100 miles, such as Leeds–Carlisle), but where a Day Return, as such, exists, the next fare up is the Saver (i.e. no SuperSaver is offered).

Passenger Transport Executives [PTEs]

Within the seven area PTEs (all function outside London), a completely independent local fares system operates, set by the relevant authority. The PTE fare systems deserve a whole paper to themselves. Generally, fares are much lower than for rural and trunk Regional Railways services. West Yorkshire *Metro*, for instance, pioneered the all bus-and-train countrywide Season ticket – the MetroCard – and the then unified London and SouthEast arm of BR – *Network SouthEast* – quickly followed with a suitably more expensive TravelCard, including combined BR and tube travel. Off-peak travel in West Yorkshire is a bargain. The maximum single at such times is currently £1.10 (that will take you from Walsden in Calderdale to South Elmsall near Doncaster!) and the bus and train Day Rover (available only after 09.30 Mondays–Fridays, but otherwise unrestricted) at £2.30 is outstanding. Where there is a large urban population on which to draw and where services are frequent, reliable and improving, a substantial shift to rail can be achieved. Of course, complications and Byzantine rules apply where train services operate partly within and partly outside PTE boundaries. Fares from boundary stations to the next non-PTE station are invariably 'end-loaded' – to prevent two-stage ticket purchases being cheaper than the through fare! Steeton & Silsden–Skipton Day Return (two stops) is £2.20!

The aim of all PTEs has been to ensure that rail helps to relieve road congestion and improve the quality of life in our major cities by offering attractive season ticket deals to the committed, regular traveller. To secure that commitment, the authorities have, in most cases, charged 'economic' fares (i.e. fares set at the prices which would apply over the rest of BR) during peak periods. The notable exception was South Yorkshire. That authority's 'anywhere-anytime for 5p' on the buses and correspondingly low fares on its sponsored train services (Sheffield–Barnsley cost 36p in the late 1970s) merely increased exponentially the cost of providing vehicles and crews to meet the demand. Where 'economic' peak fares are charged, the resulting increase in pre-paid travel guarantees regular income and helps reduce staffing costs (because less station ticket office staff are needed). Greater use of pre-paid tickets also facilitates on-train ticket checks and reduces fraudulent travel. Despite latent Conservative suspicion of PTEs (most of which are formed of Labour-controlled councils), there is a tacit consensus that the PTEs have done well and given good value to the rail passenger and taxpayer alike.

Anomalies

Selective pricing, then, has continued since 1968 and every year railway business managers try to refine the mechanism in order to rake in as much money as possible. The field is, of course, littered with anomalies! Some of these are merely accidental or have survived because it has not been possible to rectify an anomaly on the occasion of a fare increase. There is, for example, no rational reason why the Saver fare (permitting Friday and other named peak-day travel) from Bradford–Nottingham should be £8.50 more than the SuperSaver, whereas the difference for the equi-distant journey to Lincoln is a matter of a fiver. Sometimes, variations in the surcharge for Friday travel *do* reflect commercial considerations. *East Coast* (providing InterCity services from Scotland, the North-East, Yorkshire, Humberside and London) charges £55 for a Bradford/Leeds–London Saver – £10 more than the SuperSaver. *InterCity CrossCountry*, however, with a heavy weekend 'VFR' trade (Visiting Friends and Relatives), including many students holding Young Persons' Railcards offering a third discount off most tickets, deliberately hikes up the weekend Saver fare in order to raise the yield from discounted tickets. Bradford–Exeter return, for instance, costs £56 SuperSaver, but a Saver journey costs £79. These examples constitute the meagrest sample!

Privatisation: The plot yet thickens

The former Secretary of State for Transport, Mr John Macgregor, baffled the entire railway industry and travelling public when he told the Commons that 'I look forward to an even greater variety of fares after rail privatisation.' Computer technology has enabled the railways to segment the market and to sell long-distance travel just like the airlines. You pay so much according to how old you are, when and where you are travelling, when (or if) you are coming back, whether or not you have booked in advance and reserved a seat. The variations are numerous, though there is logic to the basic fares structure. Introduction of Railcards in the 1970s and 1980s has enabled the railways to popularise rail travel amongst the retired and amongst students. Even the Family Railcard makes a significant contribution to revenue; at the other end, well over four million Senior Railcards are sold each year. There are even local Railcards. Introduction of the Cornish, the Highland and (closer to home) Dales Railcard (the latter discounts travel on the Leeds–Morecambe/Carlisle routes for anybody who lives along them from Skipton onwards) enables the train operators to attract all year-round local usage. At the same time, they can raise the headline fares so as to milk the tourists! Introduction of Advanced Purchase tickets (Apex and SuperApex and SuperAdvance), of reservable and walk-on First Class upgrades (where you pay £5 or £6 to trade up on Saturdays and Sundays) such as Weekend First, Leisure First (a weekday version sold at half the full 1st class fare) and First Advance (a similar *CrossCountry* offer) has succeeded in filling spare capacity whilst (to use the jargon) retaining the revenue base.

At local level, *Regional Railways* increasingly differentiates the price of peak and off-peak travel (e.g. Bradford–York £8.90 Day Return Mon–Fri before 09.30; thereafter £6.40). This helps to spread the load – vital when you consider how scarce rolling stock is in the new contract-driven internal railway market. People travelling to work or school cannot usually choose when to travel. In the appalling case of *South and West Trains* and their Paignton–Exmouth service, the train operator seems perfectly prepared to use fare increases (in this case of up to 56%) to drive passengers away, so that it is not forced to acquire an additional diesel unit (for which there is no work for the rest of the day) at an annual leasing cost of over £200,000. In the Government's peculiar privatisation set-up, fares can be used, it seems, not merely to spread the load but to reduce it!

The problem with the Government's obsession with 'competition' and 'choice' is that, as far as rail fares are concerned, the passenger faces rather more in the way of confusion and, paradoxically, *less* choice. Already, rail fares are perceived as (and often are) very complicated. The proposal to make tickets more route-specific (solely so that revenue can be more accurately attributed to the new operating companies) removes network benefits. This, ultimately, might deter use of the railways. The emerging routeing guide is incomplete, full of anomalies and unworkable. They should let well alone! Cheaper fares are available if you use *RR North-East's* Settle–Carlisle line en route to Glasgow, but few people are likely to discover this and, even then, they may find that their journey opportunities are severely restricted. (For instance, the last train Southbound from Glasgow with a connection at Carlisle is 16.08 and there are only Sunday trains on a few occasions before 7 April 1996). InterCity *CrossCountry*, keen to increase business travellers, offers a third off the high First Class fare (Leeds–Birmingham 1st return for £49 instead of £75), provided that you book no later than 2 p.m. the previous day and provided the quota limit has not been used up. However, the ticket is only available between stations served directly by *CrossCountry* and you can only use *their* trains. In the case of Leeds–Birmingham, that limits you to just seven departures from Leeds per weekday, whereas the all-singing-all-dancing ticket at £75 allows many more journey opportunities – travel via Manchester, for instance. Furthermore, a separate ticket has to be purchased for travel by any connecting trains not operated by *CrossCountry*. A more laudable example of Mr Macgregor's 'greater variety of rail fares' is *Chiltern Trains'* 'TurboSaver' – a Saver Return valid only on the company's Turbo Class 165 diesel trains out of Marylebone and heading towards Birmingham Snow Hill, but otherwise unrestricted. Good value, indeed, at £20 (compared with *IC West Coast's* pre-11.00 arrival in Birmingham fare Mondays–Fridays of £54 – an Open Return, in other words), but how many people are prepared to take 50 minutes longer and have the choice of only one train per hour as against *West Coast's* half-hourly service to Birmingham New St? It is astonishing, too, that 'TurboSaver' is printed on the ticket! What ordinary passenger with no specialist interest in railways could possibly be expected to know what a 'Turbo' is? No-one objects to new and imaginatively-marketed bargain fares – and *Chiltern Trains'* is one such – but users are rightly concerned that the break-up of the railway is leading to loss of flexibility, increasing incoherence and, for many passengers most of the time, more real expense.

As BR finally breaks up and the Train Operators enjoy (theoretically, at least) greater commercial freedom, some consequences for the fare structure and for fare levels are already emerging. Train leasing is incredibly expensive – £200,000 per year for just one two-car diesel unit, a cost incurred before it has even left the siding – and none of the operators want trains on their books that cannot earn their keep. 'Load management' is, therefore, the name of the game. The Regulator has capped fare rises for many types of ticket, but, crucially, in respect of long-distance travel, he has protected only the Saver, NOT the *Super*Saver. *Anglia InterCity* (Norwich–London) and *West Coast* (Scotland–N.W.–West Midlands–London) have already scrapped the SuperSaver. In other words, you pay the higher Saver fare every time (nice little back-door fare increase there) and if you want to pay the SuperSaver fare, you book ahead and get a SuperAdvance. Like the Apex, that ticket restricts you to a specific train, there and back (the SuperSaver is a walk-on fare), so the train operators are able to spread the load and force 'optional' travellers onto less busy trains (meaning that they will need to lease fewer vehicles). The unsuspecting, unprepared traveller, meanwhile, will just turn up and be forced to pay the higher Saver fare. And we have seen already that *South and West Trains* is more than content to raise fares in order to lose passengers altogether, rather than be left with rolling stock that it cannot profitably use for most of the time. Of course, *South and West* are unable to transfer the train to the many operators who *could* use it, since it must stay with the train operator to which it has been leased!

Within a unified system, selective pricing has, perhaps, served the rail user well. Most European railways are moving towards market-pricing, but it is very unlikely that they will develop anything so exquisitely complicated or amusing as ours! Or, that they will throw away (as we seem gaily happy to do) the benefits of a *national* rail network and a sound commercial and socially-responsible *national* fares structure. When all the accountants and lawyers have made their mint out of this privatisation (and it is an eternal and lucrative earner for them), we shall see whether or not the Railways Act (1993) has succeeded in its declared aim of 'promoting wider use of the railway network'. As of today, whilst the shake-up has produced some fringe benefits, the pressures of the contract-driven railway and the associated tariffs mean that the train operators will be hard-put to make any money (though some directors and managers might be able to make lots of money for themselves). They certainly cannot generate any money for capital investment (whether Railtrack can generate sufficient is also open to doubt). The Regulator has limited increases to the prices of many ticket types, but much damage can still be done to the very sophisticated and delicate pricing mechanism which has evolved since 1968. If, as a result of meddling, revenues fall, we all know which lines are most likely to close; and who will be poorer as a result - the rail user!

Dr Robin Sisson
November 1995

The author is a member of the Rail Users' Consultative Committee for North-Eastern England. The views here expressed are personal. (Prepared for the Economics and Business Studies Departments of Bradford Grammar School and for Mr Malcolm Greenwood.

The following appendix gives an example of a typical long-distance fares structure: Bradford–London.

Appendix

A typical InterCity fares structure, Bradford–London

These fares are set by *InterCity East Coast*

Single	£48	
Cheap Single	£44	(sold when SuperSaver available)
SuperSaver	£45	
*SuperAdvance	£45	(like Apex, but sold less than 7 days prior to travel)
Saver	£55	
*Leisure First Return	£71	

Open Return (Std)   £96
Full 1st Return   £142 (single fare is £71)
*Apex (Std)   £28 (also promotional day return version on
                           Saturdays: £20)

* All these tickets require advance booking and reservation of outward and return journey on specific trains. The other fares are available on demand for immediate travel (subject to validity at the time).

Plus Railcard discounts for Young Persons (under 26), old persons (over 60), HM Forces, Families and Disabled; generally offering a third off all 'walk-on' travel tickets; plus Weekend First; plus inclusive tours with hotels and holiday firms, Executive packages, etc!
Half fare for kids under 16.

There are something like 20 return fares if you count all the railcard permutations.

Dr Robin Sisson
November 1995

(This paper was written in a personal capacity.)

Questions

1 What are the characteristics of the railway travel which lend themselves to the use of price discrimination?
2 The use of a uniform rate per mile appears to both equitable and commercially sensible even where elementary price discrimination is used. Why do you think BR have abandoned that principle?
3 What market segments have BR identified in order to use price discrimination (*selective pricing*)?
4 Can you find an example in the section entitled 'Is it blue or is it white?' where market segmentation failed because the two segments could not be ring fenced?
5 In the section entitled 'Passenger transport executives' can you find an example where Regional Railways have used price as a means of *ring fencing* a market segment imposed on them from the outside?
6 What logistical problems might arise in the above example if customers act rationally?
7 Is SW Trains acting logically in using price discrimination to discourage travellers from using trains?
8 Does the customer lose more from increased confusion and reduced choice of trains, than he or she gains from a variety of discounted prices? (This now occurs in some routes where more than one franchise exists.)

9 Dr Sissons argues that *selective pricing* within a unified system has served the rail user well, and implies that in the privatized network it will work less well. Do you agree?

10 Could it be argued that selective pricing on the railway will only maximize benefit to users, and revenue to the train operators, if customers have perfect knowledge of the market? If so how might the complexity of the fare structure be reduced?

11 What would be a *game theory* explanation of this pricing strategy?

12 What pricing strategy would game theory suggest for the privatized railway operating franchise?

PRICE DISCRIMINATION: AN EXPLANATORY NOTE

In practice

1 Occurs where demand is *Non-uniform*, i.e. market can be divided into *segments* each with its own *customer profile* and *buyer characteristics*.

2 Such market segments must be clearly capable of being fenced off from each other. There must be no likelihood of a buyer paying a low price in one market-place and selling on at a higher price in another market-place.

3 Market segmentation and price differentiation can occur in both product and service markets, but are more likely in the latter where the service is consumed at the time of scale and cannot be sold on.

4 Price discrimination is viable where market segments exhibit different *price elasticities*. Where demand (D) is price *in*elastic, higher prices can be charged, and lower prices where demand (D) is price elastic.

Such variations in demand elasticities may be the result of genuine differences in the needs of customers, e.g. a business passenger on an airline flight *has* to travel and the cost of his journey is trivial for his company. Whereas a tourist wanting the same journey may switch to a different destination if the price is too high. In the first case D is *inelastic* and in the second, *elastic*.

However, market segments can be created artificially by variation in packaging, means of distribution and other value adding items – such as customer service, of an essentially standardized product such as a lager beer.

5 Price discrimination is often associated with monopoly conditions, but clearly occurs in oligopoly markets which are much more common. Here, however, the decisions of companies are *interdependent*. Brewers and airline companies are likely to segment markets in similar ways, and charge similar prices in those market segments (colluding overtly or covertly on price; or accepting price leadership of a key player).

The theory of price discrimination

1 A competitive firm sets price equal to its marginal cost. If the MC is aggregated across all firms the curve then is the supply curve which tells us how much the *industry* would supply at each price.

Add the D curve and we can establish equilibrium and output.

A monopolist (*or* a group of colluding oligopolistic firms) recognizes that output affects MC & MR *simultaneously*. Output depends not only on MC but on demand and marginal revenue. The monopolist sets MR = MC and does *not* have a supply curve independent of demand conditions.

2 If we assume all consumers must be charged the same price, price will depend on output and the position of the AR/demand curve. (Look back in your notes at the model of monopoly.)

But monopolists (*or* price-colluding oligopolists) are not faced by price competition between firms and so can charge *different prices to different customers*. This will happen where *market segmentation* is possible, i.e. different groups of customers exist with different D curves (and price elasticities) for the same product.

3 For example, tourists' demand for a particular airline flight is *elastic* (substitutes are available – go to a different resort); therefore the D curve is flatter and so is the MR curve.

The more *inelastic* the D curve, the more MR curve must lie below the D curve because the greater will be the reduction in revenue from existing output units. Business travellers would have a more inelastic D curve for the same journey than a tourist (he or she has to travel, and no substitute journey will do.) Therefore, if both are paying the *same* price, *the marginal revenue obtained from the last business traveller must be* lower *than the MR from the last tourist*.

4 The airline will be carrying the wrong *mix* of travellers so long as the MR from the last tourist exceeds the MR from the last business traveller. Revenue would be gained without adding to cost by carrying the same number of travellers but more tourists and less business travellers until *the marginal revenue of the two groups is equated*.

5 *To do this the two groups* must *be charged* different *prices*. Tourist D is elastic, therefore charge a low fare; business traveller D is inelastic, charge a high fare.

6 Therefore profit maximizing output must satisfy two conditions:
(a) Business travellers (inelastic D) will pay a sufficiently higher fare than tourists (elastic D) *that the MR from the two groups is equated* – ensuring correct *mix*.
(b) The general level of prices and total number of passengers will be determined to equate the MC of carrying passengers to both these marginal revenues – which ensures the most profitable *scale of operation*.

7 Uniform and discriminatory pricing will lead to *different outputs* because they affect the MR obtained from any given total D curve facing a monopolist.

8 The monopolist will need to be aware that changes in market conditions may change the elasticity of D and extent of D in any given market segment.

For example, economic recovery might increase D at all prices for tourist flights and cause D to become more inelastic, whilst new technology (e.g. video conferencing, Email) may cause a fall in D at all prices for business travel, and an increase in price elasticity. Thus the optimum mix and output of flights may change over time.

Chapter 7

Oligopoly

We have now developed models which help us to understand the probable behaviour of firms in the limiting cases of perfect competition, and single firm monopoly, which in practice rarely if ever exist. We have also seen how the models may be adapted to explain market sectors with which we are more familiar on the high street – monopolistic competition.

However in reality most market sectors can be described as *oligopoly*. In Case study 1, the small firm sector, we examined data which suggests that 3,000 businesses in the UK, which is 0.1 per cent of the total number of businesses, generates 41.6 per cent of turnover and 34.2 per cent of all employment. We may infer from this that many industrial sectors show very high levels of *concentration*. This may be measured by the *n firm concentration ratio*, where n is perhaps the five biggest firms, which may generate 80 per cent or more of the output in that sector. Since this is the predominant market situation in many industrial economies, most of the remainder of this book is concerned with aspects of the behaviour of firms in such markets.

At this stage we propose to develop our theoretical models of market structure to encompass oligopoly. We can identify a number of key characteristics of oligopoly. Oligopoly may exist in a variety of market sectors, from basic commodities such as oil, metals, plasterboard, chemicals, or consumer goods with high levels of product differentiation, such as newspapers or coffee. Despite these differences there are *key characteristics* in common. These are:

1 *A small number of firms* dominate a market sector.
2 *Barriers to entry*. Unlike perfect competition and monopolistic competition, where entry is free, in oligopoly barriers to entry are usually considerable. These might stem from the high cost of plant where minimum efficient scale is very large, or from artificial barriers erected by incumbent firms, such as very high advertising costs to establish a new brand. Because of sunk costs in, say, specialist plant, exit costs are also high.

3 *Interdependence*. The actions of one firm affect all the others. All must therefore be intensely aware of their rivals, and be ready to respond. Such actions and responses are potentially numerous. No single theory of oligopoly can explain the behaviour of interdependent firms. For example, if a market leader decides on aggressive price-cutting to increase market share, competitors have choices: to match the cuts blow for blow, do nothing, or even increase prices. In chapter 11 we examine the use of game theory in this context. For the moment we will limit our analysis to the predictions which conventional theory of the firm might make about the two basic strategies available to an oligopolistic firm. These are:

- *Compete* with rivals to gain market share, possibly by driving rivals out of the business.
- *Collude* with rivals on price and or output quotas, restricting competition to non-price areas such as promotion or product development.

THE COMPETITION OPTION

This is a dangerous gamble, even for the market leader. In this book we invite you to examine the case study of the price war in the UK newspaper industry during 1995–96. News International used its global resources to back its subsidiary, Times Newspapers, in a vicious price war, presumably with the intention of winning market share permanently from the other broadsheets, especially the *Telegraph*, its major rival. The campaign seems to have only been partially successful. The *Independent* was seriously hurt, and its survival is doubtful. *The Times* did greatly increase its circulation, both with new readers as well as converts from the other broadsheets. The *Telegraph* did not follow suit with price cuts, but lost few of its readers. This case shows how unpredictable the outcomes of price war cuts are; because there are so many possible responses, and consumers are not necessarily rational.

What our model can indicate is that if price competition is persisted with by firms in an oligopoly, the outcome will be the same as in the monopolistic competition. Supernormal profits will be competed away, weaker firms will exit, remaining firms will earn only normal profit.

THE COLLUSION OPTION

The dangers of unrestricted competition between a handful of firms who are all aware of each other actions inevitably makes collusion an attractive option. Collusion may be open, or tacit. *Open collusion* on prices, and market sharing by formal agreement is illegal in most advanced economies. A formal agreement to collude on price is called a **cartel**. In effect the conditions created are similar to single firm monopoly, except that the members of the cartel may use non-price competition to seek an increase of market share within the total output determined for the industry by the agreed price set. The industry supply curve (see Figure 7.1) is the horizontal sum of the MC curves of cartel members. Profits are maximized at Q_1 where MC = MR, requiring a cartel price of P_1.

Any non-price competition would redistribute market shares of members, and reduce supernormal profits (due to increased costs of promotion for example).

Tacit collusion may occur when firms in an oligopoly follow the price leadership of a dominant firm, or the one which has over time been seen as the best barometer of market conditions. In practice the price leader can only guesstimate what its profit maximizing price and output will be.

Where price leadership does not occur there may emerge a set of rules of thumb followed by all. Such rules might be based on *average cost pricing* where no attempt is made to equate MC and MR, but firms simply add a percentage for profit on top of average costs. Alternatively *price benchmarks* might be established, as appears to be the case in consumer electrical goods.

Whichever form of collusion is adopted we can say with some (but not complete) certainty, that price will be higher and output lower than under perfect competition. Collusion is most likely to happen if:

- There are very few firms.
- There are similar products and production methods.
- A dominant firm exists.
- Barriers to entry make disruption unlikely.
- The market is stable.

It is worth noting that rapid technological change and the globalization of markets has made the last two conditions much rarer. Markets have become

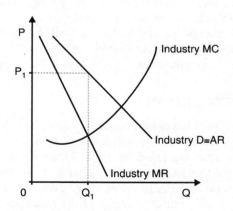

Figure 7.1 A profit maximizing cartel

much more contestable in recent years and collusion of any kind is much more difficult to maintain. Several of our case studies demonstrate this point.

NON-COLLUSION OLIGOPOLY: THE KINKED DEMAND CURVE

Even when no collusion occurs in an oligopoly market, prices may still remain stable. This variation on our model is based on two assumptions:

- If an oligopolist cuts prices his or her rivals will also do so to avoid losing market share.
- If an oligopolist raises prices rivals will keep their prices as before to gain market share at the price cutter's expense.

The implication will be that a rise in price causes a large loss of customers to rivals whose prices are now lower. Conversely a fall in prices will produce little gain in sales since rivals cut their prices. The demand curve for the firm is therefore kinked at the present price point, being more elastic above and less elastic below that price (see Figure 7.2). This model cannot explain how price is set in the first place, but it can be shown to predict a high degree of price stability, even where considerable changes in costs occur.

OLIGOPOLY AND THE PUBLIC INTEREST

Governments are concerned to monitor and influence situations where monopoly or oligopoly develops on the basis that price will be higher, output lower, and choice and possibly quality diminished. Oligopoly may be even more disadvantageous than monopoly:

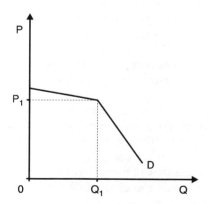

Figure 7.2 A kinked demand curve, with stable price at P_1

- There may be less scope for economies of scale to offset market power.
- More resources are likely to be wasted on advertising.

On the other hand there may be advantages to be had from oligopoly.

- An oligopolist has both resources (from supernormal profit) to use on R&D and product improvement, and the incentive (non-price competition) to do so.
- They are often also faced by a countervailing power, in the form of large retail buyers.

The conclusion so far is that the oligopolistic industry is likely to behave more competitively (and so benefit consumers) if entry and exit barriers are low, that is, the market is contestable. This is increasingly so in many oligopoly industries. Either entry or the threat of entry by new firms prevents the oligopolist from acting against the public interest.

CASE STUDY 8: THE SUPERMARKET BUSINESS

Some of Britain's supermarkets have colluded with manufacturers in price-fixing deals that have restricted competition for a decade, senior industry sources allege.

The arrangements, known within food industry circles as 'club pricing', involved assurances from suppliers to supermarket buying executives that the prices they set for certain brands would be in line with those of rival stores. This enabled them to achieve maximum profits on a number of basic foods, safe in the knowledge they would not be undercut.

The sources allege that participating manufacturers have been happy to support the arrangements to maintain their own profits. Retailers who undermined the status quo by discounting were sometimes threatened with sanctions, ranging from the loss of special terms to refusal to supply.

Some suppliers, the sources say, even agreed to underwrite any drop in prices incurred by stores that were forced to match reductions by maverick retailers.

A senior supermarket executive alleges the arrangements were made between a select group of supermarkets and manufacturers and had existed since the early 1980s. It is not a new phenomenon. 'It stopped one multiple having a price advantage over another', he said.

One retailer alleges that 18 months ago he was told by a manufacturer he was selling its goods too cheaply. We were too far below the club price. They said we were out of line with the rest of the market. The retailer said he was threatened with the removal of special terms.

A second source, who until recently was an executive with a major multiple, said some manufacturers would tell stores they intended to talk to individual retailers who cut their prices too sharply to 'make them see sense'.

He added: 'Manufacturers would come to us and say, "Look you are going to have to stop this because other retailers are complaining". They thought we were getting cheaper supplies, but we weren't. We were taking lower margins to get higher volumes.'

A third source – a former sales director of a leading food company who was involved in such arrangements – also revealed that clients were given details verbally of their rivals' intended selling prices. 'Nothing was written down. It was a series of arrangements that were informal. One buyer would ask you what the others would be selling at. We would suggest a figure so that everyone was happy.'

A fourth source, a supermarket buyer, said 'It's a fact of life that this goes on.'

The sources say the alleged pricing arrangements were at their peak four years ago but are now under threat with the emergence of discount stores. 'They are breaking down but have not gone away,' one insider said.

The Office of Fair Trading (OFT) said last week that firms had a legal duty to tell the watch-dog body about any written or spoken agreement that restricted their freedom of action. 'However, where there is a covert agreement, the assumption must be that it is anti-competitive,' it said.

There have also been renewed calls by MPs for a government investigation into pricing after revelations that Safeway, Sainsbury and Tesco initiated a secret study to counter criticisms about the high cost of food in Britain. The OFT said it would be contacting the retailers to ask for the study.

The disclosure followed concerted action by Safeway, Sainsbury and Tesco to challenge Costco, an American discount chain that is attempting to open in Britain. The stores have hired consultants to co-ordinate their campaign against the 'warehouse club', prompting accusations of a 'cabal' against free competition.

A report published recently by one City broker says share prices suggest an industry facing a 'profit collapse' amid worries that there are too many stores chasing too few customers and predictions of management panic. The report adds that although the chances of government intervention are small, the big three are not helping their case. 'Joint action, no matter how legal and proper, is bad news for grocer share prices' the report says.

Leading supermarkets denied last week there were any price-fixing arrangements. Sainsbury said staff check rival stores' prices to ensure the firm remains competitive. It added that all supermarkets negotiated with suppliers in a similar fashion to get the best deals for their customers. Tesco also denied the allegations, which it described as 'muck-raking'.

Shoprite, a discounter with more than 50 stores in Scotland, says it will begin importing Kellogg's cornflakes from abroad to keep the product on sale at 96p a packet, well below the price charged by rivals. The store complained to the OFT earlier this year when the manufacturer refused to supply it because of its discount policy.

The OFT ruled that Kellogg was entitled to withhold supplies because Shropite was said to be using the brand as a 'loss-leader'. However, Deryck Nicholson, the store's chairman, said 'Kellogg can't stop us selling at 96p. We have told the company we will go to China to bring it in by the boat-load if we have to. The customer is the one we serve, not the supplier.'

Kellogg said its actions were within the 1976 Resale Prices Act. 'We will discontinue supplies to retailers or wholesalers that sell Kellogg's cornflakes below cost for the purpose of loss-leading,' it said.

(Skipworth and Victor, 1993)

Questions

1 To what extent can the large supermarket chains act collectively like a monopoly supplier?
2 What are the likely effects of competition from new market entrants like discount stores?
3 What entry barriers could established supermarket chains erect to forestall market entry?
4 What are the main arguments (a) for and (b) against resale price maintenance (RPM)?

Case study feedback

There are no definitive right or wrong answers, as they depend partly on judgement and personal opinion. You should first aim to use the evidence provided in the question as the basis for your answers, and then to add further ideas or knowledge if you can. The main thing we would look for is an attempt to combine some economic analysis with evidence in the article. You might have included some of the following, but we would not expect you to think of all these things. You may also have good ideas which we haven't thought of.

1 *To what extent can the large supermarket chains act collectively like a monopoly supplier?*

- The major supermarket multiples jointly have a large share of the market, so potentially have a significant amount of *market power* (that is, together they face a downward sloping demand curve which represents a large part of the total market demand). Club pricing principally acts to limit price competition among the multiples, so that they can price above the pure competitive level. It probably also acts to raise the costs of rivals who are not in the club.
- Various factors limit their ability to act jointly as a pure monopolist:
    - They do not control the whole market: consumers can choose to go to retailers not in the club. However, these retailers may be getting some of their supplies on less favourable terms.
    - They still compete in other areas: store location, product range, service quality, prices of products not covered by the club arrangements etc.
    - Potential instability of the collusion: those who get a relatively low share of the supernormal profits have a temptation to break ranks. An example of a firm choosing lower margins is reported in the article.
    - The threat of entry.
    - The risk of intervention by the Office of Fair Trading.
- More subtly, it is not in the interest of the *suppliers* to allow the supermarkets to charge pure monopoly prices, as this would limit the suppliers' sales too much. Club pricing will therefore be somewhat above the pure competitive price, but below the pure monopoly price. (Why do you think that the suppliers are prepared to participate in the arrangement? One reason may be that it is a way for *suppliers* also to avoid price competition: if they know that retailers can rely on stable prices, there is less incentive for the suppliers to offer secret discounts against each other.)

2 *What are the likely effects of competition from new market entrants like discount stores?*

- One possibility is that price competition between the club and the discounters becomes intense and the club ceases to function. (There is some evidence for this in the extract: 'They are breaking down but have not gone away'). For example, if the discounters gained sufficient market share, it might no longer suit suppliers to participate in the club. But suppliers may not want their premium brands to be available at discount prices.
- Club members may just shave their prices to some extent, while trying to keep a significant differential, as well as introducing other entry barriers (see below).

- If the discounters gain a significant share, we think the most likely outcome would be *segmentation* of the market, with price-sensitive consumers buying in the discount segment and perhaps the majority still using the big chains. The big chains would lose some volume, and there may be closures or mergers. It is perhaps more likely that one of the major retailers might leave the industry than that the price-fixing practice would disappear altogether. However, there may be a period of price competition while the retailers fight to determine which would close.

3 What barriers to entry could established supermarket chains erect to forestall market entry?
- The club scheme may already act as a barrier to some extent, although the new discounters referred to in the article tend to buy from different suppliers.
- The 'campaign' referred to in the article was concerned with objecting to *planning permission* in order to prevent the construction of the new discount stores.
- Increased advertising, emphasizing the importance of quality and choice in the overall value-for-money decision.
- Improve levels of service, choice, product range etc. This may not forestall entry as such, but strengthens the position in the premium segment of the market.
- Build new stores such as hyperstores which encourage one-stop shopping so that customers don't want an extra trip to a separate discount store for some of their purchases.
- Loyalty schemes such as club cards.
- Introduce own-label brands at discount prices, particularly if supported by quality promises (although this might upset the suppliers of premium brands and so threaten the club arrangement).
- Engage directly in price competition, abandoning the club scheme.

4 What are the arguments (a) for and (b) against resale price maintenance (RPM)?
The club scheme acts somewhat like RPM and so this question is implicitly asking whether or not price-fixing can act in the interests of consumers. It is fair to say that the article doesn't give you much guidance here.
(a) Arguments for:
- Pass and Lowes (1994: 192) mention the convenience of the consumer as an argument for.
- An example would be protection of margins for small stores, so that village stores and corner shops remain viable. This doesn't apply here, since these types of stores are not members of the club.

- Another case is where the premium retailer supplies a level of information and service which supports the quality of the product and which a discounter would not provide (So consumers may go to the premium shop for advice, but would buy from the discounter unless RPM is allowed.) This doesn't apply directly to club pricing, which covers standard branded goods. However, it might be argued that higher prices on standard goods do allow stores to offer higher levels of general service, decor etc. which is valued by consumers.
- The net book agreement (which has just collapsed) was an example, where publishers claimed that they could publish a much larger range of titles as a result of RPM, and also that it helped to protect small booksellers. The question is whether readers of popular books *should* subsidize both the readers of minority interest books *and* inefficient bookshops!
- There is a case for RPM if *both* supplier and retailer are monopolists, because monopolists acting separately in a *vertical chain* raise prices even higher than a single one. (This is called the double marginalization problem). If *one* (say, the supplier) fixes prices, the price to the consumer is lower. However, this does not really apply to club pricing which is a device for *limiting* price competition at both levels and therefore *creating* a vertical chain of partial monopolists.
- An argument that might apply to club pricing is one of providing price *stability*. If price competition were too severe it is possible that some retailers would exit the market, leaving consumers with reduced choice of retailers and *higher* prices in the long run.

(b) Arguments against:

- By limiting price competition, consumers pay a higher price and do not get the benefits of price competition. This is a pretty powerful argument, and might be expected to be the usual conclusion unless there is some special reason for justifying RPM or price fixing.

Chapter 8

Market structure, conduct and performance

We have now seen how economists have developed a series of theoretical models which seek to at least partially explain the operation of markets, and the spectrum of market structures which may develop. The models of perfect competition and monopoly are limiting cases, which rarely if ever emerge in the real world. Between them on the spectrum lie monopolistic competition and oligopoly. These models are much closer to reality and offer us powerful predictive tools with which to analyse the behaviour of firms. They do have serious limitations. The models are static in nature, being based on assumptions about the surrounding economic environment of the firm which may be unrealistic. Further the form in which the models are expressed permits relationships between only two variables, price and output, to be examined. Other important variables must be taken as *ceteris paribus* – remaining unchanged.

From the point of view of the business manager, charged with the responsibility of formulating and carrying out a series of strategic decisions in a dynamic environment, they are not obviously helpful. Later we will examine other theoretical developments (game theory, and the economics of total quality management), which provide a better understanding of decision making in a dynamic business environment. At this point what we need is a more practical toolkit of ideas which will enable the manager to evaluate strengths and weaknesses, opportunities and threats (SWOT) for his or her business in the market in which he or she operates, or wishes to enter. This is provided for us by the *structure, conduct, performance schema*. As the name suggests this is not a set of theoretical models, logically developed in an *a priori* manner. It is rather a set of criteria which builds on both the theoretical models and empirical observation of the business world, and acts as a lens through which to derive the information and understanding of the chosen market on which decisions might be based. It enables the business manager to:

- formulate a business *strategy* i.e. which market to be in
- understand the *nature* of a market and the forces driving it

- assess the relative *attraction* of a market i.e. profit potential
- carry out a *SWOT analysis* of potential/actual competitors.

This schema starts from the premise that the way a market is *organized* – its structure – influences the *behaviour* of suppliers and buyers in that market, and the *conduct* of firms operating in that market. These patterns of behaviour will determine the *performance* (on accepted criteria) of firms in the market. It should however be noted that markets are inherently dynamic (fast changing), and becoming more so. Thus the causal links also run the other way. Performance influences conduct, which in turn affects structure. This relationship is summarized in Figure 8.1.

MARKET STRUCTURE

In this chapter we shall examine the key features of market ·structure. In doing so we shall build on theoretical concepts developed in earlier chapters. The important features of market structure may be summarized as follows:

- seller concentration
- buyer concentration

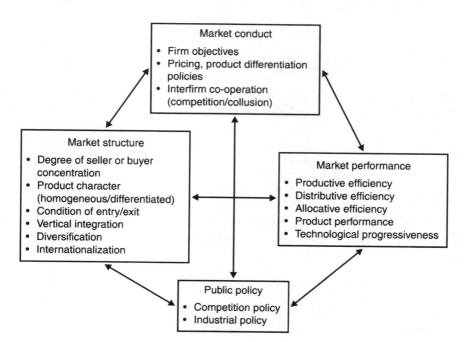

Figure 8.1 Market structure, conduct and performance schema

- nature of product
- barriers to entry
- barriers to exit
- degree of vertical integration
- degree of diversification
- degree of international operation.

If we are to discuss the degree of concentration, we need an accepted measure. This is provided by the concept of the *n firm concentration ratio'*. To calculate this we need to decide on an appropriate number of firms (n). This may be perhaps the three, five, or as many as ten, biggest firms in the industry. We then calculate the percentage of total sales in the industry controlled by the n biggest firms. We have set out some examples of concentration ratios (CRs):

1 *Very high* concentration ratios
   a) Detergents: P&G   45%
                       Unilever   44%
                       (2 firms CR = 89%)
   A *duopoly*: two dominant firms

   b) Plasterboard: BPB   76%
                       RPL   12.2%
                       Knauf   6.2%
                       (3 firms CR = 94%)
   Oligopoly: with a dominant firm

2 *High* buyer concentration ratio
   Supermarkets: Sainsbury
                      Tesco
                      Safeways
                      ASDA
                      (4 firms CR = 70%)
   Oligopoly:

3 *Fairly high* seller concentration ratio
   Frozen Foods: Birds Eye   22%
                      Ross Young   29%
                      Findus   5%
   Monopolistic competition – (3 firms CR = 56%)

4 *Fragmented market*
   Printing: *no* dominant firms
   Competitive market

If we assume that the owners of a company set out to maximize a stream of profits over a period of time for which plans may realistically be made, then they will seek to increase the control which they can exercise in their chosen market. If the owner of all firms in the market charge their managers with the task of profit maximization by growth of market share and control, then it is likely that increasing concentration will occur in the market-place – to the extent that certain important conditions exist. Fifty years ago both food retailing and printing were extremely fragmented markets, coming very close to our theoretical model of perfect competition (see Chapter 6), a situation in which all firms were small, were price takers and earned only normal profits. Before reading on, attempt the following activity.

Activity 8.1

List as many reasons as you can think of why food retailing is now dominated by four large national, and several big regional supermarket companies, while large parts of the printing industry are still in the hands of very small firms.

When you have read the next section check how many of your reasons seem to be correct.

The reasons for the development of the high CR in a market sector may be summarized as follows:

- economies of scale
- desire to dominate a market
- ability to exclude new entrants
- ability to grow horizontally/vertically by acquisition
- ability to grow organically through product improvement and successful competition
- abuse of market dominance by restrictive practices to maintain dominance.

The ability to reduce unit costs in relation to attainable market prices is a powerful driving force behind increasing concentration. In Chapter 5 we discussed the concept of economies of scale. Unit costs fall as output rises until a most efficient output level is reached for a plant (minimum efficient scale, see Figure 8.2).

As output increases up to OQ, costs per unit fall. At OQ unit costs reach their lowest point and this is the most efficient output for the firm. Beyond OQ costs per unit rise as diseconomies of scale set in.

Economies of scale derive in large part from the operation of plant in the production process. Advances in technology drive the capacity of plant in producing standardized products even higher. The bigger the size (and cost)

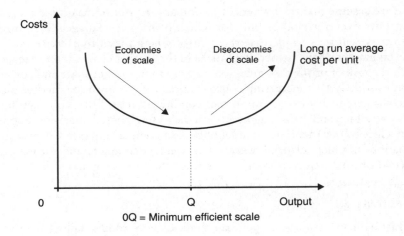

Figure 8.2 Minimum efficient scale

of the plant, the greater the quantity to be produced if efficiency is to be achieved. This leads inevitably to the need for greater market share for an individual firm. Firms which are able to finance such large plant will tend to drive out smaller players. In Chapter 12 we examine the consequences for a market when some firms develop the ability to operate very large plant with economies of large scale, while at the same time becoming capable of ever-increasing numbers of product variants without losing scale economies. However, in many industries where products are standardized, such as plasterboard, ice-cream, coffee or tobacco products, the MES (minimum efficient scale) is now so large that a very high concentration ratio is inevitable.

The pressure to increasing the size of firms through economies of scale comes also from the benefits of size on other business functions such as marketing (as in detergents), research and development (R&D) (as in pharmaceuticals) as well as, even, service functions such as distribution (supermarkets), training (motor industry), and finance and accounting.

Activity 8.2

Choose one of the case studies in this book and answer the following question.

In what ways and to what extent did (Company X) grow as a consequence of the driving force of economies of scale?

If the opportunities presented by ever-increasing scale economies are theoretically available to all companies in a new market, the question remains, why did some firms take advantage of them but not others? The answer must lie in the vision and ability of the entrepreneurs who founded the firms, and their professional managers. In particular we would point to their willingness to accept risk, grasp opportunities, plus an element of luck and chance.

If we refer back to Figure 8.2, we note that beyond output OQ, diseconomies of scale set in. These might include: overuse and breakdown of plant; loss of product quality; problems of co-ordination and control within a firm operating several plants on geographically dispersed sites.

Activity 8.3

To what extent, and how, did diseconomies of scale cause the recent problems suffered by IBM?

Once a firm has expanded money and effort to develop a strong market position, it will turn its attention to the possibility of excluding new entrants from its markets. As minimum efficient scale increases due to either the changing technology, or the marketing costs of developing and maintaining a presence in the market, entry becomes progressively more difficult.

Organic growth through product development and promotion reinforces market dominance for the successful firm. This is, however, a slow and long-term process which is most commonly observed in Germany, Japan and the tiger economies of Asia. In the USA and UK market dominance is more often actively sought by the acquisition of related companies. Such acquisitions may be vertical, horizontal or diversified. Vertical integration involves moving back down the chain of production to acquire suppliers of materials, or forward to control retail distribution. British Plasterboard Products is a good example of a company developing a new product and market and then barring entry by acquiring the principal source of supply of the key raw materials. Until recently the major UK brewers were able to defend market share by controlling most of the outlets for their products.

Horizontal integration involves the acquisition of competitors in order to take over their market share, using the opportunity to rationalize production in order to operate all remaining plant as near to MES as possible. British Plasterboard Products again offer a good example of this process.

Growth by diversification into other market areas through acquisition is only justified in this context where economies of scale may be obtained in management, marketing, acquisition of finance (perhaps by asset stripping), or in R&D of related products. British Aerospace originally acquired Rover

Cars on this basis, but later found that the supposed synergy leading to these economies of scale did not exist. Rover was therefore sold to BMW.

Once a high concentration ratio has been established in a market, the few remaining firms will do all they can to exclude new entrants. The possibilities of co-operative and non-co-operative behaviours available for this purpose are examined in Chapter 11 in the context of game theory.

The high concentration ratio will persist until technological change and the arrival of (a) new products, (b) new methods of trading, or (c) arrival of a foreign firm with strong financial backing in a formerly national market begins to erode the dominant firm's market share.

Activity 8.4

Can you think of examples of points (a), (b) and (c) above?

The direction of concentration is not all one way. Circumstances may change in such a way as to bring about a fall in the concentration ratio. A statutory monopoly may be broken up as a result of privatization – as is now belatedly happening in the case of British Gas. Decisions of the Monopoly and Mergers Commission may weaken the ability of dominant firms to erect barriers to entry, as in the case of the Sara Lee, Reckitt & Colman merger. Barriers to exit (in the form of the sunk costs of plant which has no other use) may be reduced by an increase in the value of the land and buildings occupied by obsolete plant for some other development use. New competitors may enter the market with a new version of an old product, for example Mars entering the ice cream industry on the back of the brand image of the Mars Bar, or RPL and Knauf entering the UK plasterboard market with low-cost up-to-date greenfield plant and strong financial backing.

Our definition of concentration ratio may lead us to misinterpret the degree of concentration in a market. We may define the market too narrowly/widely in the first place, for example mail order catalogues which are produced in huge volumes may be dominated by a few large firms, while the printing industry as a whole may appear to have a relatively low level of concentration.

We may observe a high concentration ratio, for example in the car industry in the UK, but the apparent market dominance of Ford, GM, Toyota and Nissan and Rover is much less strong than it appears because of the many imports from foreign-based companies such as Renault, Mercedes, Hyundai, etc. Where a market appears to be entirely fragmented we are probably being misled by defining the market too widely.

Another problem is buyer concentration – where *monopsony* exists. Food processing may appear to be highly concentrated, but the power of the companies concerned may be more than offset by the power of the supermarket oligopoly.

Product characteristics also determine the possibility of increased concentration, and the routes to it. Products may be broadly classified as standardized or commodity products, or differentiated. Coffee appears to have the characteristics of a commodity good, where consumers are likely to be indifferent between suppliers, except on price. Yet in this as in many other cases it is possible to differentiate or brand such a product either by changing/improving the characteristics of the product (granule instant instead of powder), or by creating an image appealing to categories of customer by high-powered promotion and advertising (e.g. Nescafé Gold Blend). Another example might be transistor radios, which thirty years ago were differentiated products, with a high price premium, but which have now been largely superseded by new technology (personal stereos) and now have the characteristics of a commodity product, sold on price.

Once a dominant market position has been achieved by a few companies, they are likely to work hard to maintain their position by creating and sustaining barriers to entry, and the extent to which circumstances have created barriers to exit for weaker firms. These conditions of entry/exit are summarized in Table 8.1.

Conventional theories of the firm suggest that firms will continue in business at a loss so long as they cover their variable costs (see Chapter 5). If the plant is old and written off, and has no other viable use, the firm is spending little on fixed costs and can appear viable. Its difficulty in exiting the industry helps to maintain an artificially low CR which may be damaging to the industry as a whole, since it is difficult for more ambitious companies to invest in plant and product improvements which while increasing the CR might make the remaining firms viable and competitive in an international market. This scenario occurred in the UK wool and worsted industry in the 1960s and 1970s. The barriers to exit which may prevent the modernization of a whole industry sector may be summarized as follows:

Table 8.1 Barriers to entry

Economies of scale	
Product differentiation	NATURE OF THE INDUSTRY
Capital requirements	
Patents	
Predatory pricing	ACTIVITIES OF FIRM
Exclusive dealing	
No niche markets available	
Size of firm prevents take-over danger	SIZE OF FIRM

- whether production assets are owned or leased
- age of assets
- specificity of use of assets
- plant resale possibility
- investment needed to remain competitive
- extent of excess capacity
- extent of firm's diversification.

Conclusion

From the point of view of the manager planning a decision on whether to enter a particular market, it is important to know what the concentration ratio is. Care must be taken in using such data which in increasingly global markets may mislead. It is important to know the extent of the market power of existing firms, and the nature of actual and potential barriers to entry and exit. Where barriers are low and the market is mature, it is likely to approach perfect competition and be driven by price and, therefore, entry is unlikely to be very profitable. Entry would not be attractive. If barriers are high but surmountable, entry may be possible, and desirable. The strategies which may be adopted by firms operating in high concentration ratios (oligopolistic) markets are examined in Chapter 11.

Activity 8.5

Select one of the case studies in this book. Identify and list barriers to entry and barriers to exit which exist in that industry market.

MARKET CONDUCT

The structure, conduct and performance schema suggests a largely one-way progression. In this schema it is argued that market conduct, the patterns of behaviour exhibited by firms, is influenced by market structure. The appropriateness of patterns of behaviour adopted by firms in a market-place as suppliers and buyers, will determine the ultimate performance of firms on certain criteria. If this is so, then observation of the structure of a market should permit prediction of the probable range of behaviours likely to be exhibited by firms, and the likely performance outcomes.

A number of key elements of conduct need to be examined. These may be summarized thus:

- objectives of suppliers (profit, sales growth)
- product requirements of buyers (price, performance)

- marketing strategies available (depend on market and product)
- mutual interdependency of suppliers (may lead to collusion)
- relationship between supplier and buyer (relative power).

Most markets exhibit both *competitive* and *co-operative* tendencies between suppliers. A tension exists between these two alternative strategies which is best explained by *game theory* (see Chapter 11). The conventional economies of the theory of the firm depends on the assumption of profit maximizing behaviour. No other possible goals are taken into account. In reality other goals may predominate, with profit as an ultimate (but desirable) residual factor. These other goals may be, for example, maximizing sales growth, market share or growth of asset value. In Chapter 12 we will examine the serious implications for the conventional western firm, which seeks to maximize short-term profit, of the new approach developed by Japanese companies and their imitators, the pursuit of growth of market share through maximization of customer value by a process of continuous improvement. At this stage it is sufficient to observe that the goals set by firms will determine strategic and operational policies.

The goals of a firm may be single or multiple objectives, pursued in either the short or long run. They may be operationalized as *maximizing* or *satisfying* targets. Decisions will be taken in the context of institutional, financial, legal and environmental constraints.

There is considerable disagreement between schools of economists as to the predominant goals or objectives of firms:

1 *Conventional economic theory* emphasizes *profit maximization* in owner controlled firms. The implications of the divorce of ownership and control in large modern public companies is ignored.
2 *Financial theory* emphasizes maximization of the *value* of the *firm* (shareholders' wealth) over the long term.
3 *Baumol (1967) and Marris (1964)* suggest that management controlled firms will seek to *maximize sales revenue* as a means to asset growth maximization. The purpose being to maximize management rewards (rather than shareholders) as the firm expands.
4 *Behavioural theory* suggests that maximization objectives are unattainable in an uncertain and volatile business environment. Objectives are therefore *couched in satisfying terms* on the basis of bargaining between operational departments.
5 *Modern management theory* in which a *mission statement* sets out a perception of the firm's general objective. *Targets* for explicit criteria are set, for example earnings per share, return on investment (in a conventional western firm), or maximization of customer value (in a Japanese style company).

We have remarked that in most markets a tension will exist between the need to compete with other suppliers, and the possibly greater advantages of *cooperation* or *collusion* with other suppliers. Where many suppliers exist, competition will predominate. Where there are few enough suppliers for each to be aware of the others' decisions, there will be pressure to cooperate to create an orderly market. The implications of the latter for firm's behaviour is examined in Chapter 11.

Competition may be defined as **the attempt to win and retain buyer demand**. It may be approached in five ways:

- cost effectiveness
- price competition
- advertising and promotion (non-price competition)
- new product competition
- continuous improvement of product and process (differentiation).

The competitive forces operating in a market are summed up in Figure 8.3. Any firm must develop a *competitive strategy*. This is defined by Pass and Lowes (1994) after Porter (1980; 1985) as: **'The formulation of strategic plans to meet/beat competitors in supplying a particular product market within its business portfolio.'** The aim of the competitive strategy is to identify and respond to the following factors:

- strengths/weaknesses of own firm and competitors
- the nature of competitive forces in specific markets
- understand the derived product attributes in that market.

Having done that, it is possible to seek to establish a competitive advantage:

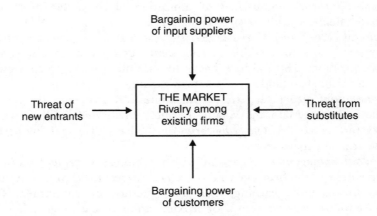

Figure 8.3 Competitive forces in a market

- possessing assets and attributes giving a competitive edge (low-cost plant, innovative products, brands)
- offering products desired by the market, cost effectively
- winning customers on a profitable and long-term basis.

Cost advantages may be *absolute* (lower at all levels than rivals), or *relative* (related to economies of scale and experience curve effects). Product advantages may stem from *differentiation* through unique functional or perceived characteristics. These are likely to stem from R&D activities and new technology, or from the use of advertising to create a new perception of a greater need for the product among potential buyers.

Analysis of the possibilities of these advantages by the firm are likely to lead to the development of one of the following *strategies*. In commodity markets, where differentiation of the product is difficult (for example bulk chemicals, or plasterboard), low cost is likely to be the chosen strategy. This emphasizes the pursuit of economies of scale and technical improvement of the production process. Where the product may be *differentiated* from that of rivals, on the basis of product characteristics (e.g. records, photocopiers), or perceived quality (coffee), it may be possible to prevent defection of buyers to rival products. Where a firm is a smaller player, competitive advantage may be sought by focusing on a niche market which is too small for consideration by the bigger players (e.g. classical records). This strategic behaviour pattern may be illustrated by reference to the market for cars as in Figure 8.4.

In the conventional western model of the firm *price competition* is seen as the most important element of the marketing mix. This is because price generates corporate income while the other elements of the marketing mix

	STRATEGIC ADVANTAGE	
STRATEGIC TARGET	UNIQUENESS AS PERCEIVED BY CUSTOMER	LOW-COST POSITION
INDUSTRY-WIDE	Differentiation GENERAL MOTORS	Cost leadership NISSAN
PARTICULAR SEGMENT ONLY	Differentiation focus MERCEDES	Cost focus SKODA

Figure 8.4 Competitive strategy in cars

Source: Pass and Lowes, 1994

are seen as costs. In Chapter 12 we discuss the alternative paradigm within which Japanese style firms operate when continuous improvement of product and process are not seen as costs to be included, but as the prime source of competitive advantage. For the moment we will concentrate on the conventional model.

Within this model we will consider how price might be set, and on what basis it might be adjusted. Price might be set on one of three approaches:

- *cost-based pricing* (relates price to cost – mark up)
- *demand-based pricing* (relates price to intensity of demand, possibly leading to price discrimination)
- *competitive-based pricing* (relates price to rivals' prices).

In practice all three may be used. Price may be adjusted to reflect market conditions:

- general increase in industry costs
- falling/rising demand
- increased competitive pressure.

From the conventional economists' point of view price competition is seen as being conducive to both allocative and technical efficiency.

In markets where there are few suppliers, and where the nature of the product permits, competition may be partly on the basis of non-price competition. The situation often results from the overt or tacit collusion on price levels which occurs in oligopolistic markets. Game theory explanations of such decisions on a degree of collusion on price and use of non-price competition are discussed in Chapter 11. The elements of non-price competition may be summarized as follows:

- product differentiation
- advertising and promotion
- product quality and service
- brand leadership
- new product variants
- continuous improvements of the products' design and reliability
- creation of a portfolio of products.

Product differentiation may be achieved by either product characteristics, or by using advertising to create an illusion of differentiation leading to brand loyalty (all three were used in our coffee industry case). Advertising may be used to inform buyers of unique product characteristics (as in photocopiers) or to persuade potential buyers (as in the Gold Blend coffee advertising series). Product functional quality and after sales service are important in many markets.

The production of new product variants is increasingly important in line with the shortening of product life cycles and the threat of new entrants (as in the Mars ice cream bar case). In order to respond to increasingly sophisticated customer tastes, it is increasingly necessary to develop a portfolio of related products to fit in a number of niches in the market (as in the coffee case).

Development of a portfolio of products helps to establish market leadership across the whole market and may force a smaller supplier to leave large sections of the market to concentrate on leadership in a newer market niche (as in the photocopier case).

While economists (and some politicians) may see unrestrained price competition as leading to allocative and technical efficiency, maximizing welfare for all (see Chapters 1–3), from the firm's perspective, orderly (i.e. controlled and predictable) markets are always to be preferred to competitive markets. Conventional economic theory suggests that orderly markets are likely to reduce 'welfare', and permit firms to make long-term abnormal profits, rather than only normal profits covering only the opportunity cost of the capital and the entrepreneurial skill invested in the business. Why this is so is explained in Chapter 3. In reality firms will always seek to control competitive forces to their advantage. This will be done by some combination of the following methods.

- monopolize a market by structural means (mergers and acquisitions), e.g. plasterboard case.
- collusive arrangements (cartels, retail price maintenance, price leadership), e.g. supermarkets
- restrictive trade practices to disadvantage competitors (exclusive dealing, tie in sales, full time forcing), e.g. ice cream, photocopiers
- information agreement.

Game theory (set out in Chapter 11) provides an explanation of why such practices are likely to arise where firms are interdependent – operating in an oligopolistic market.

MARKET PERFORMANCE

We have argued so far that examination of the *structure* of an industry sector, and the *conduct* patterns of firms within the industry enable business decision-makers to assess the desirability and possibility of entry or exit from the sector under review. This analysis will also enable predictions to be made of the *performance* of firms in the industry, or which might enter the sector. Examination of performance permits the economist to *evaluate* the condition of the industry from the wider perspective of economic welfare for society. These considerations are likely to influence government policy with regard to the regulation of industry, through (in the UK) Monopolies and Mergers Commission rules. References and decisions at this level will in turn influence entry and exit decisions by business decision-makers.

Our first task must be to consider market performance factors in relation to structure and conduct from an economist's point of view. An economist might define the ultimate criterion of market performance as follows: **The effectiveness of suppliers in using scarce resources to their maximum efficiency to the ultimate benefit of customers.** We need to examine this criterion more closely within the structure, conduct and performance framework (see Figure 8.5). We can develop this framework further using the basic economic theory developed in Chapters 1–3 (see Figure 8.6).

Conventional economic theory suggests that perfect competition, were it present in all markets, would maximize welfare through allocative efficiency. We saw that the assumptions underlying this model are unrealistic, and that some degree of concentration is likely to occur in all markets. The assumption that firms will always seek to maximize profits drives firms to exploit consumer's lack of complete market knowledge, and irrationality of behaviour, to capture their loyalty in order to be able to earn supernormal profits at MR = MC, even if only in the short run.

Where firms are able to make this advantage more permanent by erecting barriers to entry, it is likely that a *dead weight loss of welfare* to the economy will occur, stemming from the restriction of output below, and price above, the conditions which would prevail in a perfectly competitive market. On this simplistic level, greater competition would seem *always* to be more advantageous to consumers than concentration.

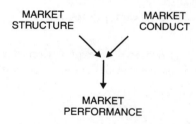

Figure 8.5 Structure, conduct and performance framework

Figure 8.6 A simple market model

(At this point the reader is advised to reread Chapters 1–6 quickly before proceeding.)

In reality the story is more complicated. A more detailed look at the structure and conduct within the industry might lead us to a different conclusion once we relate these elements to performance criteria. First we should summarize our analysis structure and conduct so far – see Figure 8.7.

What then are the key elements which might provide us with criteria through which to evaluate the performance of a market? The key elements are:

- Cost: is it the lowest possible?
- Price: is it consistent with cost and normal profit?
- Advertising and promotion: is cost of distribution and selling wasteful of resources?
- Product performance: is choice, variety and quality satisfactory?
- Technological progressiveness: is the market generating the available gains in product quality and lower cost that are possible?

We will now examine each of these elements in turn, using the tools of economic theory developed earlier.

Costs

Ideally the market may be said to be performing well if production is taking place at minimum average cost, on the lowest long run average cost curve possible given present technology. For this to be achieved, firms within the industry should be taking full advantage of **economies of scale**, and the *capacity* of the whole industry should be equivalent to the current likely demand for the product.

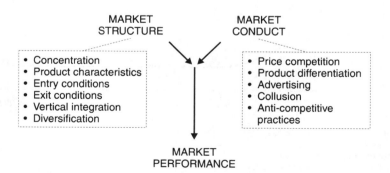

Figure 8.7 More realistic markets

The ability of the industry to reach this appropriate performance may be inhibited by the presence of the problem of **x inefficiency**. This is a broad concept which covers all the possibilities for inefficient use of resources *within* a firm stemming from management failure (see later). Performance may be further inhibited relative to our initial principle of cost minimization by the inability or unwillingness of firms to take advantage of *dynamic* cost reductions made possible by advances in the technology of materials and processes (see later). An economist would evaluate the cost performance of an industry in the following way, again using the tools developed earlier in the book.

If the industry is to maximize its performance in terms of economies of scale and industry capacity then its output should be at or above minimum efficient scale – the lowest point on the long-run average cost curve (LRAC). Refer at this point to Figure 8.8. Ideally each plant within the industry will be operating at the lowest point on its short-run average cost curve (SRAC$_2$) which is where it is equal to the LRAC for the industry at an output above minimum efficient scale (Q$_*$). If output exceeds Q$_*$, say Q$_1$, insufficient capacity is available in the industry since plant are being operated at an output where short-run average cost exceeds that at Q$_*$. That is to say diseconomies of scale have set in. If output is at a level below Q$_*$,

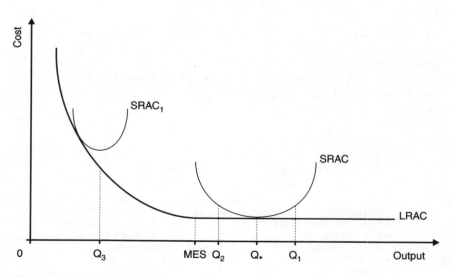

Want production above MES
Ideally each plant at Q$_*$
Industry under capacity at Q$_1$
Industry over capacity at Q$_2$ or Q$_3$

Figure 8.8 Economies of scale/industry capacity

say Q_2, then overcapacity exists, since the plant in the industry are being operated with a short-run average cost above that at Q_*, that is to say, further economies of scale are available if demand were higher, or if there were less plant in operation.

If conditions of demand and supply in the industry do not allow it to reach MES or some output above it where LRAC is still constant, allocative inefficiency in the use of resources is said to exist.

It may be the case that only large firms are able to offer economies of scale, so minimizing costs of production. Remember that this implies concentration, with lower output and higher prices than in a competitive market. Nevertheless the gains from lower costs, even though not entirely passed on in lower prices, may still be advantageous to the consumer.

However, a further source of inefficiency may develop as a result of the market power stemming from concentration. This is termed **x inefficiency**. These additions to cost which stem from complacent management, may offset the possible gains from lower costs due to economies of scale. This form of inefficiency has been for example exposed and in part corrected when public utilities in the UK have been privatized. Thus in electricity generation and delivery, the apparent loss of scale economies appears to have been more that offset by reductions in x inefficiency, resulting in large reductions in price to customers. X inefficiency stems from ineffective competition, which induces management complacency. It may take the following forms:

- excessive bureaucracy
- restrictive labour practices
- high overheads (prestige HQ, directors' perks etc.)
- poor management of systems and quality.

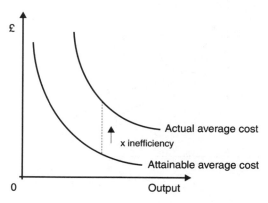

Figure 8.9 X inefficiency and cost

The impact of x inefficiency may be illustrated graphically, as in Figure 8.9. At all levels of output actual average unit cost exceeds attainable average unit cost. A further gain made as a result of concentration which might offset the loss of competition lies in the area of *dynamic* cost gains. These essentially stem from two sources: experience and learning effects, and innovation effects.

Long-established large firms have the advantage of the experience gained over much greater *cumulative* volumes of production. This should lead to cost reductions giving an advantage over new entrants with less experience. However this presumes that learning is *effective*. Long experience leading to inability to recognize that production methods are outmoded may be a disadvantage – as Ford have learned from competition with Toyota (see Chapter 12).

Large long-established firms, with great market power are likely over time to generate large supernormal profits, which may be ploughed back into the research and development of new products and new production techniques, as in the case of the coffee industry, leading to better products at lower cost. These gains may again be illustrated in terms of our conventional theoretical tools (see Figure 8.10).

Price

In evaluating the performance of an industry in terms of price, the basic principle is as follows: *Prices should be consistent with the real economic costs of supplying the product, including a normal economic profit.* Conventional theory suggests that welfare will be maximized for consumers

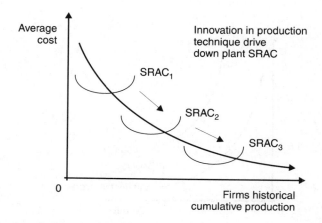

Figure 8.10 Innovation in production methods and costs

where price = marginal cost = minimum average cost (including normal profit). This can *only* occur in the conditions of perfect competition which as we have seen are an unattainable limiting case. In reality markets are more or less concentrated in the hands of relatively few larger firms. Where this is so (even if only temporarily as in the case of monopolistic competition where few entry barriers exist) price will exceed marginal cost and minimum average cost. Production will be lower and price higher than in perfect competition. Supernormal profits will be earned, and dead weight loss of welfare suffered by consumers. This situation may be illustrated graphically using conventional theoretical tools (see Figure 8.11).

Profits

The apparent superiority of a perfectly competitive market over a monopoly or concentrated market depends on the simplistic terms, normal profit and excess (or supernormal) profit. Normal profit is regarded in the conventional models of market structures as a cost of production. It is seen as the **opportunity cost** of the capital and entrepreneurial skill invested in the business. Supernormal profit (as in Figure 8.11) is seen as a residual sum resulting from the price and output decisions of a firm in a concentrated market, and removed from the firm by its owners. In reality things are not so straightforward.

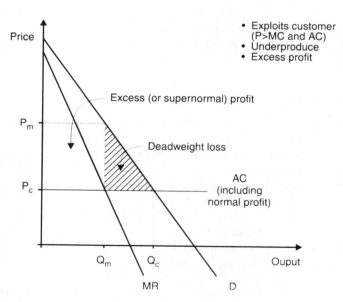

Figure 8.11 Simple model of a monopoly or concentrated market

From the dynamic perspective on the firm these concepts of profit are more complex. Normal profit may vary with the business cycle, being lower in recession and higher in the boom. It can depend on the risk profile of the market sector, being for example higher in maritime insurance at Lloyds, than in household general insurance, the former being more risk based than the latter. It may depend on the level of R&D required to innovate a succession of new products being higher in an industry where product life cycles are short, such as pharmaceuticals, and lower in more stable markets, such as plasterboard.

Excess profit may be a temporary phenomenon, accruing to existing firms in a growing market with insufficient capacity, such as photocopiers in the 1970s. In this situation it plays a key role in attracting new entrants, and so facilitating reallocation of resources in line with changes in customer requirements.

Excess profit may be a reward for innovation or risk taking, for example the development of complex colour photocopiers. Thus in one firm excess profits may be siphoned off by the owner/shareholders, while in a similar firm in the same industry much of the excess profit may be ploughed back in R&D, or in process improvement to gain a long-term competitive advantage.

Profit differences between similar firms in an industry may reflect differences in the effectiveness of resource use, in costs, or in product performance (e.g. Nescafé in the coffee case study).

It is clearly not sufficient to judge the performance of firms in a market on the basis of more or less reported profit. This is so even if it were possible to interpret profit as expressed as an accounting entity, in terms of an economic perspective. Are there other useful criteria on which to base a judgement?

Advertising and promotion

In some highly concentrated markets where tacit collusion on price, or price leadership of the leading player, prevails non-price competition to gain or defend market share is based on advantage and promotion. The detergent market is a good example, where the two dominant companies, Unilever, and Proctor and Gamble, spend up to 40 per cent of sales revenue on promoting wide ranges of similar products. For most of the last twenty years the major supermarket chains have spent heavily on promoting an image and level of service provided while tacitly colluding on price.

There are arguments for and against such heavy spending on advertising and promotion. It may replace price competition, wasting resources by encouraging brand switching by consumers. Costs and prices may be raised with no new benefit to the consumer. It may act as a barrier to entry, raising new entrants' selling costs due to established brand loyalty, and the incumbent firms' scale economies in selling. On the other hand it provides valuable information for consumers, which may help to expand the whole market sector. This may promote scale economies in production, lowering costs and price. It may actually aid new entrants by informing a wider audience of the benefits of that type of product. Examples of these pros and cons of advertising may be found within the case studies in this book, particularly those of the supermarkets and ice cream.

Product performance

From the economist's perspective the ability of a market sector to deliver to customers a variety of product types, differing in functional and perceived attributes and price category, and appealing to varying tastes and income levels may justify the market structure. A further element of product performance which is of increasing importance is the quality of customer service before and after sales which surrounds each alternative brand (see Nicholas Smith's (Garages) Ltd case study). The increasing sophistication of customer choice which has highlighted this element has also increased the importance of continuous improvement of the product and service, both incremental and in terms of more rapid development of new variants. The competitive advantage gained by firms in these ways is examined in detail in Chapter 12.

The availability of a wide choice of alternatives at a range of prices is then as important a criteria as the simple one of prices in the evaluation of market performance. Criteria for the evaluation of market power are:

- *Consumer choice (more choice/good less choice/bad)*: concentrated market may generate many competing products from few firms, e.g. coffee, or few competing products from few firms, e.g. plasterboard.
- *Entry conditions*: may be prohibitive, e.g. plasterboard pre-1989, or easy, e.g. printing.
- *Collusion*: may be strong, e.g. supermarkets, or absent, e.g. photocopiers.
- *Restrictive practices*: may be strong, e.g. book publishing pre-1995, or absent, e.g. publishing post-1995.
- *Price competition*: may be intense even where few firms, e.g. newspapers, supermarkets 1994/95.
- *Advertising/promotion*: may replace price competition, waste resources, raise costs and prices, create barriers to entry through brand loyalty and economies of scale in selling *or* may expand market by providing more information, aiding new entrants, and through economies of scale in production lower costs and prices.

There are however two important qualifications to this generalization. It is possible for there to be available an excessive variety, i.e. *product proliferation*. This may be the case for detergent products and breakfast cereals. Such proliferation may be wasteful of resources, both in terms of production costs and advertising expenditure. There may further be no objective measure of quality, leaving the way open for *deception* and false claims. These must be reduced by trades descriptions and technical standards legislation. Nevertheless difficult cases may arise, e.g. in the coffee industry. It may be argued that from the customers' perspective it does not really matter whether many suppliers provide variety of choice (e.g. printing), or few suppliers sell many brands (e.g. coffee).

Technological progressiveness

We discussed earlier some examples of *dynamic gains* which cannot be easily represented in the conventional static model of the firm. These were the possibility of reduced costs and prices, superior products and greater variety of choice, all stemming from technological change. Such advances in technology have had two effects. First, to greatly reduce the real cost of a product to the customer (e.g. colour TV), secondly, to greatly improve the performance of the product (e.g. photocopiers are now both much more reliable and faster than early models, as well as relatively cheaper).

Furthermore technological advances may lead to breakthroughs which produce a new product which delivers a function much more efficiently than its predecessor. An example might be CD as against vinyl records or audio tapes. This breakthrough may be so radical as to generate a completely new market sector. CD multimedia products are now generating a whole new publishing sector, at the expense of both conventional software producers and book publishers.

A strong argument in favour of high levels of industry concentration is the ability of very large firms to spend large sums on R&D. Firms with at least temporary market power have greater resources for this purpose from retained supernormal profits, and they are able in this way to earn greater rewards than a small firm, perpetuating their advantage. This situation is very evident in the pharmaceutical industry and may also be observed in our photocopier case.

We have outlined above some of the advantages available to firms in dynamic and highly concentrated industries, and to their customers. There are, however, some disadvantages to be observed in such industries.

The constant need to stay ahead of competitors (either by continuous improvement, or technological breakthrough) may cause very short product life cycles, with a consequent need for excessive R&D spending. In such cases, market power is likely to be only temporary, creating an imperative to be *first mover*. This excessive R&D cost increases the need for supernormal profit, causing an increased likelihood of increased concentration (as in the case of pharmaceuticals).

CONCLUSION

We have examined five aspects of market performance, bearing in mind always that our ultimate criterion is the need (as seen by the economist) for *effective and efficient use of resources in the interests of the consumer*. The degree of market concentration present is less important than the provision of a range of choice of product to suit differing tastes and incomes, and the availability of the capability for improvement and replacement of products over time at declining real cost to the consumer. Where there exist the parallel possibility of excessive market power, leading to exploitation of the consumer through higher prices, lower output and inferior product than in a more competitive market, it is necessary for government to put in place mechanisms to regulate both market conduct of firms and the process of acquisition, the latter, for example, in the case of privatized water companies. Most advanced economies have such regulatory arrangements in place. Those used in the UK and EU are discussed in Chapter 13.

The following cases (Pass and Lowes, 1994) provide an opportunity to analyse the forces driving competition in a market and the interrelationships between market structure, conduct and performance. The United Kingdom plasterboard industry supplies an intermediate or producers' good and has become highly price competitive with the recent entry of two new manufacturers; the United Kingdom coffee industry supplies a final or consumers' product and is characterized by product differentiation competition between brand manufacturers and price-based competition between own label suppliers.

CASE STUDY 9: THE COFFEE INDUSTRY

(This case study and questions have been extracted from Pass and Lowes (1994).)

The United Kingdom coffee market is characterized by product differentiation competition between manufacturers of branded products who have been increasingly exposed to competition from cheaper own label brands offered by the leading supermarket groups. In 1991 the Monopolies and Mergers Commission (MMC) reported on the industry and concluded that the consumer had benefited from the availability of a very large number of brands providing a wide choice of price and quality combinations.

Products and customers

Coffee is supplied in two main forms: 'roast and ground' which needs to be prepared in a percolator, filter machine or cappuccino/espresso machine; and 'instant' or 'soluble' coffee which requires the user merely to add hot water in a cup. Instant coffee accounts for around 90 per cent of United Kingdom consumption of coffee, a figure which is much higher than for most other countries. The types of instant coffee consumed in the United Kingdom comprise spray-dried granules, freeze-dried granules and powders (Table 8.2), these being supplied in both caffeinated and decaffeinated form. Freeze-dried granules have become more popular in recent years (freeze-drying preserves more of a coffee's flavour) as has the decaffeinated form (reflecting some customers 'healthier' life-style). In 1990 there were over 200 coffee brands available on the market.

Table 8.2 Sector share of the instant coffee market

	%	
	1986	1990
Spray-dried granules	58	58
Freeze-dried granules	18	28
Powders	24	14

Source: MMC

In 1990 the United Kingdom retail instant coffee market was worth around £600m., having peaked in the late 1980s. Although coffee has gained ground at the expense of tea in recent years (in 1970 3.7 cups of tea were drunk for every cup of coffee; in 1989 the ratio was around 2 to 1) the market for coffee is now mature. Although the share of sales between suppliers is determined by the pattern of primary demand, in part the availability of brands is influenced by the procurement and stocking policies of the major supermarket groups, who account for around 80 per cent of purchases from manufacturers, supplying either manufacturers' branded items or providing retailers with own label brands.

Market structure

Suppliers

The supply of instant coffee in the United Kingdom is dominated by Nestlé, whose 'Nescafé' portfolio of brands accounted for some 47 per cent by volume and 56 per cent by value of total retail sales in 1990. For a while in the 1960s and 1970s the company's market share came under threat from other brand suppliers, in particular by General Food's 'Maxwell House' and Brooke Bond's 'Red Mountain', and the emergence of a plethora of retailers' own label brands. At the end of the 1970s Nestlé's market share had been reduced to under 40 per cent, but it has since regained its preponderant position in the market by astute marketing and new product launches. In contrast to the experiences of many other branded grocery products, Nestlé has managed to reverse the trend towards cheaper retailers' own label brands, whose collective market share has been reduced from around 33 per cent by volume in 1980 to around 25 per cent of the market by volume, and 15 per cent by value in 1990.

Table 8.3 gives details of the overall market shares of the suppliers of instant coffee and their main brand shares in 1990. As indicated above, instant coffee is supplied both under the brand name of the manufacturer and also to retailers for sale as an own label brand. Nestlé produces only for

Table 8.3 Market shares by suppliers and major brands, 1990: UK coffee market

	%	
	Value	Volume
Nestlé	56.0	47.5
Nescafé	40.8	35.7
Nescafé decaffeinated	2.9	2.4
Nescafé Gold Blend	7.1	5.3
Nescafé Gold Blend decaffeinated	2.4	1.7
Nescafé Blend 37	1.3	1.0
Others	1.5	1.4
GFL (General Foods)	24.7	24.9
Branded sales:	19.5	18.0
Maxwell House	8.7	8.7
Maxwell House decaffeinated	0.5	0.5
Kenco	2.3	1.8
Kenco decaffeinated	1.1	0.8
Café Hag	4.0	3.3
Other	2.9	2.9
Own label	5.2	6.9
Brooke Bond	5.7	5.7
Red Mountain	4.6	4.6
Red Mountain decaffeinated	0.7	0.7
Other	0.4	0.4
Lyons Tetley	8.3	12.8
Own label	8.3	12.8
Other suppliers	5.3	9.1
Total	100.0	100.0
Brand Analysis		
Nestlé	56.0	47.5
GFL	19.5	18.0
Brooke Bond	5.7	5.7
Other branded	3.5	4.7
Own label	15.3	24.1

Source: MMC

itself, as does Brooke Bond. Around three-quarters of GFL's coffee is sold under its brand name, the remainder being supplied as own label. Lyons Tetley supplies almost exclusively own label brands.

- *Nestlé*: the company, which is Swiss-owned, pioneered the establishment of the industry in the United Kingdom in 1939 when it launched its original 'Nescafé' brand. Over the years it has added to its brand portfolio and is represented in all the main market segments (brands: Nescafé; Nescafé Gold Blend; Nescafé Blend 37; Nescafé Alta Rica; Nescafé Cap Colombie; Nescafé Fine Blend; Nescafé Elevenses; Nescafé Nescore). The company has production plants at Hayes and Tutbury.
- *GFL*: General Foods, which is American-owned, entered the United Kingdom market in 1947 with the acquisition of an established coffee producer, Alfred Bird. In 1954, it launched its main US brand, 'Maxwell House', in the United Kingdom. In 1981 it added to its United Kingdom brands by acquiring Hag AG, the Dutch supplier. The company became a subsidiary of the tobacco group Philip Morris in 1985 and was reconstituted in 1989, following Morris's acquisition of the Kraft food group (brands: Maxwell House; Café Hag; Masterblend; Mellow Bird; Brim). The company has a production plant at Banbury.
- *Brooke Bond*: the company, an established United Kingdom supplier of tea, entered the coffee market in 1965 with the launch of 'Crown Cup'. In 1985 Brooke Bond was acquired by the Anglo-Dutch food and detergents group, Unilever. The company's main brand is 'Red Mountain', launched in 1982 (other brands: Café Mountain; Brazilian Choice). Brooke Bond imports made-up coffee from Europe and Brazil which it then packages for retail sale at its Redbourn and Trafford Park factories.
- *Lyons Tetley*: the company is a subsidiary of Allied Lyons, the United Kingdom brewing and food group. Lyons entered the market in 1961 with 'Lyons Instant Coffee'. The product failed, however, and in order to use the spare capacity at its Greenford plant, the company turned to supplying own label brands. In 1965 Lyons acquired Sol Café, another own label supplier, and in 1982 it purchased Tenco, an American-owned company, which packaged own label brands. The company is now the largest United Kingdom own label supplier, although it also supplies some branded coffee for sale in cash-and-carry outlets.
- *Other suppliers*: Fine Foods International (German owned) is the largest of the minor suppliers; it sources coffee from its parent company ready packed and supplies own label retailers. Gold Crown Foods (United Kingdom) imports coffee which it packages at its Liverpool factory for sale as own label. S. Daniels entered the market in 1978 selling under the brand name of 'Vendona'; the company imports coffee, which since 1989 it has packed in its United Kingdom factories. The Food Brands Group supplies coffee under the 'Percol' brand name, which was launched in the

United Kingdom in 1989; coffee supplies are sourced from the Swiss company Jacobs Suchard (now owned by Philip Morris). Douwe Egberts is a subsidiary of the Dutch concern Sara Lee/DE NV (itself owned by Sara Lee of the USA); the company entered the United Kingdom market in 1984 with its 'Moccona' brand. McCormick supplies 'Camp', the only liquid coffee brand.

- *Own label retailers*: the main own label retailers are the leading supermarket groups – Sainsbury, Tesco, Safeway, Gateway and Asda.

The condition of entry

As noted above, a number of new suppliers have entered the market, the latest being Douwe Egberts and Food Brands, as well as an increasing number of own label brands (for example, Aldi of Germany, a recent entrant to the United Kingdom market, offers four types of own label).

The ease of entry into the industry depends on the method of entry adopted. Entry by establishing a new greenfield instant coffee plant would require a capital investment of some £30–£50m. for a spray-dried coffee plant and some £35–£60m. for a freeze-dried coffee plant, although these figures would be reduced if a plant was installed at an existing food manufacturing site. These sums would not be a problem for a 'deep-pocket' entrant. Nestlé indicated that the minimum efficient scale of operation for a spray-dried plant was in the order of 5,000 tonnes per annum, equivalent to around 10 per cent of the United Kingdom market. An alternative entry strategy would be to import ready-made coffee for packaging in the United Kingdom or importation of the complete product, as have Food Brands and Douwe Egberts.

In either case, large-scale entry into the main market segments would (given a relatively static overall demand for coffee) require an entrant to win market share from established firms. In this context, it was suggested to the MMC that advertising posed a particularly serious problem for entrants. Advertising and promotional costs for a typical national launch were in the order of £4.5m., but this in itself would not be a particular problem for a 'deep-pocket' entrant, nor is it out of line with those for any other branded grocery product. Smaller newcomers such as Food Brands and Douwe Egberts have not sought to compete head to head with Nestlé in the main market segments but have focused on the premium sector, obtaining widespread distribution for their brands without heavy television advertising. At the other end of the market, major food retailers have launched their 'captive' own label brands into mainly the low-price sector. The development of the own label sector has provided coffee producers with greater opportunities for entry as a specialist supplier of own labels, as was the case with Sol Café (now part of Lyons Tetley).

The MMC concluded that it was not so much the high level of advertising in the industry *per se* which represented a serious barrier to entry, but the need for entrants' brands to match or exceed the quality of Nescafé's brands which was the key factor in successful entry. The fact that major new brands such as 'Red Mountain' and 'Maxwell House' had failed to undermine the dominant position of Nescafé, despite heavy advertising support, was due to their inability to outperform Nescafé in terms of quality and value-for-money attributes. A number of coffee suppliers indicated that there were proprietary methods of manufacture which enabled some existing suppliers to produce coffee of superior quality: 'Most suppliers agreed that the quality of Nescafé products could not be easily replicated by other manufacturers' (para. 2.117).

The MMC concluded:

> In our view there are several means of entry to the market. Entry has indeed occurred and, although new entrants may be reluctant to compete directly with Nestlé for a large market share, there is no evidence that entry has been deterred by Nestlé's strong position in the market, or that Nestlé has taken action to prevent such entry.
>
> (para. 7.51)

Market conduct

Pricing policies

A number of stages are involved in pricing instant coffee. Suppliers set a wholesale list price for their products; their customers, in the main retailers, purchase at these prices less a discount; retailers, in turn, set retail prices to customers.

It was suggested to the MMC that competition between suppliers could be described 'as being on the basis of value-for-money rather than price alone' (para. 2.65).

The pricing system adopted by the leading suppliers is similar. Suppliers' price lists show the price per case for each product, with customers qualifying for discounts off this list price according to quantities purchased and other factors. Most suppliers offer a 'basic' discount related to quantity purchased, but there are variations based on product size (200 gram jars v. 100 gram jars) and type of product (freeze-dried v. spray-dried). Discounts can also reflect 'allowances' to retailers for providing in-store displays and promotions and special rebates (so-called 'overriders' and 'retrospective bonuses') may be paid to encourage the placing of large orders. The MMC found that the extent of these discounts varied substantially between suppliers: 'The discount off list price for Maxwell House, for example, was more than double the discount for Nescafé' (para. 2.77).

Table 8.4 lists the average retail prices of manufacturers' brands of 100-gram jars and a sample of own label brands sold in major supermarkets in June 1990. It can be seen that there is a very wide range of prices available. In the regular granulated sector the brand leader, 'Nescafé', was priced at £1.39, 5p more expensive than its chief competitor, 'Maxwell House'; 'Café Mountain' was similarly priced at £1.39. Retailers' own label brands, of varying qualities, cost between 20p and 30p less than 'Nescafé'. In the freeze-dried sector the brand leader 'Nescafé Gold Blend' was priced at £1.69, as were its main competitors, 'Nescafé Blend 37', 'Kenco' and 'Continental Gold'.

Retail surveys indicate that because instant coffee is part of many consumers' regular grocery shopping, consumers are highly aware of coffee prices and are in a position to compare the prices of different brands both within and between stores. As a consequence, retail prices for equivalent brands tend to be very similar in all the major supermarkets. The keenness of coffee pricing by these groups is reflected in the fact that the coffee brands sold in these outlets are priced only marginally higher than those to be found in the stores of 'cut-price' retailers such as Kwik-Save and Budgens.

The MMC duly noted that the price structure for coffee reflected gradations in the quality of product supplied and that consumers' perceptions of differences in quality between brands offered suppliers scope to 'add value' to their brands. Thus, as noted above, the brand leader 'Nescafé' has been able to sustain a 5p price premium over its closest branded competitor, 'Maxwell House', and a 20–30p price premium over own label while *increasing* its market share. 'Nescafé's market share by value increased from 37 per cent to 56 per cent over the period 1980–90, while over the same period 'Maxwell House' market share fell from 17 per cent to under 10 per cent. The MMC was satisfied that there was vigorous price competition between coffee brands and that given the wide spectrum of price–quality combinations available, ranging from 'basic' own label brands to premium-priced 'specialities', there was no question but that consumers had been given sufficient freedom of choice to make their preferences felt in the market-place. The MMC concluded: 'Consumer preference for the leading Nestlé brands, particularly for Nescafé, reflects therefore the outcome of consumer choice among a wide range of alternatives and a preference for a perceived higher quality at a somewhat higher price' (para. 7.64).

Product differentiation

The leading coffee products are strongly branded and their successful marketing has required a substantial investment and expertise in developing an appropriate brand: 'The branding of the product is a complex mixture of

Table 8.4 Prices for 100-gram jars, June 1990 (£s): UK coffee market

Average at major supermarkets	Nestlé	GFL	Brooke Bond	Other manufacturers	Own label (OL)
0.52				Vendona Chicory (S. Daniel – O)	
0.53					OL – O
0.59				Vendona S/B Powder (S. Daniel – P)	
0.68					OL – O
0.73				Vendona Classic Granules (S. Daniel – G)	
0.79				Grandos Instant (FFL – G)	
0.86					OL – P
0.89					OL – PD
0.92				Camp Chicory (McCormick – L)	
0.94				Vendona Gold (S. Daniel – F)	
1.09					OL – F
1.15				Grandos Expresso (FFL – F)	
1.19			Choice (P)		OL – G
1.27	Nescafé Fine Blend (P)				
1.29		Birds Mellow (P)			OL – G OL – GD
		Maxwell House (G)			
1.34		Maxwell House (P)			
1.39	Nescafé (G)		Café Mountain (G)		
1.47		Master Blend (G)			
1.49					OL – FD
1.59			Red Mountain (F)		
	Nescafé Decaffeinated (GD)	Café Hag (GD)		Continental Gold (Douwe-F)	
	Nescafé Gold Blend (F)	Maxwell House Decaffeinated (GD)		Percol Decaffeinated (Food Brands – GD)	
1.69	Nescafé Blend 37 (F)	Kenco (F)			
1.72				Percol Café Mocha (Food Brands – P)	
1.74				Percol Café Expresso (Food Brands – P)	
1.89		Café Hag Select (FD)	Red Mountain Decaffeinated (FD)	Percol SP Decaffeinated (Food Brands – FD)	
1.95	Nescafé Gold Blend Decaffeinated (FD)	Kenco Decaffeinated (FD)			
	Nescafé Cap Colombie (F)				
2.55	Nescafé Alta Rica (F)				

Type Code:	F	(Freeze-dried)	P	(Powder)
	FD	(Freeze-dried decaffeinated)	PD	(Powder decaffeinated)
	G	(Granules)	O	(Other mixtures)
	GD	(Granules decaffeinated)	L	(Liquid)

Source: MMC

taste positioning, advertising, packaging, pricing, trade and promotional terms in order to develop a differentiated product' (para. 2.49).

Advertising plays a key role in developing a brand, by serving to communicate the qualities and characteristics of the brand, to create favourable associations in the consumer's mind and to communicate the benefits of the brand compared with competitors' products. The two main coffee suppliers rely extensively on advertising and promotions to support their brands. Table 8.5 shows the total amount spent on advertising and promotion by Nestlé, GFL and Brooke Bond over the period 1985–9 and the amount spent on television advertising in 1989. Television advertising accounts for about half of the advertising and promotional spending at Nestlé and GFL. The remainder is taken up by various 'value added' promotions, a substantial proportion of which consist of lump-sum payments to retailers for providing in-store displays and special promotions. Nestlé spends only slightly more on advertising than GFL, though it has twice the market share. Nestlé, it will be noted, sells all its brands using the 'umbrella' name of 'Nescafé' which it feels confers 'considerable spillover gains between advertising different Nescafé brands' (para. 2.60). GFL's brands, by contrast, are promoted on a stand-alone basis.

Table 8.5 Advertising and promotion spending, 1985–9 (£ million): UK coffee market

	Date launched	1985	1986	1987	1988	1989 TV	1989 Total	Cumulative 1985–9
Nestlé		14.7	19.3	24.5	29.3	15.3	29.9	117.7
Nescafé	1939	9.3	12.3	15.7	18.4	6.9	18.5	74.2
Blend 37	1955	0.7	1.0	1.3	1.3	1.4	1.8	6.1
Gold Blend	1965	4.2	5.1	6.4	8.3	6.6	8.4	32.4
Fine Blend	1973	0.3	0.5	0.6	0.6	—	0.4	2.4
Nescore	1975	0.1	0.1	0.1	—	—	—	0.3
Elevenses	1977	0.1	0.1	0.1	0.1	—	—	0.4
Alta Rica/Cap Colombie	1985	—	0.2	0.3	0.6	0.4	0.8	1.9
GFL		10.6	19.1	21.1	28.2	17.5	27.6	106.6
Maxwell House	1954	8.1	11.4	14.2	16.8	8.2	14.5	65.0
Café Hag	1979	1.5	1.9	2.2	4.7	4.1	5.9	16.2
Mellow Birds	1972	1.0	1.8	1.8	1.8	0.5	1.3	7.7
Kenco	1988	—	—	—	2.7	4.7	5.6	8.3
Master Blend	1986	—	4.0	2.9	2.2	—	0.3	9.4
Brooke Bond		2.1	3.2	4.5	6.3	2.7	5.8	21.9
Red Mountain	1982	1.4	2.7	4.4	6.2	2.7	5.6	20.2
Other		0.7	0.5	0.1	0.2	—	0.2	1.7

Source: MMC

Maintaining the market position of established brands requires close attention to marketing mix details. A good illustration of the branding process is provided by 'Nescafé'. Nestlé told the MMC that in the 1960s it had 'set about developing the instant coffee market away from a commodity milk modifier to a more discerning appreciation of coffee quality' (para. 2.52). Its marketing department was charged with making 'Nescafé' synonymous with 'quality' in terms of its physical properties, its presentation and the perception of the brand by consumers. In 1981 a 'new improved' Nescafé was developed, containing a more expensive, higher-quality blend of coffee beans. The relaunch in 1981 was combined with a new label and a new advertising campaign. Nestlé indicated that it strongly believed that 'long-term advertising campaigns were a cumulative investment that made a major contribution to the establishment of the brand in the minds of consumers' (para. 2.52).

Over the longer term, the maintenance and extension of a company's market position requires it to pay particular attention to product updates, repositioning opportunities, withdrawal and the introduction of new brands. Table 8.6 gives details of product launches, relaunches, etc. in the coffee market. 'Nescafé' was launched in 1939 and its major rival, 'Maxwell House' was introduced into the United Kingdom market in 1954. In 1970 both Nestlé and GFL brought out spray-dried granular versions of these brands. In 1981, as noted above, a quality-enhanced version of 'Nescafé' was introduced.

In the freeze-dried sector, 'Nescafé Gold Blend' was introduced in 1965. It was not until 1982 that a branded rival appeared with the launch of Brooke Bond's 'Red Mountain'. GFL entered this sector only in 1988 with its 'Kenco' brand. In the late 1980s several new freeze-dried products were launched, including various 'Percol' brands (from Food Brands) and two brands by Douwe Egberts.

The powdered sector is more heterogeneous. GFL offers a powdered version of Maxwell House and introduced Mellow Birds in 1972, while Nestlé is represented by 'Nescafé Fine Blend' (launched in 1973) and 'Nescafé Elevenses' (launched in 1977); Brooke Bond introduced 'Brazilian Blend' in 1972 and launched a reformulated version of this product in 1982 under a new brand name 'Brazilian Choice'. The leading suppliers have withdrawn a number of unsuccessful brands in this sector, for example, 'Good Day' (in 1985) and 'Coffee Time' (in 1989).

In the decaffeinated sector, Nestlé launched 'Nescafé Gold Blend' in 1978. GFL, having acquired Hag AG in 1979, introduced the company's leading brand 'Café Hag' nationally in 1981. This brand is now market leader. Decaffeinated versions of established brands have been introduced by Nestlé ('Nescafé' in 1986), Brooke Bond ('Red Mountain' in 1988) and GFL ('Maxwell House' in 1989).

Table 8.6 Brand developments, major suppliers, 1939–90: UK coffee market

	Nestlé	GFL	Brooke Bond	Other
1939	L Nescafé			
1947		GF acquires Alfred Bird brands		
1954		L Maxwell House		
1955	L Blend 37			
1960				L Lyons Instant Coffee
1963				W Lyons Instant
1965	L Gold Blend		L Crown Cup	Lyons acquires Sol Café (own label)
1970	R Nescafé Granulated	R Maxwell House Granulated		
1972		L Mellow Birds	L Brazilian Blend	
1973	L Fine Blend			
1975	L Nescore			
1976		L Coffee Time		
1977	L Elevenses			
1978	L Gold Blend Decaffeinated	L Brim		L Vendona brands (S. Daniels)
1979		GF acquires Hag brands		
1981	R Nescafé	L Café Hag for general distribution		
1982	L Good Day		L Red Mountain R Brazilian Choice (Blend)	Lyons acquires Tenco (own label)
1984	L Gold Blend roast and ground	L Master Blend roast and ground		L Douwe Egberts Moccona
1985	W Good Day			
1986	L Nescafé Decaffeinated R Blend 37/Gold Blend	L Master Blend light and rich		
1987	L Blend 37 roast and ground	GF acquires Kenco	R Red Mountain	
1988		L Kenco Regular and Decaffeinated	L Red Mountain Decaffeinated	
1989	R Nescore Decaffeinated	L Maxwell House Decaffeinated		L Percol brands (Food Brands) L Douwe Egberts Continental Gold
1990		L Maxwell House Classic		

Key: L = Launch
R = Relaunch
W = Withdrawal

Source: MMC

Market performance

Prices and selling costs

The conventional market theory objection to product differentiation is that it is used by suppliers as a substitute for price competition, since product differentiation offers a more permanent and 'safer' way of improving a company's market position and profitability than price competition, which if pursued aggressively reduces everybody's profits. This view, however, needs to be tempered by the fact that in many markets, including that for coffee, advertising and price are used in combination as part of a broader-based marketing-mix strategy; that is, they are not either/or options, but are deployed *in tandem* to support 'value-for-money' competition. The leading coffee producers supply a range of brands serving particular market segments and operate a price structure to reflect gradations in quality and different types of coffee. Advertising of established brands is used as a means of 'competitive maintenance', reminding customers of the quality of the brand and reassuring customers of the value of the product to them. In this sense advertising is pro-competitive, rather than restrictive of competition. Similarly, although conventional market analysis depicts advertising as a barrier to entry, in reality it is an essential means of supporting the launch of a new brand onto the market. Again, advertising can have a pro-competitive impact, in this case serving as an 'entry facilitator'. As emphasized earlier [see Pass and Lowes, 1994: ch. 8], studies indicate that it is not advertising *per se* which acts as a major barrier to entry. A more critical element in the entry equation is the need for entrants to offer customers innovative new brands which will induce them to switch their purchases away from established brands in sufficient numbers so as to enable the entrant to win a viable market share. Outperforming efficient, innovative established producers is difficult, as the experiences of Lyons Tetley and Brooke Bond bear out.

Coffee producers spend large sums of money on advertising their products, but the amount leading suppliers spend on advertising *per se* is much less than for many other consumer-product industries. Table 8.7 shows advertising–sales ratios for a number of branded consumer goods markets in 1990. The MMC did not consider the amount of expenditure on coffee advertising to be excessive, and was satisfied that it was a manifestation of 'workable competition'.

Choice and product quality

Overall, the MMC was of the opinion that the thrust of competition in the coffee market had benefited consumers by providing them with an extensive variety of brands and improvements in product quality. The MMC concluded:

Table 8.7 Advertising–sales ratios: selected markets, 1990

	%
Toothpaste	15.2
Shampoos	14.1
Washing powder	11.0
Breakfast cereals	10.3
Cough remedies	9.2
Margarine	8.5
Sauces and pickles	8.2
Coffee	7.6
Soup	7.0

Source: Advertising Statistics Yearbook

The market research studies we have seen confirm that quality has improved over time, and that most participants in the market are continuing to improve the quality of their products. Given the continuing choice available to customers, with a wide spectrum of price and quality alternatives, these improvements in quality would appear to accord with consumer preferences. Nestlé has indeed increased its market share at the expense of own label by offering higher quality and better value-for-money, despite higher prices. The increasing success of its brands, particularly of Nescafé, given the extent of choice available, reflects Nestlé's success as a competitor in offering a reliable product at a quality and price in accordance with consumer preferences.

(para. 7.66)

Profitability

Table 8.8 provides details of the rate of return on capital employed achieved by the leading suppliers for the period 1985–9. Nestlé's profits were considerably higher than the average rate of profitability for manufacturing industry in general and for food companies in particular. High rates of profitability may be justified by superior efficiency, the need to generate funds to finance capital investment and research and development, and to reward suppliers for taking risks. The MMC is required to assess whether a particular dominant company's profit rate is indeed a 'reasonable' reward in this regard, or whether it has 'abused' its market power by overcharging customers. In practice, of course, it is difficult to draw a fine distinction between what is reasonable or unreasonable. As regards Nestlé, the MMC was 'satisfied' that the company's profits had been earned in the context of a highly competitive market and reflected its commercial success in out-performing its rivals, rather than its ability to exploit a monopoly position protected from competition. The company's profitability 'has arisen in a market with a wide degree of consumer-choice and effective competition' (para. 7.87);

> there is sufficient competition on prices to set a ceiling to the prices that can be charged by Nestlé. Nestlé's only advantages stem from its success as a competitor; it has increased its market share by offering a good quality product, its advertising is more effective, its leading brands are stronger, and in a number of ways it appears to have been more efficient than its competitors.
>
> (para. 7.78)

The MMC concluded:

> It may be regretted that no other firm has to date proved as effective a competitor as Nestlé, but this is no reason, we feel, to conclude that Nestlé's performance is against the public interest and Nestlé is, in our view, a highly effective and successful competitor in their market: its high profitability need not lead us to penalise that success in a market characterised by such a wide degree of choice. Its high profitability should indeed be seen as an incentive for other firms to compete in this lucrative market.
>
> (para. 7.79)

Even so, in other cases where profits have been similarly high (for example, colour film, household detergents, salt, contraceptives) the MMC has recommended price cuts or the imposition of price controls to ensure 'fair' prices. The MMC did in fact consider the possible impact of such a course of action in the coffee case, but rejected it, observing that although this 'could offer some short-term benefits in the form of price reductions' it would carry the considerable risk (given the lower profitability of Nestlé's competitors) 'of there being less choice, poorer quality and weaker competition in the long run. The interests of consumers who already have the option of purchasing cheaper coffee should they so choose, are in our view best served by the maintenance of competition' (para. 7.80). Whether

Table 8.8 Return on capital employed, 1985–9: UK coffee market

	1985	1986	1987	1988	1989
			%		
Nestlé	49.5	64.9	98.9	118.1	113.7
GFL	27.6	35.7	37.2	33.0	29.2
Lyons Tetley	47.3	35.3	33.1	22.2	10.0
Brooke Bond	(loss)	(loss)	(loss)	8.9	2.6

Source: MMC

or not lower prices by Nestlé would serve to eliminate such competition is, of course, a moot point. (In the colour film case, following the instigation of price cuts by the dominant supplier, Kodak, that company's only United Kingdom rival at the time, Ilford, was forced to exit the market as a brand supplier, leaving Kodak as monopoly supplier facing limited competition (at the time) from imports and own label brands.)

Postscript

In February 1994 Allied Lyons withdrew from the UK coffee market, selling its soluble coffee interests to General Foods. Allied's decision to exit from the coffee market followed a strategic decision to concentrate its resources on its larger branded tea business.

Questions

1 Account for the continuing dominance of Nestlé in the coffee market.
2 (a) Examine the proposition that advertising can act as a barrier to entry.
   (b) What evidence is there that advertising by established firms is a strong barrier to entry in the coffee market?
3 Why do oligopolists tend to prefer product differentiation competition to price competition?
4 Examine the role advertising and sales promotion as a source of competitive advantage (a) generally and (b) in the particular case of coffee.
5 Examine the role of new product development in maintaining competitive advantage (a) generally and (b) in the particular case of coffee.
6 Evaluate the MMC view that competition in the coffee market was strong and had benefited consumers as evidenced by the wide spectrum of coffee brands and prices on offer.
7 Is there a case for imposing price cuts/controls on Nestlé in view of the company's extremely high level of profitability?

Feedback to case study

1 (a) Astute marketing and
   (b) New product launches (Gold Blend adverts etc.)
   (c) Refusing to supply own label products
   (d) High minimum efficient scale (10% UK market) as barrier to entry
   (e) Static overall demand for coffee
   (f) Advertising as a barrier to entry – especially since Nescafé is the benchmark brand for quality.
2 Expensive to:
   (a) maintain brand presence
   (b) launch new brands.

Can be up to 40% sales revenue in some duopoly/oligopoly situations.

Note advertising to sales ratios – evidence of high cost of advertising. Therefore barrier to entry to all but *very* large conglomerates. The fact that Nescafé has regained market share lost to own label products despite its higher prices, indicates success of advertising.

3 Oligopoly involves few players in the market, each aware of the other's actions. A price cut by one would lead to tit for tat response by the others, eliminating most of supernormal profit and forcing out weakest players.

Much better to collude on price and compete on non-price characteristics, new product launches, advertising, free gifts, etc.

4 See (2) above

5 A new product displaces demand from other products from that company, but may attract some customers from a rival company's products, thus increasing market share. Also necessary in view of product life cycle – maintain a suitable portfolio of products (see pp. 146–7).

Tit for tat new product launches are expensive, but not so much as a price war, and can be controlled and planned.

6 Arrival of 'own brands' ensured a wide range of price, while a small number of companies with high profits and so development funds, ensured wide range of choice of products, and consistently high quality standards.

MMC view seems justified despite high profits.

7

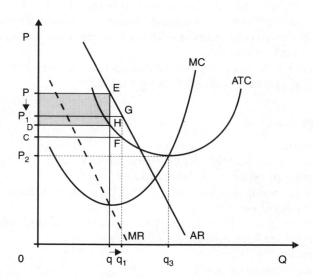

Figure 8.12 Feedback model to question 7

If price reduced by decreasing from OP to OP_1 (see Figure 8.12) profits fall from PCFE to PICHE. Because demand is inelastic, big price fall produces small increase in demand OQ to OQ_1. What would happen if demand for Nescafé is more elastic, i.e. other products seen as stronger substitutes?

How might Nestlé respond?

What if the government forced price cut to OP_2 – the price which would be set in perfect competition? OQ_3 would be demanded, but Nestlé make no supernormal profit and *if possible*, exit the industry (in the UK).

Would it be reasonable to treat *one* company in an oligopoly in this way?

CASE STUDY 10: THE PLASTERBOARD INDUSTRY

(This case study and questions have been extracted from Pass and Lowes (1994).)

Introduction

The United Kingdom plasterboard industry was transformed in the late 1980s from one dominated by a single supplier facing limited competition from imports, to one characterised by more competitive supply conditions with the entry of two new producers. The industry was investigated by the Monopolies and Mergers Commission (MMC) in 1990, which concluded that the industry had become highly competitive and that 'there are no facts which currently operate, or may be expected to operate, against the public interest' (para. 1.8). A previous report by the Commission on the industry in 1974 had found certain practices of BPB, the monopoly supplier of plasterboard, to operate against the public interest. In particular, BPB was forced to abandon its zonal system of uniform delivered prices and various restrictions on customers who wished to buy direct rather than through builders' merchants. In 1988 BPB was fined ECU 3m. (around £2m.) by the European Commission under Article 86 of the EC Treaty for impeding imports into the United Kingdom by offering financial inducements to builders' merchants who agreed to buy their plasterboard *exclusively* from BPB.

Materials, products and customers

Plasterboard is a flat sheet which consists of a core containing gypsum plaster, sandwiched between two sheets of heavy paper known as plasterboard liner. A number of standardised types of plasterboard are produced (baseboard, wallboard, etc.), varying in thickness, width, length and texture according to particular user applications. Plasterboard is used extensively in both domestic and commercial buildings as an internal lining for walls, an internal partition within buildings, as an internal lining for walls, an internal partition within buildings, a ceiling lining material and a roof lining material. In a number of uses, plaster which is applied 'on the spot' to surfaces represents a competitive material to plasterboard, but plasterboard has been gaining market share because of its greater convenience and versatility.

Gypsum is of two types: natural gypsum, which is mined in the United Kingdom and in countries such as France and Spain, and gypsum obtained as a by-product from other processes, in particular power station desulphurisation (DSG). BPB Industries, the leading United Kingdom producer of plasterboard, is the sole United Kingdom supplier of natural gypsum, and it is also the only United Kingdom supplier of lining paper.

In 1990 United Kingdom plasterboard sales totalled £197m., having fallen from £222m. the previous year with the onset of recessionary conditions in the house-building market.

Most end-users of plasterboard make their purchases through builders' merchants, who form the largest customer group for the plasterboard producers. In 1990 there were around 1,750 builders' merchants, the largest of which operate on a nationwide multi-outlet basis. Other customers include large DIY groups, national house and factory builders and dryliner contractors who in the main buy direct from the producers. Buying power has become more concentrated in recent years and this, together with the entry of new producers, has served to increase discount competition. According to an MMC survey of builders' merchants and direct users, many of them have adopted a policy of multi-sourcing and, given the standardised nature of plasterboard products, are readily prepared to switch their custom to obtain lower prices.

Market structure

Seller concentration

Until 1989, BPB Industries was the sole United Kingdom manufacturer of plasterboard, accounting for upwards of 95 per cent of United Kingdom supplies of plasterboard. Import penetration was limited by the low value added nature of the product and relatively high shipping costs. In April 1989 and September 1989 two new producers, Knauf and RPL, respectively, opened up greenfield manufacturing plants in the United Kingdom. Table 8.9 gives market-share details and shows a deconcentration of the market as the new entrants have established a greater market presence.

Table 8.9 Market shares: UK plasterboard market

	1986/87 million sq.m	%	1987/88 million sq.m	%	1988/89 million sq.m	%	1989/90 million sq.m	%
BPB	143.3	97.0	161.0	96.3	174.6	90.6	138.4	76.0
RPL	—	—	0.4	0.2	8.5	4.4	22.2	12.2
Knauf	—	—	—	—	1.6	0.8	11.2	6.2
Others	4.4	3.0	5.8	3.5	8.0	4.2	10.2	5.6
	147.7	100.0	167.2	100.0	192.7	100.0	182.0	100.0

Source: MMC

The development of BPB's dominant position

The production of plasterboard originated in the USA. It was introduced into the United Kingdom in 1917 by British Plaster Board Ltd, now called BPB Industries plc. Initially market penetration was slow, as the building industry regarded plasterboard as an inferior substitute to traditional wet plastering, but the product gained acceptance in the 1930s.

At this time BPB expanded its interests into plaster production and gypsum-mining by acquiring seven companies. BPB also acquired three of its plasterboard competitors in 1936, 1939 and 1944, and in so doing became the United Kingdom's largest producer. The remaining producers were ICI and Plaster Products, the latter being acquired by BPB in 1955. In the 1950s a new entrant, Bellrock, appeared. By 1969 the market shares of the three producers were BPB 78 per cent, ICI 11 per cent and Bellrock 11 per cent. In 1968 BPB acquired Bellrock (this takeover was 'vetted' by the then Board of Trade under new powers contained in the 1968 Monopolies and Mergers Act, and was allowed to proceed without reference to the Monopolies Commission). Also in 1968 ICI notified the Board of Trade that it was withdrawing from the market and offered to sell its machinery to BPB. No objection was raised to this and the transaction was completed, leaving BPB as the monopoly supplier.

Over the years, BPB has expanded into mainland Europe and is a leading producer of plasterboard in Italy, Germany, France, the Netherlands, Spain and Austria, as well as having interests in gypsum-mining and plaster production. The company is now the largest plasterboard manufacturer in Europe.

The entrants

RPL is a joint venture company owned 51 per cent by Redland, a United Kingdom-based supplier of building materials (roof tiles, bricks, aggregates, etc.) and 49 per cent by CSR, which is the largest producer of plasterboard in Australia. The company's first plant, at Bristol, came on-stream in September 1989. (RPL intends to build a second plant at some future date.) RPL had already begun to build up its sales and distribution network in 1987 to 'prime' the market and supplied this operation by importing plasterboard from its joint venture companies in the Netherlands and Norway.

Knauf, with its headquarters in Germany, is the second largest plasterboard manufacturer in Europe, after BPB. It has three plants in Germany and one each in Austria, France, Greece and Spain. Knauf started importing plasterboard in August 1988 in order to prime the market before production at its first United Kingdom plant, at Sittingbourne, came on-stream in April 1989. A second plant was opened at Immingham in September 1990.

Market entry: background to the decision to set up United Kingdom capacity

RPL told the MMC that it had decided to enter the United Kingdom market 'because they believed that, given the existing high margins, unpopular monopoly conditions and prospects for future growth, there would be considerable potential for a *second* supplier to establish a sound and profitable business in the market' (para. 7.2). When RPL announced its decision to enter the market in September 1987, 'it was not aware that Knauf also intended to begin production' (para. 7.3).

RPL had intended to establish two plants to give it national coverage, but Knauf's entry put it in a dilemma by causing overcapacity and BPB to cut prices: 'RPL believed [when it had originally planned its entry] that the addition of 60 million square metres of plasterboard could be absorbed by the likely growth of the market' (para. 7.6). This had exacerbated its losses during its start-up phase and raised a question mark over the viability of setting up a second plant.

Knauf had been 'eyeing up' the market for some time, but 'the acquisition of a German competitor by BPB in 1987 had probably accelerated its decision to enter' (para. 7.27). Knauf, like RPL, was interested in establishing two United Kingdom plants. At the time of the MMC report the company's second plant had been given the go-ahead and was under construction.

Potential barriers to entry

Various possible barriers to entry were cited, including the *capital costs* required to build an optimal-sized plant (estimated at £20–30 million – see Market performance section in this study) and the need to acquire *technical expertise* in producing plasterboard. These were not particular problems for RPL or Knauf, which were both backed by 'deep pocket' parents, while in the case of Redland plasterboard know-how was provided by its joint-venture partner (with Redland providing marketing expertise and established contacts in the building materials market).

RPL and Knauf told the MMC that the main potential barrier to a new entrant concerned the availability of locally sourced materials and the marketing difficulties of persuading the large multiple merchants to stock new entrants' products.

- *Access to inputs*: the production of plasterboard requires the input of gypsum and liner paper. BPB is the only company mining natural gypsum in the United Kingdom. An alternative base material is DSG, which is produced as a by-product of power generation. BPB has contracted to buy the entire output of the first United Kingdom power station (Drax) which will produce DSG.

  RPL and Knauf currently source gypsum from abroad. According to data supplied to the MMC, RPL and Knauf are at an (undisclosed) cost disadvantage compared to BPB. RPL relies entirely on Spanish gypsum. The cost of this is around £11.30 per tonne, of which £6.80 is accounted for by shipping and port charges. Knauf uses DSG sourced from German power stations at around £10.50 per tonne (to which must be added £2 per tonne drying costs).

  RPL told the MMC it was concerned that BPB had taken a majority stake in a Spanish holding company which controlled most of the gypsum mined in Spain, including supplies to RPL. Thus, 'it would be indirectly dependent on BPB for the supply of gypsum' (para. 7.20). Additionally, RPL was concerned that BPB, having secured DSG supplies from Drax, would similarly pre-empt supplies from other power stations as they became available.

  Liner paper is the single largest element of manufacturing costs (around 22 per cent). BPB owns all the current production of liner paper in the United Kingdom. RPL obtains its liner paper from a Swedish paper producer in which it has a 51 per cent stake; Knauf imports liner paper from a German paper manufacturer, partly owned by Knauf's parent. Again, the entrants have been required to absorb the extra expense of importing liner paper compared to BPB.

- *Access to customers*: Knauf maintained that many of the larger builders' merchants purchased exclusively from BPB. Some merchants were prepared to take a proportion of their needs from Knauf and RPL but 'rarely more than 10 per cent. Merchants seemed unwilling to risk their relationship with BPB to any greater extent than that' (para 7.39).

  The MMC surveyed builders' merchants' procurement policies and concluded: 'The evidence indicates that the new entrants, pricing at levels lower than BPB, could expect to have an impact on the market provided that the quality of their product was satisfactory' (para. 4.62). This has been the case 'as shown by the number of merchants who purchase from them and by the fact that, amongst the merchants who do not, they are considered realistic alternatives to BPB'.

With regard to special project work, where large contractors bypass merchants and buy direct from the manufacturer, two factors were, according to Knauf, preventing its market penetration: loyalty to BPB's 'Gyproc' brand name, but more particularly the cross-subsidisation by BPB of the ancillary products (such as steel supports) used in special projects.

Market conduct

Pricing policies: general

Given the commodity nature of plasterboard, competition in this market (post-entry) has been largely based on price.

Plasterboard prices edged upwards between 1985 and the end of 1988, but by less than the United Kingdom's average inflation rate. BPB cut its prices in January 1989, January 1990 and again in June 1990, reflecting its attempt to limit the market penetration of the new entrants. In real terms, BPB's prices for standard wallboard and baseboard products were 25 per cent lower in January 1990 compared to January 1985. On 4 June BPB introduced a further range of discounts to merchants of between 15 and 22½ per cent as compared with the 'standard' merchant discount of 10 per cent (which itself had been increased from 5 per cent in 1989).

BPB informed the MMC that its long-term pricing strategy was to keep increases in plasterboard prices below rises in the retail price index and the building materials index in order 'to support a strategy of developing the market for new applications' (para. 4.76; note MMC's conclusion, however, that BPB's prices – prior to entry – were 'unreasonable' – see Market performance section).

BPB's pricing policy since 1974 has been conditioned by the under-takings given to the OFT, following the MMC's first investigation of the industry. The undertakings mean that BPB's ex-works prices for a given type of product are the *same* throughout the country, and that its delivered prices for these products *add* to the ex-works price a transport charge reflecting delivery costs (previously BPB had operated a zonal system of *uniform* delivered prices which meant that customers further from a given regional plant were subsidised by customers more proximate to the plant).

For pricing purposes, BPB categorises plasterboard in many different ways (by type; by thickness and width; by length; by finishing), leading to a complex pricing structure (quoting some 2,880 different prices!).

RPL's strategy had been to set its published prices at approximately 2 per cent below BPB's. Delivered prices were set to take into account delivery costs and prices charged by competitors. Until BPB's June 1990 increase in discounts, RPL's standard discount had been the same as BPB's (10 per cent), but RPL also offered 'special' rebates on larger orders and various trade promotions (e.g. reduced delivery charges, free packs). RPL responded to BPB's increased discounts of June 1990 by increasing its trade discount on all plasterboard products from 10 to 15 per cent.

Knauf also generally aims to undercut BPB's published prices 'in order to gain entry into the market' (para. 4.92). Its pricing also took into account transport costs from its Sittingbourne plant and the intensity of competition from BPB and other suppliers. Knauf offers a 'standard' merchant discount (initially 10 per cent, but increased to 15 per cent following BPB's June 1990 discount increase), but does not offer further discretionary discounts to customers.

With regard to national coverage and related delivery charges, single- or dual-plant operators (such as RPL and Knauf) are at some disadvantage compared to BPB, which is a multi-plant operator, currently servicing the British market from five major works.

BPB's reaction to entry

RPL said that BPB had responded to the new entry by increasing the prices of products not sold by the new entrants, such as specialist boards and plasters, and reducing the prices on products supplied by the new entrants.

BPB had also offered additional discounts and rebates to encourage buyers to remain loyal and offered low metal prices on mixed board/metal contracts which 'tended to suggest that BPB was cross-subsidising between products' (para. 7.9).

Moreover, RPL believed that BPB charged delivery prices which reflected transport costs from the nearest plant to the customer, rather than from the plant which in fact manufactured the product. 'This enabled BPB to supply the South of England with products made in the Midlands while charging prices as if the product originated in the South-East' (para. 7.11).

BPB introduced major price cuts on 4 June 1990 (during the course of the MMC inquiry) which RPL considered to be predatory. RPL believed

> that these price cuts had reduced BPB's average net margins on all its plasterboard products to a level such that RPL believed that BPB could not be earning an adequate return on capital employed . . . RPL did not believe that the selling prices were sustainable in the long term given that cost inflation was running at about 7 per cent and therefore concluded that the latest price cuts represented a further attempt by BPB to drive the new entrants out of the market.
>
> (para. 7.13)

As noted above, the general fall in plasterboard prices had increased RPL's losses during the start-up phase of its operations.

Knauf complained to the MMC that BPB had reacted to its entry by lowering its prices in Germany very significantly (by around 30 per cent over a period of twelve months). This, Knauf suggested, was designed to cut its cash flow, with a view to preventing Knauf from building a second United Kingdom plant. BPB also simultaneously lowered the price of plaster in Germany and raised plaster prices in the United Kingdom.

Knauf told the MMC that it had anticipated a fall in plasterboard prices in the United Kingdom in response to new entry and that its 'business plans in the short to the medium term took this expectation into account' (para. 7.31). Knauf considered that it could survive because, like itself, 'its competitors would not be operating profitably at those levels and in due course prices rise again' (para. 7.31). Knauf, as a private company with no external borrowings, took a long-term view of its investments – it did not expect a payback on investments for between twelve and fifteen years. It was, thus, not going to be 'pressurised' into leaving the market.

Overall, the MMC concluded on the entry issue:

> even in the face of keen competition by BPB, RPL and Knauf may be expected to remain viable competitors. They have invested substantial capital in starting-up manufacture; the financial position of their parents is strong; and each of them has built up a sound customer base' . . . we conclude that BPB's latest price cuts were not predatory. BPB's resulting realised prices exceed total average costs; the cuts are explicable as a competitive action by BPB in a market which is under threat, particularly at a time of excess capacity; and having regard to the structure of the market it is implausible to suppose that BPB considered that the cuts were likely to drive out either RPL or Knauf.
>
> (paras 9.84 and 9.85)

Market performance

Ideally, an industry's output should be produced in plants of optimal scale, thus allowing market supply costs to be minimised. If plant sizes are suboptimal, or because of an imbalance of market supply and demand, optimal sized plants are under-utilised, then actual supply costs may be higher than attainable cost levels. Ideally, customers should be charged prices which are consistent within the real economic costs of supplying a product, including a 'normal' profit return to suppliers for providing risk capital.

In the plasterboard market, the entry of two new United Kingdom producers has had a salutary effect on market performance by leading to lower market prices and profitability, but it has also created a problem of overcapacity.

Costs and capacity

Estimates of the minimum efficient scale for plasterboard production were provided by RPL, Knauf and BPB. Knauf suggested an annual production rate of 20 million square metres of plasterboard, while RPL cited the higher figure of 25 million square metres. BPB considered that costs per square metre of plasterboard would continue to fall as scale increased (as lower running costs offset higher capital costs), but above the capacity range of 20 to 30 million square metres, further falls in cost per square metre were considered to be 'modest'. Table 8.10 gives details of the nominal capacity of the plants operated by BPB, Knauf and RPL in 1990, together with details of the capacities of two further plants yet to come on-stream. It is apparent from these data that the industry's output is being produced in plants of minimal optimal scale.

However, because of an over-capacity problem, some of these plants were only barely breaking even. According to estimates submitted to the MMC by the companies 'the minimum economic output lies in the range of 60–70 per cent of plant capacity' (para. 9.48).

The industry's overall capacity-utilisation rate in 1989–90 was around 58–63 per cent (nominal United Kingdom plasterboard capacity = 314 million square metres compared to industry sales in 1989 of 193 million square metres and 182 million square metres in 1990).

Prices and profits

Table 8.11 gives details of BPB's turnover, profits and its return on capital employed for the financial years 1985–90. For the years 1985–9 (that is, before the entry of RPL and Knauf) BPB's profits were well in excess of the

Table 8.10 Plant capacities (9.5 mm basis), 1990: UK plasterboard market

		Million square metres
BPB	East Leake	63.0
	Kirby Thore	53.5
	Robertsbridge	36.4
	Sharpness	25.7
	Sherburn	51.1
		229.7
RPL	Bristol	38.2
Knauf	Sittingbourne	46.0
		313.9
(RPL Rainham – planned)		29.2
(Knauf Immingham – under construction)		(24.0)

Source: MMC

Table 8.11 BPB's turnover, profits and return on cpaital employed

			£ million		
	1985/86	1986/87	1987/88	1988/89	1989/90
Turnover	141.6	155.5	181.8	200.9	155.5
Profit before interest and tax	40.4	53.4	67.1	73.7	33.6
Return on average capital employed (%)	34.0	41.5	46.8	42.9	17.2

Source: MMC

norm of the building materials industry in general. The MMC commented thus:

> We accept that part of the explanation was improved efficiency, coupled with high and rapidly expanding United Kingdom demand in the last few years which has enabled BPB to run all its plasterboard plants at high levels. In part, however, we believe that the explanation was that BPB was able to charge its customers prices for plasterboard higher than would have been the case in conditions of more normal competition and this, we find, was a step taken by BPB to exploit the monopoly situation.
> (para. 9.105)

The entry of Knauf and RPL, together with recessionary conditions in the United Kingdom market after 1989, had severely dented BPB's profitability, and the MMC felt that while an upturn in demand would enable prices to rise, the ability of BPB to exploit this to the disadvantage of customers was now constrained by the presence of competitors. Some rise in prices was considered desirable in any case, it was suggested to the MMC by Knauf and RPL, to provide them with a 'reasonable' return on their investment in United Kingdom capacity.

A point of concern in the MMC inquiry was whether these new competitors could survive the price cuts imposed by BPB, which Knauf and RPL felt were instigated primarily 'to oust them from the market'. The MMC concluded, however, as noted earlier, that BPB's increased discounts to merchants introduced in June 1990 were primarily to defend its market position, rather than as a deliberate predatory act to remove competition. In particular, BPB was still trading profitably at the new price levels and had not sold plasterboard at below production cost in order to impose losses on its rivals. The MMC duly noted the 'deep-pocket' backing of the two entrants' parent companies and the fact that the entrants had quickly established a market reputation. Accordingly, the MMC was confident that the earlier monopoly conditions had now been swept away 'and that there was now no reason to suppose that they will return in the foreseeable future' (para. 9.105)

Postscript

Redland

In 1990 Redland ended its joint venture with CSR, exchanging its 51 per cent holding in RPH for a 20 per cent stake in a new joint venture company, Lafarge Plâtreurope, formed in association with Lafarge Coppée, a French building materials supplier. At the same time the new joint venture company acquired CSR's 49 per cent holding in RPH for cash. 'Our plasterboard operations could not escape being squeezed between falling demand and a marked increase in total industry capacity. In these circumstances we decided it would be preferable to broaden our competitive position in this activity [. . . by forming a joint venture with a major European-based supplier]' (Annual Report, 1990). In 1991, however, after incurring further losses, Redland sold its stake to Lafarge Coppée, thus exiting the plasterboard market.

Questions

1 (a) What factors can lead to an increase in concentration in a market?
   (b) What is a 'concentration ratio'? Why might a concentration ratio overstate or understate the degree of competition/monopolisation present in a market?
   (c) Account for the growth in concentration in the plasterboard market down to the late 1980s.
2 (a) Outline some of the main potential barriers to entry operating in a market.
   (b) What potential barriers to entry exist in the plasterboard market?
   (c) What factors encouraged RPL and Knauf to enter the United Kingdom market?
3 (a) Comment on the pricing strategies of RPL and Knauf.
   (b) How did BPB react to new entry? Do you consider BPB's behaviour to have been a 'reasonable' response, or predatory?
4 (a) What is meant by the 'minimum efficient scale' of operation?
   (b) To what extent has the addition of new capacity in the plasterboard market served to compromise the achievement of cost-effective rates of capacity utilisation?
5 (a) What is meant by the concept of 'normal' profit?
   (b) Indicate some of the difficulties in distinguishing between 'normal' and 'excessive' profits.
   (c) How do these considerations apply to BPB's profitability?

Exercise

Objectives

1 To develop further group discussion skills.
2 To develop evaluation skills using economic concepts.

Methods

1 Students to prepare in advance by reading the Plasterboard case.
2 Consider the questions set out at the end of the case.
3 Tutor to use group discussion process to evaluate the usefulness for a
   business student of the structure conduct, and performance model.

Chapter 9

Beyond the theory of the firm model

Conventional microeconomics deals with the way in which consumers and suppliers interact in a market place, through the signalling mechanism of price. It is assumed that the consumer acts rationally in the attempt to maximize satisfaction (welfare). If the consumer has perfect knowledge of market conditions, he or she can do so. If we were all able to do so we would achieve the **Pareto welfare optimum** discussed earlier. Such a market could only develop where many consumers interact with many small suppliers of very similar or identical products. These are the conditions which are presumed to occur in the conventional model of perfect competition which is discussed in Chapter 6. We discovered that the conditions for this model rarely if ever occur in reality. This is because in most markets the suppliers develop from reactive price takers into firms with a degree (often a high degree) of market power.

Conventional theory has little to say about why this happens, beyond the occurrence of technical and other economies of large-scale production. The firm is a 'black box' whose existence we take for granted. Until quite recently we had no theoretical explanation as to why firms develop, grow and change.

Having examined the conventional theory of the firm and its implications for the structure, conduct and performance of firms in particular markets, we propose to consider briefly the question as to why firms arise in the first place. The nature of this problem is best illustrated by a simple example.

A farmer decides to build a bungalow for his retirement. He acquires a plot of land at auction. He has a pile of good stone from a redundant barn. He can buy building materials from builder's merchants, and can hire professionals and tradespeople by the hour. He can assist with labouring himself, as well as co-ordinating the whole project. Once completed the property has cost say £80,000, as against a market value of, say, £180,000. By using the market he has added value of £100,000. If we could all do this no construction firms would exist. But clearly most of us buy our homes from a construction firm, or a former customer of such a firm. There must be an explanation for the existence of construction firms.

Conventional theory of the firm is (as we have seen) descriptive and static. It can only show how output and price decisions are arrived at on the assumption that firms are all entrepreneurial and seek only to maximize profits. The models developed beyond perfect competition represent apparent market failure in Pareto terms. Since most markets are oligopolistic in nature, dominated by a few large firms, the market as a resource allocator appears to fail. We need a theory which explains more precisely why and how firms develop in this way.

WHAT DO FIRMS DO?

We need to be able to answer two questions:

1 Why do we not all use the market to buy or subcontract the process of adding value to create the desired product – like the farmer in our example above?
2 What can the firm do which the market cannot do?

In essence a firm is likely to do better than an individual operating (like our farmer) in the market, at overcoming these sorts of problems.

The principal–agent problem

This arises when one person (the principal) hires another (his or her agent) to undertake a task. The outcome depends on the efforts of the agent and the information available to that agent, which can only be imperfectly observed, or even unknown to the principal. It is difficult for the principal to overcome the incentive for the 'agent' to offer less effort than that which is optimal from the point of view of the principal. (Our farmer will be busy with his own work, and unable to oversee his subcontractors most of the time.)

Transactions costs

These arise from the process of decision making, and the information required for this activity (there will be a cost to our farmer in identifying and negotiating the best subcontractors). Conventional theory assumes that consumers behave rationally, that is they are able to obtain and assess all relevant information. In reality they are not able to do so, especially when the transaction becomes more complex. (Our farmer would be much more efficient at buying a new cow for his dairy herd than he can be in hiring, say, an architect.) This problem is referred to as **bounded rationality**.

Co-ordination

The individual seeking to carry out a sequence of complex transactions with subcontractors in the market-place will find it very difficult to avoid the loss (of time and quality) caused by the difficulty in co-ordinating the activities of numerous subcontractors who have other jobs under way, and are therefore not entirely reliable.

The firm is likely to be better able to overcome these problems because: it is easier to observe, monitor and control employees (agents within the firm) than subcontractors; it will be better able to obtain and assess relevant information; and it will be better able to co-ordinate a variety of complex activities to minimize the costs of delay.

For an individual (like our farmer) seeking to acquire a new house, it is much simpler and more cost effective to allow the construction firm to overcome these problems than to do it himself. It is worth to him £100,000 (which the farmer saved by operating through the market) to not have to deal with these problems himself. As Ferguson, Ferguson and Rothschild (1993) remark: *'In an efficient economy the lowest cost method of coordinating any value adding activity would prevail.'* In a modern complex economy we can only approximate to that degree of efficiency through the domination of most markets by firms acting as suppliers. Another way of making this point would be to say that for most purposes for an individual, the costs incurred by using a firm as a supplier are less than the costs of complete self-sufficiency, or operating through a complex sequence of markets.

The provision of complex products then compels the development of firms which can overcome these transactions and co-ordination costs as well as obtaining the cost-reducing benefits of division of labour and the economies of scale and scope described in conventional theory. But we are left with another very important question.

WHAT SORT OF FIRM?

Where should the boundary of the firm be drawn, and what should its organizational architecture be like? At any given moment it will be determined by the relationship of the transaction costs of using the market to the managerial costs of carrying out specific activities in house. The perfectly efficient firm (assumed in conventional theory to be achievable) is in fact impossible to achieve because of the constraints of bounded rationality and uncertainty, combined with the constantly changing relationship between transaction and managerial costs. *For these reasons the firm must constantly review and change its boundaries and organizational architecture as its market environment changes.* Is there any generalization which we might make as to when a value adding activity should be internalized within the firm or acquired via the market (the make or buy decision)?

- A market solution is appropriate where 1) large numbers of suppliers exist, and 2) economies of scale are not available to the firm.
- Internalization is appropriate where 1) small numbers of suppliers/ buyers exist, 2) where asset specificity occurs (of site plant, human skill), and 3) even where the market solution offers financial advantages, but cannot apply sanctions to opportunistic behaviour.

Is it possible to identify the optimal boundary of the firm? It may be possible to quantify the transactions costs of using the market. However, we have until recently had no way of quantifying the managerial costs of internalizing a specific activity. We will consider the question of managerial costs in more detail later. At this point we can say that accumulated management knowledge and skill can add value in some as yet undefined way. We can also say that the further from its optimum boundaries a firm is (too big or too small), the higher the costs of adding value. *Therefore competitive advantage derives from constant revision of the firm's boundaries.*

How then can a firm adjust its boundaries? The following solutions are available:

1 *Outwards*: merger (vertical or horizontal)
   diversify (merger or organic growth)
   multinational (geographical spread in response to relative factor costs, + costs of export + government interference.
2 *Inwards*: sale of subsidiaries (downsizing to core activities)
   demerge (break up of conglomerate)
   subcontract (support services).
3 *Alternative solutions*: long-term contract with supplier contracting alliance or joint venture (economies).

CONSTRAINTS ON THE FIRM'S MAKE OR BUY DECISIONS

In the course of its activities in processing inputs into value added outputs, a firm also acts as a money processor. This involves three constraints on its behaviour:

- its ability to raise finance
- its ability to sustain cash flow
- its ability to pay tax as required.

As the firm seeks to extend its boundaries on the basis that to make is better than to buy, it is likely to need a wider capital base than the original proprietors (or entrepreneur) can provide. This leads inevitably to separation of ownership (shareholders) and control (salaried managers). The conventional theoretical model of the firm depends on unity of ownership and control in pursuit of profit maximization. In our expanding firm this no longer holds good. The question is no longer just where the boundary of the firm should be since that is determined by the organizational architecture of the firm and its effectiveness in relation to the market. We need to know more about the firm's internal transactions/managerial costs.

THE INTERNAL MANAGERIAL COSTS OF THE FIRM

The objectives of the firm

In the conventional models of perfect competition and monopolistic competition, profit maximization is a necessary condition of survival. This is not so in oligopoly (which is the most common market structure with a few firms dominant in the market), where the firm will usually make supernormal profits.

In this situation managers are likely to set sales revenue growth objectives (rather than profit maximization). This may lead to satisficing behaviour. Given the separation of ownership and control, the principal–agent problem arises inside the firm. Managers will pursue their own objectives in conflict with those of the owners, causing a further internal cost.

On the other hand, by using the surplus profits generated in oligopoly the firm has the means to modify its structure, limit competition faced, develop new business through research and development, improve processes, influence consumer demand through marketing activities and grow by acquisition.

The firm's activities

In adding value a firm seeks to be an efficient organizer of inputs through the following activities:

- Purchase factors of production in factor markets.
- Seek maximum output which can be produced from different combinations of inputs with given technology.
- Seek technical efficiency – not possible to produce a given quantity of goods with less of one factor without using more of another.
- Achieve economic efficiency – produce at **minimum efficient scale**.
- Develop organizational architecture which minimizes internal transaction costs by resolving principal–agent problems between members of the organization.
- Satisfy requirements of shareholders (owners) for relative return compared to alternative opportunities.

- Satisfy internal members requirements for a return on effort better than the opportunity cost of their efforts.
- That return on effort may be financial or emotional.
- Review internal transactions costs of doing the above activities against the transactions costs of using the market.
- Adjust both boundaries and architecture of firm constantly in light of change in the economic environment.

All these activities take place within an organization which has a history and ideology which inform its culture, which in turn relates to its organizational structure and the specific competencies developed by its managers.

The organizational structure of the firm

All firms originate in the activity of an entrepreneur who sees an information gap between the reality of availability of a product, and the perception of its availability by potential users. This enables the entrepreneur to acquire the product in one market-place and sell it in another, earning arbitrage, a margin sufficient to offset the cost of his time and the transactions costs, to earn a residual profit.

This residual will be eroded by the entry of new entrepreneurs, unless the original entrepreneur can capture it permanently by erecting a structure - a firm, which can internalize production and distribution of the good, and add perceived value sufficient to retain customer loyalty. Initially he or she will be able to do this by using organizational architecture to reduce managerial costs below the transactions costs of the market (to both customers and other intermediaries).

As we have seen, if the entrepreneur can create a brand image for his or her product, and so create customer willingness to pay a premium, he or she will earn supernormal profits – which can be ploughed back into achieving even greater domination of the market.

The broad architectural structure of the firm will then evolve in accordance with:

- the stability of the market
- the degree of standardization of the product
- the degree of importance of professionalism
- speed of technical change and innovation.

This architecture may be summarized as in Figure 9.1.

The growth of organizational structure types is a constant evolutionary process, and more complex patterns develop than indicated in Figure 9.1. For example, six accountancy partnerships have grown to dominate the market and have moved to either U or M form structures; car manufacturing

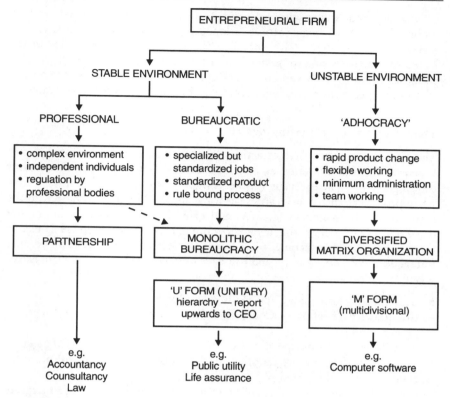

Figure 9.1 Organizational architecture

Source: after Mackintosh *et al.*, 1996

has moved from U to M form, while computer software has moved from M to U in some cases and the NHS is being forced to move from U to M.

In sum, a modern firm is likely to be:

- Large, complex
- Ownership and control separated
- Its objectives are those negotiated by individuals within the organization
- Which raises the question, who bears the risk among the stakeholders – shareholders, managers, employers or community?

If this is so, management objectives within the firm's architecture are a critical element of managerial costs which relate as we have seen to the alternative transactions costs of using the market place for some (or all) the firm's activities.

Owners face huge enforcement costs (Hay and Morris, 1991) to know about the firm's performance in relation to their objectives, whether it is satisfactory and if not why not, and how it might be improved, and by whom. Firms have been seen as 'islands of conscious power in a sea of markets' (Coase, 1937: 388), and to a large extent that power lies in the hands of managers whose power is absolute unless the firm's performance collapses below some acceptable threshold of performance as reflected in its customers' perception and behaviour, e.g. British Gas, Yorkshire Water.

The firm as a co-ordinating device

The firm may replace market activity because it eliminates to some degree transactions costs by acting as a co-ordinator. A set of market transactions centring on one entrepreneur (farmer's bungalow example) becomes a firm when producers, distributors and sales force allow a 'grant of authority' to the individual co-ordinator to organize and carry out their work at his or her discretion. They will do this if higher/more efficient production levels enable them to have a higher income, while leaving the entrepreneur better off because transactions cost, uncertainty, and risk have been reduced. Once the firm exists, it builds up 'organizational capital' (Prescott and Visscher, 1980: 353):

- firm-specific knowledge and skill of employees
- simultaneity of effort – ability to monitor and supervise employees to prevent shirking
- durable transactions specific investments – where there is a danger of being dependent on one supplier, market fails, and the firm will prefer to create its own dedicated plant
- distribution, storage and retailing costs – may lead the firm to integrate vertically by internalizing these activities.

This process is likely to lead to continuing growth by internalization of market processes until costs of co-ordination rise to the point of **control loss** where they exceed the costs of market transactions, referred to in conventional theory as **diseconomies of scale**. Thus the relative efficiency of decision taking may explain replacement of market transactions by firms, and also the tendency to increasing industrial concentration.

It has been argued that the **bounded rationality** of managers within the organizational structure of firms may lead to satisficing behaviour. The limits to the size of the firm are set by the ability of the architecture of the firm to overcome this tendency and respond to changes in the economic environment.

They further suggest that continued growth demands a move from U form to M form structure. This is because the latter is less inefficient since it separates overall integration and co-ordination problems from those of local operational control. It also permits better auditing of the performance of individual products, divisions or subsidiaries, and permits more focused investment and R&D decisions.

The economics of business process design

The increasing interest among managers in the development of new approaches to the organization of the business process – the architecture of the firm – suggests an increasing awareness of the need to manage more effectively what we have called internal transactions costs or managerial costs. Economists have in the past focused on reasons for market failure, and only recently have begun to develop a theoretical understanding of the structure and function of organizations. In Chapter 12 we consider the economic rationale for the TQM/continuous improvement movement. Here we outline the economic underpinning for the Business Process Re-engineering approach. This, like TQM, recognizes that the costs of internalization of activity in a firm are contained within the process by which value is added. But it goes further, suggesting that radical redesign of the process architecture will be more effective than seeking to improve the process within the existing architecture, which may be deeply flawed.

Transactions cost economics has identified market failures and associated transactions costs such that there is no equilibrium price at which the parties can trade. This approach can explain most of the macro-organization patterns (boundaries) to be found in modern firms. However, it is incomplete since it tacitly assumes that when external transactions are costly, internalization will occur. There are two consequences:

1 If we have no theory of the costs incurred as a result of internalization our explanation of internalization is incomplete. Internalization will only be preferable if the internal costs of doing so are less than the external costs of using the market. 'We have a theory of market failure, but not one of organization success' (Buckley and Carter, 1996).
2 We may understand the forces delineating the boundaries of firms, but not developments in the internal organization of the firm. Those writers who have most influenced internal organization (Juran, Deming, Peters etc.) have argued for leaner, flatter organizations focused on customer satisfaction through delegation of both information and decision-making powers to the lowest possible level. Drucker (1988) sees it as the replacement of the 'command and control' organization by the 'information based organisation'. Until recently economists have concentrated on the principal–agent problem of getting employees to do what modern management gurus assume they can be expected to do if the architecture and culture of the organization are right.

Two conventional views of internalization

1 *Internal market*: the firm is organized so that it functions as a series of approximations to a perfect market. Internal processes are designed to

transmit 'shadow' prices between decentralized cost centres so that overall profits are optimized. External markets are replaced by an internal market, e.g. NHS, BBC.

2 *Hierarchies*: given bounded rationality and opportunism, an internal market cannot generate appropriate shadow prices. Directives rather than prices constrain action within a hierarchical structure. The market is replaced by a different mechanism e.g. as in the case of a university.

The internal organization problem

The problem faced by the firm is the co-ordination of the actions required to carry out production, marketing, distribution, etc., in line with the objectives of the firm. These actions constitute the business process, in so far as they must be linked together in an appropriate way. Thus a collection of activities creates and adds value.

The business process: problems

1 *Motivation*: In order to overcome the principal–agent problem noted above, it will pay the firm to take measures to induce employees to act in accordance with the firm's objectives. Different inducements may be appropriate in different types of business process. We will develop this idea further a little later (see Figure 9.2).

2 *Information*: employees must act on best estimates of key information, which, due to division of labour, may be held by several individuals. The organizational architecture must therefore be designed to acquire and transmit key information to wherever it may be needed. Recognition of the most useful types of information and ways in which it may be enhanced is therefore also an important requirement of the architecture. Advocates of TQM see statistical process control techniques transferred to front-line staff via training, as the key to better management of processes, (and incidentally to improve motivation at lower levels of the firm).

3 *Co-ordination*: this creates complementarity between actions, and may be achieved by a single responsible individual or by a jointly acting team. Optimal levels of co-ordination would occur if (a) all members of the firm share the firm's objectives (perfect motivation), (b) all members had best available information (perfect information), (c) all complementary actions were chosen jointly (perfect co-ordination).

There will in reality be a trade off between the cost of preventing loss to the firm of motivation loss, information loss, and co-ordination loss. For example to prevent members pursuing their own rather than the firms objectives, there will be a cost in creating incentive schemes, supervision or resocializing by training. The firm's organizational design problem is thus to minimize the sum of these three transactions costs (motivation loss/cost, information loss/cost, co-ordination loss/cost).

Organizational design

The architecture of an organization is the way in which individuals are organized into a decision-making system to deal with information and co-ordination problems. It must also expedite the motivation of the individuals within the organization to maximize the degree to which individual members share the firm's objectives.

The modern view is that team behaviour is best for both purposes, in many but not all circumstances. Team behaviour is likely to be best when actions are complementary. Where individual goals differ, individual behaviour will be constrained through either hierarchy or market incentives. It follows that the lowest cost form of organization is that *with the lowest combination of the costs of getting information, co-ordinating actions and motivating employees, and lowest losses due to doing these things imperfectly.* 'There is no uniquely superior process or architecture. The desirable form of organisation will result from the particular parameters of technology, and market environment facing the firm' (Buckley and Carter, 1996: 22).

Hennart's organization types

	Managers have superior process knowledge	Workers have superior process knowledge
Low output monitoring costs	1. Likely to be pure internal or extenal market	3. Selective market like incentives
High output monitoring costs	2. Hierarchy	4. Workers internalize employers' values

This model suggests possible responses in organizational architecture to various combinations of the variables 'process knowledge' and 'monitoring costs'. It may be an over-simplification, but it offers a means of analysing the suitability of the architecture in use in a firm.

Figure 9.2 Hennart's organization types
Source: Hennart, 1986

1 Hennart did not discuss this combination of variables. It seems likely that in these conditions an external market would work well, but that internalization on the basis of an internal market could work.
2 Where the management closely specifies the nature of inputs, because output may be uncertain (as in the Army), internalization within a hierarchical organization is likely.
3 In a case where workers have superior information about the process, and it is easy to monitor their activities, hierarchical structures are likely to be reinforced by some form of performance-related pay.
4 Where monitoring costs are high and workers have superior process knowledge, (e.g. in a modern car plant), some attempt to cause workers to internalize the employer's values and objectives is likely to be valuable. This is also likely to be worth while in innovation-driven businesses working in very unstable environments (e.g. computer software).

CASE STUDY 11: GREEN END FARM

Green End Farm is a 300-acre tenanted dairy farm situated in the Lower Ribble Valley on the borders of North Yorkshire and North Lancashire. The land is undulating fertile grassland running alongside the river. The climate is relatively mild with wet but not excessively cold winters. The fields are mostly 15 acres or more, bounded by well-kept drystone walls with some hedgerows. There is some woodland near the river.

MB and his brother GB have farmed the land in partnership for thirty years. The landlord, Colonel J, is elderly and has no heir. The future of the estate on his death will be uncertain. The partners have decided to review their farming system and long-term business strategy.

The main enterprise of the business is milk production. Two hundred Holstein cattle are milked. The old established herd is served by a pedigree British Holstein bull and is of high quality and good reputation. Milk is sold on contract to MD dairies who have a creamery a few miles away. The milk is collected twice daily by an MD tanker. Some heifer calves are retained and reared as herd replacements. All bull calves and most heifer calves are sold off at the nearby market at under seven days old to the continental veal trade. Cull cows (milkers which are worn out) are also sold into the beef trade through the market. The subsidiary enterprise involves over-wintering sheep for a neighbouring hill farmer. These are brought down in November and taken back in March before lambing begins. A boarding fee is paid per head. The sheep fulfil a useful function in cleaning up the land before spring growth begins. Being situated on good land, and with a quality high-yielding herd, the farm is at present profitable. The farm is worked by the two brothers, one farmhand (who has been with them for twenty years) and a student.

In view of the uncertain future of the estate of which the farm is part, and the possibility of the brothers wishing to retire in a few years time, decisions have to be made.

The buildings are sound and well equipped. The machinery employed is of good quality but mostly quite old and almost written off in the books. At present the only processes undertaken on a subcontracting or bought-in basis are veterinary and chiropody service for the livestock, building maintenance, and vehicle and machinery maintenance. No hay is made and what little is needed for young stock is bought in from a neighbour. Concentrate is bought in for supplementary cattle feed.

The partners are looking at all the processes involved in the business and are considering the possibility of using contractors for some or even all of them. The principal processes involved are set out below and present methods used are indicated. Theoretically it would be possible to contract out to firms or self-employed workers all of these tasks.

Business processes at Green End Farm

Care of stock

Milking	Parlour/tank/collection
Feeding	Winter – concentrates in parlour, silage, some concentrates and straight feeds mixed in mixer wagon and trough fed in covered feed area
	Summer – concentrates in parlour, at pasture
Calf-rearing	Winter – housed in old barn fed hay and concentrates by hand
	Summer – at pasture
Stock care	Veterinary practice
	Chiropodist
Slurry	Mechanized removal to slurry tank
Veterinary	By local vet. Practice, and self-employed chiropodist

Cultivation

Grass renewal	Ploughing, cultivation, sowing in spring by contractor
Fertilizer application	Nitrate (twice per annum) slurrying (several) by tractor and spreader tank and contractor using pipe system
Silaging	Three cuts (late May, late July, September) by tractor and forage harvester
Haymaking	Not undertaken

Other

Transport   Milk collected by MD dairy tanker, stock moved by
                              landrover and trailer

Building and fence
  maintenance   Minor repairs by partners, other work by
                              contractors

Book-keeping records   Milk yield recording by computerized system,
                              correspondence etc. by partner, annual accounts
                              by local accountant

The problem

Much of the capital plant is coming due for renewal, very large outlays of
this kind are unwise in view of low resale values should the estate be broken
up, the farm sold by the landowner and the partners retire.

Question

What factors would an economist suggest that they take into account in
their review of the business and its strategy?

Chapter 10

The economics of the growth of the firm

THE GROWTH OF FIRMS

What we need to explain

We have developed an explanation of the reasons for the development of firms as a more convenient alternative to market relationships. Conventional theory of the firm concentrates on price–output decisions made by the firms in different market structures. In developing these ideas we have arrived at a partial explanation of the development of market structures and of different degrees of concentration. The structure, conduct and performance (SCP) schema provides a set of criteria by which to analyse the behaviour of firms in particular markets, and to make predictions about future behaviour.

A model of the process of growth in firms

What we need now is a theoretical model to explain the process of growth within a firm. This needs to take into account the usual price–output decisions, but also expenditure and financial decisions. If price and output decisions are successful in generating profits, then decisions must be taken with respect to payment of dividends, retention and use of profits, new finance through borrowing and the issue of new equity. Such decisions involve an implication that firms are not merely passive players in a market, but are able to manipulate the competitive environment of the markets within which they operate. Up to a point they are able to manipulate consumer preferences, actual and potential competition, costs of production, and technology. If this is so, are there any constraints on this activity?

The divorce of ownership (by shareholders) and control (by managers) of the firm's assets raises questions about the location and use of power within the firm. The threat of take-over of the firm, or by the firm of other firms, creates both threats and opportunities. The firm must not only be concerned with its performance in its product markets, but also in capital markets.

Both threats and opportunity of take-over lead to the probability of a search for growth in size of firms. Since markets are increasingly dominated by larger multiproduct firms, there seems on the surface to be no constraints on growth, or limits to the size of the firm. We have already suggested that the assumption of profit maximizing behaviour on which conventional theory of the firm rests is unsound. In reality maximization of the rate of growth of the firm is a more realistic assumption. This could be said to stem inevitably from the divorce of ownership and control, and the resulting effect on the motivation of managers.

However, attempts to establish this apparently clear difference in motivation between owner-controlled and manager-controlled firms have failed to establish such a difference or a difference in performance, measured by growth or profit. This is partly due to the technical difficulties in defining appropriate boundaries between owner control and managerial control, but this lack of clear difference may be due to two practical considerations. First, managerially controlled firms can only grow beyond the profit maximizing growth rate if the freedom and discretion to pursue growth alone exists. If an efficient capital market exists, this may not be so. Secondly taxation regimes on dividends, and on the inheritance or transfer of shares, may force owner-managers to pursue growth since they make little gain personally from profit, either in dividends, or from increases in share value. The other financial and non-financial benefits of successful management for growth may come to dominate behaviour. The relationship between motivation, location of control and performance has not been satisfactorily resolved. This being so, it must be the case that growth of firms is determined by factors other than choice of objectives, profit or growth by owners or managers. Models of growth used to analyse the relationship between ownership, profit and growth have used steady state methodology, that is, firms are assumed to set decision variables over an indefinite period. They are assumed to have management strategies aimed at pursuing a particular long-run rate of growth of the firm. This is likely to be an unrealistic assumption, except possibly in the case of firms operating on the Japanese model.

Alternative models of growth in firms

Two alternative models may be suggested, based on a life cycle pattern of growth, and evolutionary change.

Life cycle approach

The life cycle approach centres on managerial economies of scale in the use of information concerning the firm's product and market. Early in the firm's life such economies promote both accelerating growth, and profits. This leads to diversification into new products, and possibly acquisitions.

Eventually managerial diseconomies set in. At this point it may be desirable from the shareholders' point of view that the company be broken up into a number of smaller companies by demerger in order to release a fresh wave of managerial economies of scale. In reality the interests of managers may lead to pressure for further growth in size, causing over-investment combined with progressively slower growth and declining efficiency. This argument suggests that the firms growing to an excessive size are the older and slower growing firms. It also leads to the conclusion that the growth rate of a firm will vary systematically over the life of the firm.

There is some evidence that the stock market prefers profits to be paid as dividends in mature firms in slow growing or declining industries, e.g. chemicals, but be reinvested in newer firms in faster growing industries, such as electronics. It also appears to be the case that growth rates decline with the age of the firm.

Evolutionary approach

The evolutionary approach suggests that growth of the firm over time depends on a combination of technological opportunities available with the search and decision process over time in the firm. Since no static equilibrium is assumed growth rates will vary over time with no tendency to converge on a particular rate.

Similar decisions taken at different times may produce different growth consequences. It could however be argued that growth at below a competitive rate may be more likely to lead to failure due to inadequate investment in capital and R&D, and lower efficiency combined with a less non-price competitive product. In such a case lower profit and less investment, culminate in the accentuation of slower growth rates. By the same argument faster growth, perhaps stemming from R&D, and continuous improvement of product and process may lead to increasing growth rates. Comparison of specific firms' growth rates over time with the observed industry rate of concentration may enable analysis of the performance of specific firms.

A further conclusion which may be drawn is that a relationship exists between the size and age of a firm and its rate of growth. It is likely that smaller, newer firms will grow at a faster rate than larger, older ones. However, some research suggests that in a specific industry both smaller and larger firms grow faster than intermediate-sized firms.

Problems in the theory of growth of firms

Much of the work done in this area has related decisions to performance on the basis of a *ceteris paribus* assumption, ignoring the reality that firms operate in an unstable and changing environment. Firms may be able to manipulate some elements of their environment in their own interests, for example demand curves and product performance. What might be called the superenvironment is not capable of being manipulated, and is constantly changing. This superenvironment may include, for example, changing patterns of consumer taste (e.g. CDs replace LPs) or of availability of skilled labour. The same decision taken at different moments in this changing environment might produce quite different outcomes. The decision may itself produce a change in the superenvironment, for example increased advertising by one firm might lead to greater or less susceptibility to advertising throughout the market, or a large firm undertaking a large-scale training programme may change conditions in the labour market for all firms in the industry. The superenvironment is therefore largely exogenous, but with elements of endogenicity.

In the model in Figure 10.1 an attempt is made to draw together in one picture the various elements of the behaviour of firms in industrial markets which have been developed in our discussion of the conventional theory of the firm, the SCP schema, and theories of the growth of the firm. The outcome of these relationships is some trade off between profit and growth.

It is assumed that:

- the firm is a multiproduct/multidivision organization
- it has a multidivisional, M form structure
- each division operates as a quasifirm with a U form structure
- there is no limit, therefore, to the growth of the firm through the creation of new product divisions.

Such quasifirms show performance which depends on the structure, conduct, performance elements appropriate to its product market. The firm

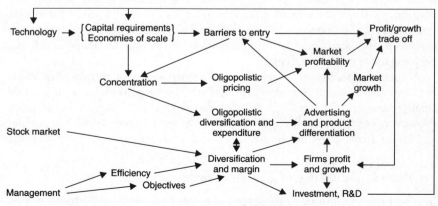

Figure 10.1 The firm and the market: an integrated framework
Source: Hay and Morris, 1991

as a whole is not constrained this way. These SCP factors only loosely constrain its performance, which is, however, constrained by exogenous factors. Its profits/growth path will be determined by its agreed objectives combined with the degree of discipline imposed by the stock market. The latter will be less effective in the different business and capital market environment of the Pacific Rim countries than in Western environments.

Figure 10.1 also encompasses the endogenous elements in the super-environment. Thus, investment, R&D and marketing decisions may induce oligopolistic conditions, and interdependence between competing firms, which in turn affects future decisions and profit–growth path taken.

Patterns of growth: changing the firm's behaviour

We have looked at some of the problems raised by the quest for a theory of the growth of the firm. In what ways might growth be achieved? Organic growth may be achieved by smaller firms entering new markets, or by successful product innovation and reinvestment of resulting profits, but research suggests that between 42 per cent and 55 per cent of growth arises from acquisition (Kumer – quoted by Hay and Morris, 1991: 370). Further, growth by acquisition was positively correlated with past growth by acquisition, which suggests that growth by acquisition tends to persist as a strategy over time. It may be that this is an inevitable feature of growth patterns in highly concentrated market sectors in western economies, but perhaps less so in Pacific Rim economies.

ROUTES TO GROWTH BY ACQUISITION

It is not difficult to identify the presumed advantages of growth by acquisition:

1 Demand side Avoids problems of market entry
              Avoids need to induce expansion of the market, or
              Take business from competitors
              Reduces the likelihood of damaging response by
              competitors
              Reduces need to develop new products
              Reduces uncertainty about future levels of market demand
2 Financial   Acquisition can be financed by issue of equity, rather than
              retained profit
3 Management Appropriate managers acquired rather than recruited and
              trained
              Synergy in research and development, and production
              capabilities, and economies of scope all may occur
4 Production   Economies of scale and scope
              Synergy in production and distribution

But the advantages may not always accrue for a number of reasons:

- problems in valuation of the company to be acquired, both tangible assets and intangible (such as brands and goodwill)
- the assets acquired may be less than ideal – in technology, or in location, for example closure and redundancy costs incurred
- clash of corporate cultures may make integration more difficult than anticipated.

The potential advantages of an acquisition may be analysed by a linkage approach which is illustrated in Figure 10.2. However, this has the limitations of a static approach, taking no account of the continuously

	COMPANY 1	COMPANY 2	COMPANY 3
PRODUCTS →	KITCHENS	WINDOWS	FINE QUALITY FURNITURE
AREAS OF LINKAGE ↓			
Customer age	25–50 ————	40–60 ————	40–60
Socioeconomic group	A/B – – –	– – B/C – – –	– – A/B
Markets	UK (DIY)	UK (DIY) Hardwood	UK/USA Retail Veneered
Product	Kitchen units – – –	– Double glazing units – –	– Dining and lounge furniture
Technology	Timberworking batch production	Timber/glass flow production	Timber working small batch and bespoke
Skills	Design/cut/ assemble – –	– Semi-skilled operative – –	– Wood working trained
R&D focus	Design	Production improvement	Design
Production base	UK/North	UK/North East	UK/ South West

Key: – – – Weak link   ——— Strong link   ▬▬ Very strong link

Figure 10.2 The linkage approach to acquisition

Source: after Ferguson, Ferguson and Rothschild, 1993

changing nature of both the exogenous (or super) environment, and its endogenous (internal) environment.

Activity 10.1

Study Figure 10.2. Consider whether the linkages indicated suggest sufficient synergy effects to make a merger a good idea between any two (or all three) companies.

The decision as to whether the growth of a firm should extend beyond the national boundaries of the company to become a multinational company will depend on the relative costs of exporting as against undertaking foreign investment. Such investment may or may not involve acquisition, but should it do so any synergy or other advantages might be outweighed by the difficulties of integrating two corporate cultures within different national business cultures.

CONCLUSIONS

The attempts to develop a dynamic approach to the questions of growth and acquisition described in this chapter suggests the following conclusions:

- The stock market (in western economies especially) may be seen as 'the major potential constraint on management' (Hay and Morris, 1991: 372).
- This pressure leads management to seek (via diversification, financial and expenditure decisions) their optimum growth/profit combination.
- Size of the firm is a by product of growth, rather than its objective.
- Performance in specific markets (in a multidivision firm) is only one element in determining the overall performance of the company.
- Pricing is only one of a number of interlocking corporate decisions.
- The true motives of firms' owners and objectives of managers, whether profit or growth remain unresolved and not clearly related to performance.
- The analysis of the behaviour of firms must go beyond the conventional SCP schema.
- Growth maximizing behaviour may generate a dead weight loss of economic welfare as compared to price competition in perfect markets.
- Net welfare benefits may arise if the social net benefit effects of R&D exceed the private benefits (which may not all be realizable by the owners).
- If faster growth of firms spills over into faster growth of GDP then national economic welfare is increased.
- If an economy has a preponderance of growth maximizing firms (like Japan) rather than valuation (of shares) growth maximizers (like USA),

then the former, being willing to pay more to acquire a firm than the latter (because of their long-term strategy), will predominate. Therefore, Japan will grow at a faster rate than the USA. This is because the limited management labour market and underdeveloped stock encourages growth maximizing behaviour rather than profit maximizing behaviour.

CASE STUDY 12: THE PACKAGE TOUR INDUSTRY

Thomson and Airtours, Britain's largest holiday companies, were yesterday referred to the Monopolies and Mergers Commission as part of an investigation of the entire travel industry that could initiate a wide-ranging shake-up.

The investigation will focus on 'vertical integration' – the owning by a few giant companies of their own tour operators, travel agencies and airlines. Thomson owns the Lunn Poly chain of high street travel agents and the charter airline Britannia, and Airtours owns the travel agents Going Places and Airtours. Among the concerns of the Office of Fair Trading that have led to the investigation are whether agents sell their own holidays in preference to those of other operators or use their dominance of the package-holiday industry to control supply and fix prices.

Thomson owns 700 Lunn Poly stores and controls 20 per cent of the £7 billion overseas market. Airtours has a £1.5 billion annual turnover and takes 2.5 million holidaymakers abroad each year. Thomas Cook sells more than four million holidays from 385 high street outlets.

John Bridgeman, the Director-General of Fair Trading, said he had decided to refer the companies to the MMC after failing to secure undertakings from Thomson and Airtours to operate with greater openness and ensure that their customers knew of the links between the firms within their groups. He was also concerned about reports that vertically integrated travel agents threatened to remove from display the brochures of smaller independent tour operators unless they agreed to pay high commissions.

If the MMC were to find that leading companies had abused their market power, there are in theory few limits to the changes it could recommend. A commission spokesman said: 'There's no limit to what we can recommend. Our recommendations can be as wide as we think necessary.' The Department of Trade and Industry, which will be responsible for acting on the commission's findings, also has few restraints on its powers.

The most extreme option would be to require the holiday companies to sell their travel agents. More likely would be some form of control over the nature of the relationship between the operators and their subsidiaries. These could be backed up by measures to allow smaller holiday firms to gain better access to the leading chains.

The brewing industry provides one of the closest parallels to the allegations faced by the travel industry. In the late 1980s the MMC found that big brewers operated a complex monopoly, allowing them to restrict competition by preventing their tied pubs from selling beers that they did not brew. The MMC recommended that the national brewers should be ordered to sell 34,000 of their pubs.

Although watered down under industry pressure, the 'Beer Orders' that resulted played a key role in the reshaping of the drinks industry over the past seven years. Grand Metropolitan, once one of the largest brewers, sold off its beer and pub interests, while several smaller companies, such as Greenalls, decided to concentrate on pubs.

Yesterday Sue Ockwell, chief executive of the Association of Independent Tour Operators, said: 'The big companies have a stranglehold on smaller companies – they demand 19 per cent commission from smaller companies to display their brochures, but only 10 per cent from their in-house companies. This cost is passed on to the customer, which makes independents seem expensive. Customers do not realise this when they walk into a shop.'

Last night Thomson, Airtours, Thomas Cook and AT Mays defended their position, claiming that the consumer gained from cheaper deals. David Crossland, chairman of Airtours, said: 'The consumer has benefited from big players like us being able to keep the cost of holidays down by buying aircraft, hotels and cruise ships. This move by the OFT has not come from customers complaining about prices.'

Martin Brackenbury, a director of Thomson, said it had given undertakings to be open about links between companies within the group, but had refused other demands being made by the Office of Fair Trading.

These, he said, included measures to stop Lunn Poly negotiating freely with operators during key periods of the year and an insistence that Thomson Holidays should deal with all retailers on the same basis.

Mr Crossland insisted that Airtours was not at fault, and blamed Thomsons' refusal to give assurances for the referral. 'Airtours was prepared to put in writing all the undertakings that the OFT was looking for,' he said. 'For the past three years we have had posters in travel agents owned by Airtours telling customers that we own hotels, cruise ships and aircraft. We also give a good width of choice – more than 70 per cent of our turnover is from non-Airtours companies.'

Mr Bridgeman said: 'The two leading travel companies with whom I have had discussions have argued that their practices are a reflection of the competition that prevails in the travel trade. My view is that they can distort the competition process.'

The Monopolies and Mergers Commission is expected to report its findings within a year.

(Farrell, Bale and Durman, 1996)

The five leading British travel companies reacted with disbelief yesterday that the Office of Fair Trading had decided to recommend the referral of the industry to the Monopolies and Mergers Commission.

Last week, at the Association of British Travel Agents' conference in Istanbul, they had listened to detailed figures showing that not only were holidaymakers switching to small tour operators and travel agents, but that the alleged problems of vertical integration caused little or no concern to the public.

In the past year the number of holidays sold by the top five tour operators – Thomson, Airtours, First Choice, Sunworld and Inspirations – fell by 5 per cent from 66 per cent of the total market of about 8.5 million to 61 per cent. This, they argued, was proof that the individual travel agent and specialist tour operator was not suffering.

More than that, the OFT had received no more than a handful of complaints from the public, they said. The big conglomerates believe there is no case to answer and they are convinced that they have been able to offer the British holidaymaker a better deal and lower price than any other country's travel industry.

The slow move towards vertical integration began in 1972 when Thomson – the biggest tour operator, with a dominant 30 per cent share of the market – bought the Lunn Poly chain of travel agencies. Since then they have built up to nearly 900 shops in almost every town centre in Britain. At about the same time Britannia Airways, and its fleet of Boeing 767 and 757 jets, became part of the group and carries virtually all Thomson holidaymakers.

The big tour operators say that owning their own travel agency and airline provides much lower prices, by using their marketing clout to gain the lowest possible rates from hoteliers and villa owners. For the small agent or tour operator, however, the dominance of the big five means they are under constant pressure to match their prices – which they cannot do. It is therefore not surprising that they have been lobbying hard for intervention.

Their main argument at the Abta conference last week was that to sell a holiday from a major tour operator in the operator's own travel agency was at best unethical and possibly illegal. Customers would get biased information and advice, they said.

If a holidaymaker asked for a particular break in a Going Places shop, for example, he was likely to be shown only an Airtours brochure because Airtours owns the 700 Going Places shops. A typical high street travel agent would have between 100 and 150 brochures on display and up to 400 in stock.

The MMC is certain to investigate the linkage of compulsory holiday insurance to particular packages. This can add up to 20 per cent to the cost of a holiday, which is often not made clear in brochures. Last week Abta reached a voluntary agreement with the Advertising Standards Authority to end the hiding of such costs, but the practice still goes on.

(Elliott, 1996)

Questions

1 What is the three-firm concentration ratio in the package tour industry?
2 In what ways do the major firms erect barriers to entry?
3 Do you think the loss of welfare resulting from the exclusion of smaller competitors, is offset by welfare gains due to economies of scale?
4 Is there any evidence to support the claim by the big companies that the industry is very competitive and open to entry?
5 If the Office of Fair Trading refers the case to the MMC, what do you think their conclusion will be?
6 In the light of your experience of the package tour and brewery industries:
  (a) Do you think the growth of market dominant companies by vertical integration causes greater, if less obvious, abuse of market power than horizontal integration?
  (b) If the MMC issued recommendations similar to those in the case of the breweries report, do you think the results would be beneficial to customers?
7 As a group exercise, write the summary, and conclusions of such an MMC report, (use the Presentation Cases in Chapter 14 as a model).

Chapter 11

Oligopoly and game theory

Conventional theory treats oligopoly, where a market is dominated by a few very large sellers (or buyers), as one case on a spectrum of market structures. This spectrum stretches from perfect competition to monopoly, the limiting cases. In the real world most markets are oligopolistic. Oligopolists are seen as very large companies which are able, at least temporarily, to earn supernormal profits by producing less and charging a higher price than would prevail in a perfectly competitive market. It is recognized that they are able to do so by differentiating the product and/or achieving such economies of scale as to present insurmountable barriers to entry and exit for newcomers to the market. But conventional theory can only discuss decisions about output and price on the basis that the individual firm can make plans in isolation. It is recognized that in reality, where only a small number of firms exist in a market, they are interdependent, and operate in conditions of uncertainty about the plans of competitors.

A search for competitive advantage by such a firm on the basis of price reduction would inevitably lead others to follow suit. If this happened all firms in the industry would compete away supernormal profits in the same way as firms in a 'monopolistic competition' market. Since this is in nobody's interests a market dominated by very few interdependent firms is likely to generate an alternative method of strategic decision-making.

Such a strategic planning process must take into account changes in the operating environment, and the possible reactions of competitors. A range of choices must be considered for different scenarios. These choices must be made on two levels, tactical day-to-day decisions, and corporate strategy decisions, in the search for long-term advantage. An example of this process may be seen in the case of the newspaper 'price war'. News International made a long-term strategic decision to terminally weaken one or more of its major competitors by fierce price cutting. Once embarked on this strategy it has needed to embark on regular tactical adjustments to this strategy, depending on the response of its competitors. Hence for example the recent decision to cut the price of *The Times* on Mondays, to only 10p.

The inadequacy of conventional theory in explaining the behaviour of oligopolistic firms has led to the application of a theoretical approach stemming from mathematical origins, and originally applied by military decision-makers in the Second World War. This is game theory, which allowed UK naval command in the war to make useful estimates of German U Boat command behaviour rather than always reacting to out-of-date information. It has since been used by many academic disciplines as a key to understanding human behaviour in situations where interdependence and uncertainty prevail, giving a range of possible choices of strategy, from collusion or co-operation, to competition.

GAMES AND GAME THEORY

Parkin (1990: 349) has defined game theory as '**a method of analysing strategic interaction**'. But what is a game. All situations where humans interact, whether on a cricket field, in a family, or in a market, have three features in common:

- rules (constraining behaviour)
- strategies (for decision-making)
- pay offs (or rewards/punishments for decisions).

The process within a game is one of strategic interaction. This involves acting in a way which takes into account the expected behaviour of others, based on a recognition of mutual interdependence. Game theory was first developed by J. Van Neumann in 1937.

Rules of the oligopoly game

These arise from the economic, social and political environment within which the firms operate.

- *Rule 1*: The number of firms operating within the market, as it is perceived by the players.
- *Rule 2*: The objective (or method of scoring). This may be perceived simply as profit or loss (if profit maximization is assumed to be the common objective of all players). The concept of profit has been redefined as value maximization, labour, capital and other assets should provide the greatest stream of net profits possible over some relevant time frame. Given the uncertainty of future outcomes, it is better to think in terms of expected value maximization. Thus the **costs of wasting** must be discounted. Thus we arrive at: **net present value of expected future net cash flow (profits) discounted back to the present at an appropriate rate of interest, to account for the fact that future profits are less valuable than currently earned profits.**

Maximization of this entity is difficult to achieve because it would involve detailed knowledge (or accurate estimates) of future revenues, costs and discount rates. Decision-making therefore involves determining the optimum course of action involving marketing, production, finance, personnel and organizational structure to produce a long-term business strategy. Day-to-day decision-making requires *partial optimization*. That is to say decisions may have to be satisfying in nature – choosing the least worst alternative.

- *Rule 3-n*: Any restrictions imposed by prevailing legal codes, e.g. Monopolies and Mergers Commission rules regarding mergers or restrictive practices, in the UK, or Anti-Trust legislation in the USA.

Strategies of the oligopoly game

All possible actions available to a player must be considered as possible strategies. There are many strategies available to a firm in an oligopoly market, of which those in Table 11.1 could be said to be the most obvious.

These strategic decisions are taken within a strategic environment. Broadly two alternatives are possible:

1 The co-operative game: collusion occurs between players on the basis of formal binding agreements, or tacit understandings.
2 The non-co-operative game: behaviour is based on self-interest alone. Co-operation arises only when it is selfishly beneficial.

Which of these situations exist will determine the choice made from the strategies in Table 11.1.

Pay offs in the oligopoly game

In game theory the players' score is called a pay off. In oligopoly we can think of this for simplicity's sake as profit and loss accruing to players. Pay offs will be determined by the strategies adopted by players, and their

Table 11.1 Strategies available in an oligopoly market

Strategic variable	Alternative strategies
Price	Raise price / lower price / keep constant price
Output	Raise output / lower output / keep constant output
Advertising	Increase advertising / cut advertising / keep advertising constant
Product	Enhance product features or quality / simplify product / leave product unchanged
Costs	Cut costs by seeking economies of scale via volume production / cut costs by seeking continuous improvement of product and process. (This strategic choice is discussed in detail in Chapter 12.)

interaction, and also by the constraints imposed on players from outside. The principle constraints may be summarized as follows:

- *Constraint 1*: the customers, who determine the demand curve for the production in the market and for the firm's product in relation to other players. This constraint is in some cases very unpredictable.
- *Constraint 2*: the production technology available. This may change suddenly and without warning.
- *Constraint 3*: the cost of inputs of materials and labour, which is much less stable than thirty years ago.
- *Constraint 4*: legal restrictions which may make collusion impossible. Whether or not such restrictions exist and to what degree they are effective will determine whether or not a market is co-operative or non-co-operative.

The range of strategies available, and the battery of constraints on action suggests the possibility of a matrix of possible strategies and pay offs. This complexity of game structures can be illustrated by the example of a simple two player (duopoly) game.

The prisoners' dilemma

Two mythical prisoners have the choice of confessing, or not confessing to their joint crime. If prisoner A confesses, and B does not, A is only lightly punished but B is heavily punished, and vice versa. If both confess they both receive heavy sentences, whereas if neither confesses, they both are lightly sentenced. This pay off matrix can be represented as in Figure 11.1.

The best solution is for neither to confess, but this choice entails risk for either player because A has to trust B. Non-trusting (non-co-operative) behaviour is likely to lead at best to both confessing, and each being sentenced to eight years!

If no communication is possible between the players an unbreakable vicious circle will develop where one non-co-operative choice will inevitably lead to retaliation. Deutsch (1960) found that in this sort of game, if the players were told that the only purpose of the game was to make money, non-co-operative behaviour increased with successive games.

NON-CO-OPERATIVE VERSUS CO-OPERATIVE BEHAVIOUR

Non-co-operative behaviour

Where each firm A, B or C seeks to maximize its pay off, given its rival's choices, behaviour is non-co-operative. This is likely to leave all firms with less profit than could be obtained by co-operative behaviour. If there are only two firms rather than several, pursuit of the dominant strategy may force both firms into this position.

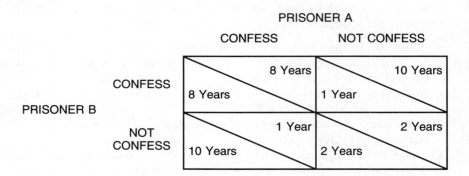

Figure 11.1 The prisoners' dilemma

Given that A, B and C dominate the market, they are likely to be aware of the actions of the others, and base their decisions on their assessment of the likely reactions of the others. In order to succeed by any performance criteria (profit, market share, etc.) a firm must seek to anticipate and direct behaviour. Competitive edge will depend on the quality of a firm's judgement as to how its competitor's actions will impact on its own outcomes, that is, success in an oligopolistic market depends on recognition of and adjustment for interdependence. Where no formal agreement between firms exists the relationship will be tacitly collusive.

Activity 11.1

Reread Case study 8 and the related feedback, and consider the contrasting behaviour of the established supermarkets and the new entrant discounters. The established retailers have devised a successful mechanism for co-operation which is being undermined by the non-co-operative policies of the new firms.

It can be shown using an adaptation of the conventional theoretical model of oligopoly that tacit collusion over price is likely to occur, and that firms will resort to non-price competition which is thought to be characteristic of oligopoly markets (see Chapter 8). This kinked demand curve model is now developed further.

The kinked demand curve

A theory of non-collusive oligopoly developed in 1939 by P. Sweezy in the USA and R. L. Hall and C. J. Hatch in the UK. It suggests that even in the absence of collusion, prices may remain stable. It is based on two assumptions:

- If an oligopolist cuts prices, rivals will follow to avoid loss of customers.
- If an oligopolist raises prices, rivals will not follow thus gaining customers.

On these assumptions the demand curve is kinked at current price and output. Demand is relatively price elastic above the kink. Demand is relatively inelastic below the kink. This is because a rise in the firm's price causes customers to switch to rivals, but a fall is countered by rivals, thus customers do not switch. This situation is shown in Figure 11.2 (see also Chapter 7).

Oligopolistic firms are likely to avoid destructive price competition, and non-price competition involves less head-on confrontation. This model does capture essential features, but is marred by inability to predict where the appropriate tacitly accepted price level will lie.

Cost-based pricing

Similar problems arise if we assume that cost-based pricing is the method likely to be adopted in such markets to determine the tacitly accepted price. This is because it is possible that average variable cost per unit is likely to be similar for all firms in the market. The price mark-up required to cover fixed overheads, profit contribution, will be likely to differ for all the firms. However, where the industry is stable, and firms are well informed about each other's behaviour, the price chosen by each firm will be similar to the median price suggested by the kinked demand curve model.

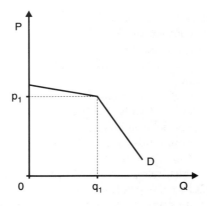

Figure 11.2 A kinked demand curve with price stable at p_1

The above situations have involved firms of similar size and influence. Where they vary in size and influence scope exists for another form of tacit collusion by price leadership. Two forms of price leadership are of particular interest.

Barometric price leadership

This occurs where one firm is the largest in the industry, or historically the most influential. Other firms have the alternatives of fully or partially matching price changes by the dominant firm, or not changing prices. Can the market find a price level which is acceptable to all? An example where this occurs is in petrol retailing in the UK, where BP and Shell are the traditional price leaders.

Dominant price leadership

This occurs where a leading firm (or firms) sets a profit maximizing price, leaving others only the possibility of maximizing profits subject to the price set by the market leader. (Supermarkets offer an example where one supermarket in an area competes with smaller shops).

In such a market a further possible strategy for the dominant firm is to act in such a way as to increase the costs of smaller and less efficient firms, for example by raising wage levels, or advertising spend. In such a case, despite raising its own average costs, higher prices as a result of raising competitor's costs actually increases profits.

Co-operative behaviour

Collusion and cartels

A cartel is a form of co-operative game where all players make a binding agreement to maintain either market shares or price. Such practices are normally made illegal since their purpose is to restrict output, raise prices and drive profits above levels which would obtain in conditions of unrestricted competition.

Members of the cartel must make best estimates of their respective marginal costs (this is more difficult in some industries than others) in order to reach a state of affairs which can be conveniently described in terms of the conventional microeconomic model of monopoly.

In Figure 11.3 MC of Q when firms act as a cartel is less than MC to each firm of producing this quantity (because of diminishing returns to inputs). By equating Cartel MC with market MR, the cartel acts as if it were a single form monopoly and makes supernormal profits as shown by the shaded area in the figure. The decision on how to share the combined profits is made by

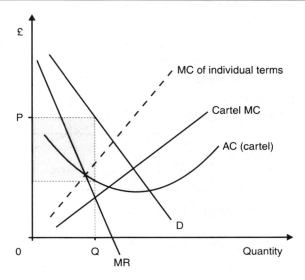

Figure 11.3 A cartel

allocating each member a share in production of Q. If all firms end up producing at the same MC no reallocation of quotas could reduce the aggregate costs of the cartel. If costs are difficult to identify or one very large firm demands a disproportionate share or firms misrepresent their costs, the cartel will not work.

An incentive always exists to cheat (as in the OPEC cartel). In a duopoly case, if one firm increases its output while the other produces the original quantity, the cheater gains, and the best response for the other is to cheat. Cheating becomes a dominant strategy and the cartel breaks down.

Repeated games

What can make co-operation sustainable, even in a non-co-operative game theory framework, is the prospect of a reward from co-operation over time. For example, suppose that two firms which were contemplating co-operation had the pay off table shown in Figure 11.4.

They can both achieve £10 million by co-operating but, by the prisoners' dilemma argument, they would both be inclined to distrust the other, who could gain an extra £2 million by cheating but be left with nothing by *not* cheating. Therefore, both firms would cheat and the predictable outcome is a disappointing £6 million each.

However, suppose that this game could continue for several periods with the same pay offs each time. If a firm cheats, then it might achieve £12

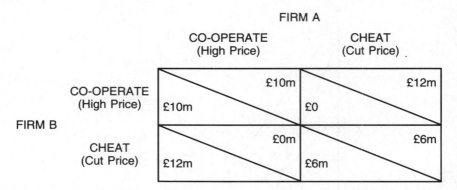

Figure 11.4 A two-firm co-operation pay off table

million the first time it does so, but after that it is unlikely that the other firm will agree to any price-fixing arrangement. So, in the year after cheating the best that could be hoped for would be £6 million – the non-co-operative outcome. Therefore the *two year* payback from cheating is a total of £18 million, but by *co-operating* in *both* years the firm would have a payback of £10 million each year, totalling £20 million over two years. It does better by co-operating, and has the prospect of continuing to do so. If either firm were to cheat, the other can punish the non-co-operative behaviour by refusing to be co-operative in the future. Provided the relationship is expected to continue into the future it pays both parties – even if they are motivated by pure self-interest – to co-operate with one another.

Contestable markets

Another threat to the stability of a cartel and its pricing arrangements may come from new entrants into a market. (This is a problem to firms in any oligopoly, even when non-co-operative behaviour is the rule e.g. BPL case study). *If it is possible for a new entrant to compete on the same cost basis as established firms, or if any firm in the market can exit without loss, a* contestable market *is said to exist*. This situation developed in the UK newspaper industry in the 1980s as a result of changes in printing technology and the collapse of the print unions.

The question then arises as to whether existing firms can implement strategies to deter such new entrants. Where markets are perfectly contestable (as in the case of the long-distance coach operation for example) the outcome in terms of output and price is likely to revert to monopolistic competition conditions (see Chapter 6). The prospect of new entrants will curb the activities of existing firms. The degree of asset specificity will determine the likelihood of entry by new firms. That is there are no sunk costs involved in entry.

It follows from this that a major barrier to new entrants is the costs of exit. Where costs of exit are low then it follows that there is little point in seeking a strategy to exclude new entrants. This is especially so if no barriers to entry can be erected. In practice no market is likely to be perfectly contestable. There are always some entry and exit barriers which can be created, or threatened. The threats (e.g. predatory pricing) must, however, be credible. Commitment to a credible threat may take the form of adding production capacity, knowing that a new entrant would be faced by a situation of overcapacity in the industry, the new entrant faced by higher MC than existing firms would be driven out of the industry. This occurred in the BPL case in the 1990s.

A future strategy for deterring entry is undertakings to customers, as may be seen, for example, in the supermarket industry where the response of UK companies to the threat of entry from Aldi and Netto was to promise to match their price competition by offering guarantees of lower prices than Aldi and Netto. Such action is not simply done to retain customer goodwill, but to ensure that higher prices prevail. This can be shown by game theory.

Game theory of entry deterrence

An incumbent firm can deter an entrant provided it can establish a credible reputation for fighting entry and if, by fighting, it can force the entrant into a loss-making position without too great a cost to itself. Figure 11.5 shows the possible actions of each firm in a two-player entry game and the pay offs that would result.

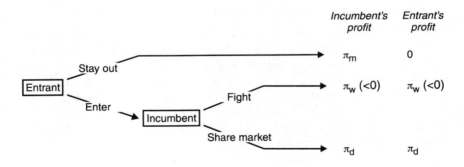

Key: π_m = monopoly profit: high prices

π_d = duopoly profit from shared market: lower prices

π_w = profit from a price war: probably negative for both

Figure 11.5 Possible actions and pay offs for firms in a two-player entry game

As long as the entrant *believes* that the incumbent will fight entry then it will do better to stay out of the market. But a simple threat from the incumbent to fight entry may not be enough. This may not be a credible threat, since it would mean the incumbent choosing to fight a price war for profits π_w which would be even lower than if it shared the market (π_d). The incumbent must make a *credible commitment* to fight *before* the entrant makes a move into the market. A public announcement to customers to match the entrant's price – as in the supermarket case – *may* be enough to make the entrant think twice before coming into the market.

Game theory and price wars

Even where an oligopoly market appears to revert to price war conditions, apparently due to the collapse of tacit or cartel collusion, game theory predicts the outcome. A large cut in price by one firm resulting from market conditions will provoke a response from the other firms as if the price cutting firm had cheated (rather than responding to a change in the conditions of demand for its product). This is the only way a credible threat can be maintained against a price cutter. However, where market conditions cause an increase in price, firms are likely to revert to co-operative behaviour.

CONCLUSION

There are many types of oligopolistic market in which the way in which firms interact depends on:

- individual firm's perceptions of the competitive environment
- for every set of perceptions, outcomes in terms of prices, outputs and profits – (performance indicators), are different.

Oligopolistic markets therefore are characterized by interdependence between member firms in an inherently uncertain and risky environment.

Game theory offers a logical framework within which to assess competitive and co-operative situations. Thus analysis of the structure, conduct and performance of markets can be informed to a greater degree than is possible using only conventional tools of the theory of the firm, which are based on a static rather than dynamic form of analysis. It can also offer a more useful toolkit for strategic business decision-making.

CASE STUDY 13: THE NEWSPAPER PRICE WAR

Exercise

Objectives

1 To encourage students to use their experience so far to look at a current issue of interest.
2 To develop group discussion skills in the whole group.

Methods

1 Students to prepare by
   (a) looking at current prices of main newspapers
   (b) reading issued articles
2 Tutor to lead group discussion around the following questions:
   (a) When did price cutting begin?
   (b) By what methods and to what degree?
   (c) Which group led the process and why?
   (d) Why did others follow suit?
   (e) Can anyone win such a price war and what happens to losers?
   (f) What are the implications for the public?
   (g) What might be done about it?

The intention here is to make use of concepts developed in Chapters 6 and 11 on structure, conduct and performance, and game theory respectively.

The pressure in the national newspaper price war eased a little yesterday as Mr Rupert Murdoch's News International announced that the price of The Times will rise by 5p on Monday.

The rise to 25p on weekdays and 35p on Saturdays is a reflection of sharply rising costs, particularly of newsprint, and in no way represents the end of Mr Murdoch's strategy of selling The Times at a discount to the rest of the broadsheet market.

The rise should give a little headroom to The Daily Telegraph and The Independent to increase their prices in line with rising costs. Mr Stephen Grabiner, the managing director of the Telegraph group, last night welcomed the move by The Times and said he would meet the rest of his management team today to consider a response.

All the signs are that The Daily Telegraph will soon increase its price by 5p. It cut its price to 30p only to protect its circulation in the face of the 20p Times. As a result the Telegraph has held its circulation and is now selling an average of 1,075,000 copies a day.

It has been clear for some time that the cover price of The Independent, which was also cut to 30p, would rise as soon as the paper had been redesigned and its editorial quality strengthened. The board of Newspaper Publishing, the holding company of The Independent, has a routine board meeting tomorrow and a 5p increase is considered likely.

By moving to 25p The Times has caught up with the price of The Sun, its tabloid stablemate – but it is still 7p cheaper than The Guardian and 40p cheaper than the Financial Times.

Mr Murdoch, the News International chairman, has made it clear that the aim is to use discounting as a long term strategy to try to take The Times to the 1m circulation of The Daily Telegraph.

Mr Peter Stothard, the editor of The Times, said yesterday that the price cutting strategy had been 'a huge triumph' for the paper. Sales for June are expected to have averaged more than 680,000 copies a day compared with 354,000 in September 1993, before the price cuts were introduced.

None of us has seen newspaper growth quite like this before,' said Mr Stothard, who added that new readers liked the paper and stayed with it.

(Snoddy, 1995)

When the fiercest price war in Fleet Street's history started nearly two years ago, most of the pundits and many editors believed that the effect of this gimmick – alien to newspapers if not to supermarkets – would be sharp but short. All previous marketing tactics – new games or serialisations backed by costly advertising on television – achieved sharp boosts in sales followed by sharp slumps once they ended, as promiscuous readers sought new thrills elsewhere. So why should cutting prices be any different?

Yet two years on, cutting the cost of newspapers is continuing to boost circulations. In the quality broadsheet market, where readers can now buy two daily papers for 50p, it is a strategy that is still expanding the overall market – up almost 300,000 copies a day, an increase of 15 per cent, compared with 2.6 per cent for the tabloids. As a result, about 90 million more quality papers will be bought this year than two years ago.

The success of the new strategy is shown by a comparison of sales in August 1993, the month before *The Times* first reduced its cover price, with circulations last month. The main beneficiary has been *The Times*, with sales up by 310,000, an increase of 88 per cent in 20 months that must set a record in the broadsheet market. Yet *The Daily Telegraph* is selling 45,000 more copies – although only since it, too, reduced its price – and the two broadsheets that did not cut their cover price are also selling more copies. The *Financial Times* is up by 25,000 and *The Guardian* by nearly 6,000. The chief casualty has been the *Independent*, now starting to recover sales. It relaunched itself this week in a new format.

What *The Times* has also achieved [Table 11.2] is a significant increase in its share of the quality market, which is up by nearly 10 per cent. On market share, the chief casualty has been *The Daily Telegraph*, down by 4 per cent, and the *Independent*, whose share is down by almost 3 per cent. Since August 1993, the sales gap between *The Daily Telegraph* and *The Times* has been cut from 670,000 to just over 400,000.

Overall sales of the tabloids [Table 11.3] have also expanded but only thanks to *The Sun*. If prices had not been cut, sales would almost certainly by now be sharply down on two years ago. The *Daily Mirror*, chief target of *The Sun*'s price cut, has done well to hold its loss of sales at only 1 per cent and its sale has increased every month

Table 11.2 Daily broadsheets

	Sale May '95	inc over Aug '93	Mkt share	Inc over Aug '93
Telegraph	1,073,463	+45,807	39.29	−3.99
Times	664,501	+310,221	24.32	+9.40
Guardian	397,388	+5,862	14.54	−1.95
Independent	296,397	−29,459	10.85	−2.87
FT	300,593	+25,277	11.00	−0.59

Total: 2,732,342 + 357,708

Source: ABC August 1993, May 1995

Table 11.3 Daily tabloids

	Sale May '95	Inc over June '93	Market share	Inc over June '93
Sun	4,055,476	+590,526	34.64	+4.27
Mirror	2,581,017	−58,298	22.04	−1.09
Star	732,985	−33,017	6.26	−0.45
Mail	1,783,754	+38,217	15.23	−0.07
Express	1,270,877	−218,084	10.86	−2.19
Today	544,772	−7,340	4.65	−0.19

Total: 10,968,981 + 298,476

Source: ABC June 1993, May 1995

this year, but *The Sun* has achieved an increase in sales of almost 600,000 in 22 months and increased its lead over the *Daily Mirror* by 336,000.

A sense of triumph is also in order at the *Daily Mail*, which *increased* its price but is still selling nearly 40,000 more copies than in 1993. Among the daily tabloids the chief casualty has been the *Daily Express*.

With the price of paper about to increase sharply for the second time this year, the cost of producing newspapers is rising sharply. Yet all the signals from News International, which publishes *The Sun*, *The Times* and *Today* on weekdays, are that the price war is not about to end.

(MacArthur, 1995)

Rupert Murdoch's admission on January 31st that newspaper prices will probably have to be corrected to some extent may not bring much relief to other national newspapers. They are about to be hit by a cost squeeze even tougher than the one imposed on them by Mr Murdoch's decision in 1993 to cut the prices of two of his titles, *The Times* and the *Sun* (though not of the profitable *Sunday Times*). Meanwhile Mr Murdoch has just negotiated a deal that will bring him bigger gains than his competitors can enjoy, if prices do rise.

The cut in prices by the two News International papers has been followed by only two other titles: the *Daily Telegraph*, whose attempt to match *The Times* at 30p was foiled by a further 10p cut by the latter, and the *Independent*, fighting for its life. But most papers are spending more on promotion; and none can now afford to raise its price until Mr Murdoch moves.

Some of the factors that made price cuts desirable for News International have disappeared. The group has grabbed readers, especially from United, publishers of the *Daily Express*, and Mirror Group, publishers of the *Sun*'s main rival. Indeed, the whole market for quality papers has expanded. But as Richard Dale and David Forster, media analysts at Smith New Court, a stockbroker, point out. News International's market share has slipped, from 36.9 per cent in June 1994 to 36.6 per cent in November.

Moreover, the price cuts came after a decade in which, as Peter Ingram, publisher of *Paper Market Digest*, a trade paper, points out, newsprint prices had declined sharply in real terms. The cash price per tonne at the end of 1994 was the same as it had been in 1982. Yet, overall, quality broadsheets were 50% dearer in 1992 than they had been at the start of the 1980s.

Now world newsprint prices are soaring, driven by buoyant demand in America and a growing newspaper market in Asia. Further increases are likely in the summer. Mr Murdoch, whose group is Britain's biggest buyer of newsprint, talks of a 30–40% rise in newsprint costs, which are 20–25% of News International's total costs.

At the same time, News International has negotiated a new contract with distributors that increases its gains from a price rise. Under the previous contract, distributors received a proportion of the cover price. When the prices of *The Times* and the *Sun* were cut, News International maintained the absolute level of payments to distributors, and absorbed the loss, leaving it with almost no revenue from the cover price.

Under the new contract, which came into effect in most parts of the country this week, distributors such as John Menzies and W.H. Smith will take a flat fee. Their share of current cover-price revenues will be smaller, and they will get no more if the cover price is raised. Because of the rise in News International's sales, and because it has halved the number of wholesalers it uses, the distributors nevertheless think they can recover the loss of revenue by boosting volumes.

Other groups may negotiate similar terms when their own contracts run out. For the moment, they will be able to keep a smaller slice of any cover-price increase they make. They also face a further challenge. On the back of their circulation rise, News International papers are increasing advertising rates, static since 1991. Their managers claim to be narrowing the gap between *The Times* and the rival *Telegraph*. Some advertising agencies are sceptical, but agree that *The Times*'s advertising revenues do not yet fully reflect its 50% increase in sales since the price cut.

Mr Murdoch has most to gain by raising the *Sun*'s price, thanks to its 4m circulation and dependence on cover-price revenue. But a small price rise – say, to 25p – for *The Times* would offset higher newsprint prices, while leaving weaker rivals, already charging more, with little room to follow suit.

(Economist, 1995)

Mr Rupert Murdoch, chairman of News International, the media group which publishes The Sun and The Times and instigated the UK's bitter newspaper price war, yesterday indicated that he may raise the prices of his titles. Prices 'will probably have to be corrected' in response to a 30–40 per cent increase this year in newsprint costs which had 'changed the economics of the industry', he said. News International had not yet decided on any specific price increases, he told the World Economic Forum in the Swiss Alpine resort of Davos.

Mr Conrad Black, chairman of the Telegraph publishing group, said at the meeting that 'the objective conditions for a de-escalation of the war now exist'.

He said the steep price cuts initiated 18 months ago by News International had achieved Mr Murdoch's purpose of restoring News International's competitive position. But Telegraph prices would continue to respond to Mr Murdoch's pricing policies.

The price war has cost News International about £45m across all its titles estimated Mr Tim Rothwell, BZW's media analyst. 'The price wars were made possible by low raw materials prices,' he said. 'But the paper cycle turned with a vengeance last year and it has only now filtered through to newspapers. Mr Murdoch can't absorb it any longer, margins have to be restored.'

The price war was launched by Mr Murdoch in July 1993, when he cut The Sun's price from 25p to 20p. Two months later, he cut the price of The Times from 45p to 30p and then to 20p last June. This staunched circulation losses and took The Times's sales to more than 600,000 and The Sun's to more than 4m. The competition from The Times hit other national broadsheet newspapers, especially The Independent and Mr Black's Daily Telegraph, which were forced to cut prices.

Mr Sergio Cellini, managing director of Newspaper Publishing, which owns The Independent, said he was content to 'wait and see' what Mr Murdoch's remarks may mean in practical terms.

The Daily Mirror, which costs 5p more than The Sun, is estimated to have felt the worst of the circulation losses. Mr David Montgomery, Mirror Group Newspaper's chief executive, was unavailable for comment.

On the stock market yesterday, the Telegraph group rose 3p to 359p a share and Mirror Group Newspapers by 2½p to 124½p. News International was unchanged at 211p.

(De Jonquieres and Davos, 1995)

The warning by Mr Rupert Murdoch that the rise in newsprint prices means he may raise the price of his titles could sound an eventual end to the newspaper price war. Newsprint counts for about 20 per cent of newspaper costs and January's 15 per cent rise in newsprint prices would cost News International over £20m a year. However, this standard cyclical phenomenon should hardly warrant an abrupt change in strategy.

Newsprint manufacturing profits usually peak at the same time as newspaper publishers': rising costs coincide with increasing advertising revenue and higher cover prices. Advertising revenues are forecast to rise by 8 per cent this year. The only marked change in this latest cycle is reduced cover prices – a factor directly attributable to Mr Murdoch.

However, Mr Murdoch may consider it a convenient time to raise The Sun's cover price. Close to 70 per cent of its revenue is from the cover price, compared with less than half for The Times. And its readership has stabilised at higher levels. Moreover, having raised The Times' advertising rates on the back of readership gains, News International may want to maintain price pressure in the quality market. Greater hope for the Daily Telegraph and The Independent could come from News International's efforts to cut distribution costs, which have not fallen with the cover price. Passing on at least some of the cost of the price cuts to distributors would alleviate the pain from the price war. And with marginal rises in newspaper sales, retailers could afford to carry some of the costs.

Copyright © The Financial Times

(Lex Column, 1995)

Postscript

November 1996. *Daily Telegraph* beginning to feel the effects of *The Times* price cuts, Mailshots A.B.C_1 households with a special offer – copies of *Daily Telegraph* for three months at 10p weekdays (20p Saturday, 25p Sunday).

Questions

1 How might market share be better expressed? (pie chart, graph).
2 Work out three firm concentration ratios for (a) broadsheets, (b) tabloids.
3 Calculate the change in monthly revenue (June 1993 and May 1995) for
 (a) *The Times*
 (b) *Sun*
 What does this suggest about price elasticity of demand for newspapers?
4 Which broadsheet has been the biggest loser and why?
5 Calculate percentage increase in sales for (a) broadsheets and (b) tabloids, 1993–5.
6 Why do you think the overall sales of broadsheets have risen so much?
7 Why do you think the overall sales of tabloids have risen by much less?
8 Do you think News International will be able to raise the price of *The Times* and *Sun* to counter rising costs by 5p *without* losing market share? If so why?
9 Why was News International able to cut its prices so dramatically?
10 Murdoch says price discounting is 'a long term strategy'. Does this make business sense?
11 What would be a game theory explanation of News International's behaviour?

Case study 13 feedback

Table 11.4 Current newspaper prices (pence)

	Weekday	Saturday
Broadsheets		
The Times	25	35
Guardian	45	50
Telegraph	35	70
Financial Times	65	
Independent	35	
Tabloids		
Sun	25	
Mirror	27	
Mail	35	
Star	25	
Today	27	

Proposed rise in News International prices

A 5p rise still leaves *The Times below* others and will offset increased newsprint costs. Others cannot follow suit – or can they? Latest suggestions are that the *Telegraph* will go up 5p. *The Times* will still be 10p less than the *Guardian*, and 40p cheaper than the *Financial Times*.

Can increased costs be passed on to distributors and retailers?

Price cuts

July 1993	*Sun*	25–20p
Sept. 1993	*The Times*	45–30p
June 1994	*The Times*	30–20p

Murdoch says discounting on price is long-term strategy: the aim was to reach *Telegraph*'s 1 million circulation (now achieved, October 1995). What is the impact on advertising price and revenue? Advertising revenues 1995 expected to rise by 8 per cent. Half the revenue for *The Times* comes from the cover price, while the *Sun* achieves 70 per cent.

Revenues

Change in revenue for whole broadsheet market: −£70,523 per month. Newspaper demand would appear to be price *inelastic*.

Table 11.5 Change in revenue for the broadsheet market, June 1993–May 1995

Newspaper	June 1993			May 1995			
	Price	Sales	Revenue	Price	Sales	Revenue	ΔRevenue
The Times	45p	354,280	£159,426	20p	664,501	£132,900	−£26,526
Telegraph	35p	1,027,656	£359,680	30p	1,073,463	£322,039	−£37,641
Independent	35p	325,856	£114,050	30p	296,397	£88,919	−£25,131
Guardian	40p	391,526	£156,610	40p	397,388	£158,955	+£2,345
Fin. Times	65p	275,316	£178,955	65p	300,593	£195,385	+£16,430
Sun	25p	3,464,950	£866,238	20p	4,055,476	£811,095	−£55,143

In 1993–5 *The Times* lost about 16 per cent of its *cover price revenue*, which is itself about half its total revenue. An equivalent increase (16 per cent) in advertising revenue in the same period would leave its total revenue unchanged. We might *guess* that advertising would grow roughly in line with market share, which has increased from about 14.9 per cent to 24.3 per cent. This is a 63 per cent increase in its share of the market. If advertising revenues grew at this rate, the net effect on *The Times'* revenue would be roughly:

- total revenue lost from cover price: − 8%
- total revenue gained from advertising: +30%
- net revenue change: +22%

(This is only a guess. We have no data on *The Times'* advertising income.)

Total cost must have increased in the period due to a near 88 per cent increase of output.

Chapter 12

The economics of total quality management

INTRODUCTION

Our understanding of the behaviour of firms in a market has so far been based on the conventional theory of the firm, to which we have added the refinement of the application of game theory. This approach has provided us with powerful insights. However in a sense these insights have been self-fulfilling. The theory of the firm has itself contributed to the development of a management paradigm which has come to predominate in western economies which might be called the mass production/scientific management paradigm (Cole and Mogab, 1995).

Definition of paradigm

'Theoretical principles which function as the dominant interpretation of behaviour' (Cole and Mogab, 1995).

Such principles are based on:

- *Science* – economic theory.
- *Repetitive behaviour* – experience.
- *Logical argument* – later endorsed by practice.

Such principles *furnish a vision to guide progress, but once out of date, hinder progress via a new paradigm.*
As Keynes remarked:

> the ideas of economists and political philosophers, both when they are right and when they are wrong, are more powerful than is commonly understood. Indeed the world is ruled by little else. Practical men, who believe themselves to be quite exempt from any intellectual influences, are usually the slaves of some defunct economist. Madmen in authority, who hear voices in the air, are distilling their frenzy from some academic scribbler of a few years back.
>
> (Keynes, 1973: 383)

We have seen the overwhelming success in global markets of Japanese and other Far Eastern manufacturing companies over the last thirty years. This has accelerated the process of deindustrialization in many western economies, notably the UK and USA. Only since 1980 have western companies begun to recognize that these successful companies, such as Toyota, operate in a quite different way to familiar big names like Ford or General Motors. Attempts to emulate the Japanese models have not always been entirely successful. This has led to a belief that the difference is to be found in sociology or culture rather than in management style. Until recently economics has had little to offer by way of explanation. Cole and Mogab argue that the explanation is to be found in the differences between the underpinning paradigms which explains the apparently unstoppable progress of the Japanese and other 'Tiger' economies. They go further and argue that the difference in structure, conduct and performance of Japanese firms can be explained with the familiar tool-kit of the theory of the firm. In their view the development of what they call the continuous improvement firm (CIF) in contrast to the mass production/scientific management (MP/SM) firm constitutes much more than simply a new approach to management technique, but rather a new industrial revolution. In this brief chapter it is impossible to do full justice to their arguments, only to provide a summary which may help you to see the business world in a different way, with the legitimization of conventional economic analysis. The basic contrast between the two paradigms is illustrated in Figure 12.1.

Attempts to understand the CIF through the lens of the mass production/scientific management paradigm fail. The CIF may only be understood through the lens of its own quite different paradigm. However, we can make some sense of the CIF through the tool-kit of conventional economic theory just as we can with the MP/SF firm.

The CIF sets out to achieve endogenous, incremental technological improvement of product and process, via a management style which motivates all employees and suppliers to promote change and supports these efforts. Change is seen as essential to constantly respond to changing customer requirements. The dynamic of a continuous improvement culture leads inevitably to a condition where the plant is capable of the flexibility of jobbing production in response to immediate customer requirement, with the low unit costs normally associated with the economies of scale of mass production. This flexibility and low unit cost is achieved by the creation through training of a generalized rather than specialized workforce, which is empowered to work in teams towards the goal of zero defects. Market share is the objective rather than immediate profit maximization. This permits the maintenance of lifetime employment for employees despite the ever-increasing productivity of labour. The resulting market domination inevitably leads to increasing profits, but the shareholders have to be prepared to take their gains in the long term, since the interests of the other

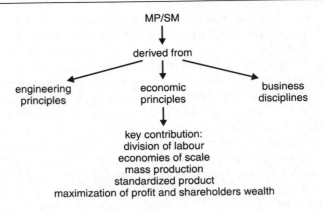

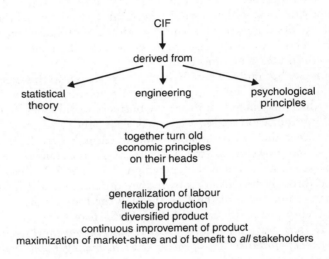

Figure 12.1 Mass production/scientific management firm contrasted with continuous improvement firm

stakeholders, i.e. employees, suppliers and above all customers, have priority over shareholders in the short run.

In complete contrast the MP/SM firm uses highly specialized and often low skill labour to produce very large quantities of standardized products in anticipation of demand rather than in response to demand. Quality is secondary to output volumes in the pursuit of low unit costs, with the result that up to 30 per cent of output is scrap waste and rework. Since this is also true of suppliers, the system is buttressed by very large and costly inventories of materials, parts, work in progress and finished product.

The fundamental contrast is this. For the MP/SM firm, improved quality in the product implies a higher cost (more inspection plus more costly inputs), and long-term investment in new technology. The CIF seeks successfully to both improve quality and achieve lower unit cost in the short term, without massive investment in new technology being a prerequisite (although it may be a consequence).

The MP/SM firm sees technology as an *exogenous factor*, which it is assumed managers will acquire if it increases the *net present value of the firm*. This will only take place over the long term and be adopted only if cost benefit analysis suggests that it will add to profits. In contrast in the CIF product and process are *continuously improved*. This constitutes what might be called *soft technology*, which is improved constantly in the short term. Long-term investment in new hard technology will of course take place, which gives the CIF a double advantage. Technology is endogenous, and is generated by highly trained multiskilled workers whose tasks are specialized, but whose skills are generalized.

The assumption in the MP/SM firm that technology is exogenous leads to the further assumption that some *optimal* organization is possible around imported technology. Whereas in the CIF a constant search takes place through *organizational learning* for the best fit between internal organization and imported technology. This search is the essence of technological change and so we should perhaps consider the CIF management methods as a *soft technology* in their own right which gives the CIF an overpowering advantage in the market place.

The MP/SM firm seeks to maximize profits for shareholders, whereas the CIF seeks to increase *customer value*, gaining profit as a *residual*. In the process it seeks to *reward* all stakeholders rather than *exploiting* all but the shareholders. The CIF approach requires a *culture change* of enormous magnitude which takes time. Thus while this soft technology of continuous improvement may be capable of transfer to an MP/SM firm, it will be extremely difficult, and will carry large costs – as many western companies have discovered. It is not possible to isolate apparently critical elements in CIF practice such as just in time (JIT) inventory management and apply them in the old context. Just in time is the *consequence* of countless incremental and small changes to working practice.

In Figure 12.2 we have summarized the discussion of the CIF thus far. To understand in more detail how the CIF works in practice read J. S. Oakland's *Total Quality Management* (1993). Next we can see how this paradigm might be explained in the technology of conventional economic theory.

Textbook models of the theory of the firm give no consideration to the economic impact of organizational structure or management practices, or the origin and nature of technological change.

In the MP/SM paradigm it is assumed that each firm will choose the most appropriate organizational structure, management style and technology for

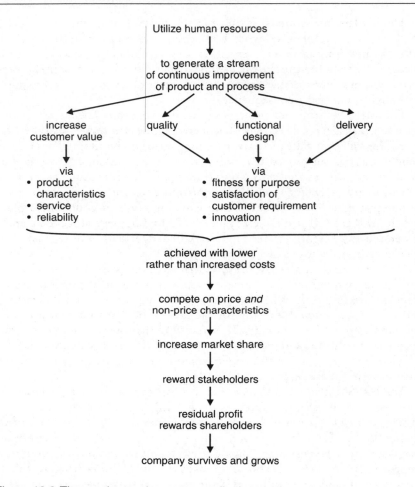

Figure 12.2 The continuous improvement firm's process

the maximization of profit. The firm will adopt new technologies *automatically* if the discounted stream of future net benefits derived from the change is positive. We may now go on to examine in more detail the operation of the MP/SM firm through the eyes of an economist.

THE ECONOMICS OF THE MASS PRODUCTION/SCIENTIFIC MANAGEMENT FIRM

The MP/SM firm appears to base its operation on several key economic assumptions:

- the nature of the product is given
- price is the main source of competitive advantage
- profit maximization is the only motive
- technology is exogenous and long term
- technological change carries costs
- with technology given, some optimal quantity mix and organizational use of inputs is achievable
- if this is done, costs are minimized and
- profits and shareholder value are maximized
- only response to increased competition is reduced price via lower input costs
- which often involves downsizing, reduced labour force, reduced product range, lower quality.

While it may be true that modern manufacturing companies in the West have moved some way from this model in the direction of greater awareness of customer requirements, the model remains an accurate representation of the behaviour of such firms.

We can now examine the way in which firms operate within this set of assumptions. The operational practice of the MP/SM firm is represented from an economist's point of view in Figure 12.3. The principles of specialization and division of labour have also been applied to the non-production functions within the organization, e.g. accounts, purchasing, logistics, marketing and design. Specialists in these departments are highly trained in the specialism, but are not expected to communicate with each other, even though all would be required to contribute for example to new product development. In this case the process would *push* a new idea from design, through production to marketing, who would be expected to sell the product to the customer, whose exact requirements have not been sought. Purchasing, logistics, accounts and personnel departments would also input a view, but co-ordination would occur only via the budgeting process, and the overall co-ordination would be the province of the Chief Executive Officer, who him or herself would be trained and experienced in only one specialism, probably accounting.

If a new product line is agreed, it can only go into production if a new line is installed, which involves a long-term and large investment in new technology. Flexibility of response to customer requirements as they change can only be achieved slowly through growth of the firm, or by acquisition.

Thus conventional theory of the firm models suggest that the firm may only respond to short-term changes in its markets by cost cutting to restore price competitiveness or, if demand for the product in the market is in decline, by either downsizing or possibly the acquisition of competitors in order to close them down. The product is given, and price is the only measure of value. It may respond to change in the long term by acquiring

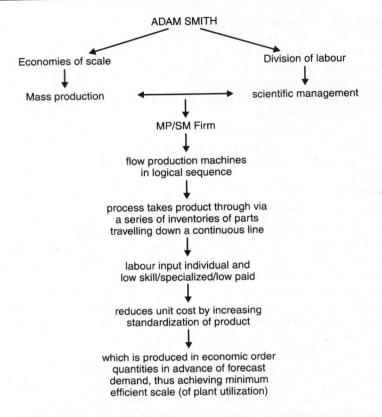

Figure 12.3 Economics of mass production/scientific management production

better technology to produce the same product, or new technology to produce a replacement product, but only if it can be predicted that the benefits of doing so outweigh the costs.

The theory of the firm has little to say about the internal dynamics of the firm, although the production process based on mass production and scientific management implies a top-down system of control and direction. This is reinforced by the conclusions of agency theory, (see Chapters 8 and 9). This model suggests that management of the internal processes of a firm consists of the identification of contract alternatives which are most efficient for principals (owners/managers) to monitor agents (managers/workers) to carry out their instructions in pursuit of the maximization of profits and shareholder value. The motives of managers as both agents for the owners, and as principals to the workers, and of the workers themselves, may not always be consistent with the achievement of the principal's (owner's) objectives of profit maximization. This conflict of interest reinforces the need for top-down authoritarian management in the MP/SM firm.

Further problems arise due to the **transactions costs** involved within a firm's processes. These costs arise from the need to collect and use information in decision-making. The strictly specialized functional organizational structure increases these transactions costs. Successful MP/SM firms minimize them by becoming efficient bureaucracies. This view implies that if it is prepared to pay the transactions costs, an MP/SM firm could achieve the same gains commonly achieved in the cross-functional organization of the CIF. This is not so, since the CIF is able to generate information costlessly which would incur a transactions cost in the MP/SM firm.

Agency theory and the concept of transactions costs does get us beyond the market for the product and for inputs, and into internal buy/sell relationships for factors of production, but not into the dynamics of technological improvement, which are *endogenous* in the CIF.

We may summarize the economics of the MP/SM firm thus: product, technology and organizational structure are given in the short run, and largely exogenous to the production process. The only management decisions left then are the quantity to be produced and the price at which to sell, which are determined by the profit maximization motive. New products and improved technology may only be introduced in the long run, with high costs. Competitive advantage may only be achieved via price. Quality considerations are costly and subsidiary to the achievement of economies of scale and minimized unit costs.

The weaknesses of the MP/SM firm may be summarized as follows. The pursuit of econmies of scale requires standardized products. Output decisions must be made on the basis of speculative demand forecasts which are subject to failure for various external microeconomic and macroeconomic reasons, resulting in very high inventory costs. Design and development of new products is slow and costly because of internal functional specialization. Quality is a cost and can only be inspected into the product at the end of the line, incurring high scrap waste and rework as well as internal inventory costs.

THE ECONOMICS OF THE CONTINUOUS IMPROVEMENT FIRM

We have seen (Figure 12.1) that the MP/SM firm is centred around the principles of conventional economic theory, supported by engineering principles and practice, such as work study. In contrast the CIF firm is centred around statistical theory (variance) and psychological principles (worker empowerment and management by familiarization not control).

Thus there are three key features of the CIF firm:

- Technological change is endogenous (generated from within).
- Workers at all levels know best how to improve product and process.
- Hierarchies are flat, causing information flows to be horizontal across functions, or bottom-up, rather than top-down only as in the MP/SM model.

Within this organizational architecture, *continuous improvement* of product and process is not seen as a cost, to be avoided, but the central theme of management, bringing about *reductions* in costs per unit. Change is therefore *incremental* and *small scale*, but may lead to large investments in new technology. Small improvements lead to major break throughs in cost reduction and greater flexibility of response to customer requirements. Innovation is the combination of existing elements. It is achieved by empowering front-line workers with skills, problem-solving techniques, and information, which in an MP/SM firm would be the province of senior management. Workers, in teams, are better able to improve their part of the process if they understand the whole. Generalization of the workers through training enhances creativity in response to changing customer requirements, which pulls product through the process. Processes remain standardized, but are flexible. Such a firm builds an organizational structure which promotes technological innovation through a highly trained and motivated workforce. This is what the Japanese call *kaizen*.

The particular advantage enjoyed by Japanese firms which is not easily created outside the Pacific Rim culture, is *keiretsu* – cross-holding of shares between banks, manufacturers and trading companies. This makes it easier to concentrate on *long-run* growth of market share, rather than *short-term* profit maximization. Shareholders cannot interfere in management, and the company can promote the interests of *all* its *stakeholders* – including customers, suppliers and employees.

The total quality management (TQM) paradigm enables the firm to simultaneously improve quality, productivity, flexibility, unit costs and price. This paradigm also turns on its head the principal/agent concept. In the MP/SM firm, management is the principal and labour the agent. The latter must be controlled, because his interests are in conflict with those of the manager. In the CIF firm management and labour are collectively the principal, acting through capital, which is the agent. The principal/agent conflict of interest is eliminated, since labour and management together bring about improvement in which they have a mutual interest. Investment is then added in machines. Employees are seen as human capital not as a cost. Their training is seen as a gain, not a cost to be minimized. Workers and managers alike have their long-term value enhanced by job rotation ('experience looping'). Life time employment for core employees is the logical consequence. Relationships with suppliers are likewise developed on a co-operative long-term basis rather than the adversarial relationships based on price competition which prevail in the MP/SM paradigm.

PRODUCTIVITY AND COST IN THE CONTINUOUS IMPROVEMENT FIRM

The model of the firm in the MP/SM paradigm stems from the mindset of the conventional theory of the firm. This is to search for the lowest long-run average unit cost – the minimum efficient scale. This is achieved by the pursuit of economies of scale centring around appropriate investment in plant, to which inputs of labour and materials are added. The technology is a given factor in the short run. Massive investments are possible in the long run, but there is no possibility of short-term improvements in productivity beyond the optimum output from the fixed plant. The product is also given in the short and medium term, and can only be substantially improved by major investment. Volume of output in relation to plant, and sales in relation to output, alone determine profitability.

In contrast the CIF has major advantages. Product process, and technology are capable of immediate change, at little cost, in response to changing market conditions. Massive investment may occur, but as a *response* to gains in market share, not in anticipation of possible increased demand. Continuous improvement of the process permits greater flexibility of response *without the loss of economies of scale*. This is the essence of JIT and *kanban* systems.

Labour productivity can be improved not just by increased output from fixed plant, but by improved quality systems which eliminate scrap waste and rework. The ultimate goal towards which CIF firms are steadily moving can be summed up thus: 'to produce on a customised basis for immediate delivery at a unit cost equal to that which is possible by mass production' (Cole and Mogab, 1995: 109). Conventional economies cannot yet think of productivity in these terms. This is because it thinks always in terms of **opportunity cost**. For any gain, there must be some cost, something foregone. Thus Daimler Benz accepted 30 per cent scrap waste and rework as an acceptable cost of maintaining their reputation for engineering quality. In the CIF improvement of product and process comes *cost free* – any expenditure on training is more than offset by elimination of the costs of quality – the scrap waste and rework and associated inventory costs.

Conventional industrial economics would challenge this assertion that continuous improvement is cost free, arguing that an *information cost* is involved (worker time, training etc.). But this is not so because gathering, learning, and problem solving are *integral parts of the operation of the production process*. Since improvement is continuous and productivity increasing daily, there would be an opportunity cost to the CIF if it concentrated on production and stopped thinking about improvement!

THE ECONOMICS OF FLEXIBILITY

It can be argued that the competitive advantage of a CIF lies in continuous improvement. This is demonstrated in Table 12.1.

Table 12.1 Costs of flexible response

Stages of response	MP/SM firm	CIF firm
Conceptualization	High cost in house or bought in R&D	Quality circles etc., little cost
Implementation	Large investment in new production plant. Production costs high till MES output achieved	Some cost, but minimal relative to technological advance and cuts in cost of production
Learning	After installation, high initial unit costs and machine downtime costs	Continuous part of operation, precedes changes. No cost.

The general propositions outlined in Table 12.1 are equally relevant to the processing of insurance claims (service sector) as to engineering (manufacturing sector). In sum we have suggested that continuous improvement provides an important competitive advantage to the CIF firm, which is virtually cost free. Can we now go on to demonstrate this proposition using the familiar tools of the conventional theory of the firm?

Conventional theory and the continuous improvement firm

Assume two firms, A and B, producing identical products, and with identical cost functions. Both are operating as MP/SM firms with short-run average cost represented by the curve SAC in Figure 12.4. At optimum capacity unit costs are C_1 and output Q_1. Firm B then adopts a TQM programme of continuous improvement. Scrap, waste, and rework are steadily reduced, which also leads to lower buffer stocks of parts, and work in progress. Unit costs fall over the first period, bringing the short run average cost curve down to SAC_2. At optimum output, unit cost is now C_2 and output rises to Q_2. Lower market prices plus improved quality lead to increased market share. The result of this process can be summarized thus:

- A given amount of resources can produce a larger output in a given time period.
- The percentage of throughput which is effective (saleable) product is increased.
- Market share is increased via lower price and improved quality.

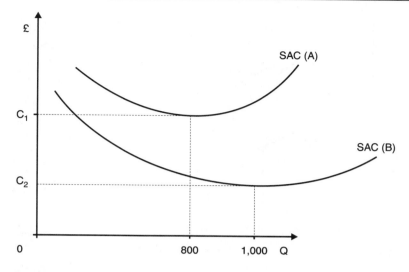

Firm B forces SAC down and to the left by continuous improvement. It can now produce an optimum output of 1,000 units of one product variant at unit cost C_2, whereas Firm A is still able to produce only 800 at unit cost C_1. Firm B wins market share and extra profit via lower price and better quality product.

Figure 12.4 Continuous improvement firm gains from cost reductions: 1

- The capacity (but *not* the size) of the plant is increased to cope with increased market share.

Firm B has achieved advances in the short run which would normally require the economies of scale resulting from investment in larger plant. These advantages continue in the long run when all factors of production become variable for both firms.

Thus in Figure 12.5 firm A is able to acquire new plant as required and achieves a minimum efficient scale (MES) range of output $QMES_1$ to $QMES_2$, after which diseconomies of scale set in due to management and co-ordination difficulties. A similar programme of plant expansion by firm B will generate lower unit costs at all outputs. However the process of continuous improvement will also cause unit costs to continue to fall. This process is reinforced because firm B can use extra profits gained from increased market share to invest in more improvements or extensions to the plant. Firm A can only react by major and costly restructuring of both plant and organizational architecture, or a belated and possibly unsuccessful switch to a TQM programme.

The CIF firm, once ahead is unlikely ever to be overhauled in the race with MP/SM firms for market share and profit.

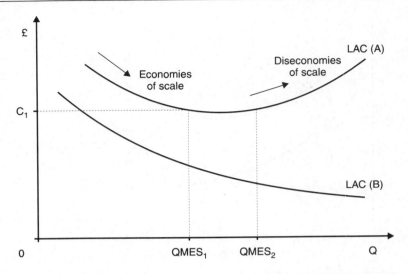

In the long run, firm A invests in new plant and gains economies of scale. It can produce a range of output of one product variant from $QMES_1$ to $QMES_2$ at its lowest unit costs. Firm B has also invested in plant, but continues to drive down unit costs via continuous improvement. Its unit cost is below that of A at any output. There is no MES because the problem of diseconomies of scale has been overcome.

Figure 12.5 Continuous improvement firm gains from cost reductions: 2

Firm B gains from flexibility

In Figure 12.6 CIF firm B has lower unit costs in the short run than MP/SM firm A at all levels of output, and a higher optimum output of 1,000 units as against 800. At this stage both A and B are producing only one product variant.

In order to increase market share by greater responsiveness to the needs of specific groups of customers, firm B decides to increase the number of variants of this product from one to ten. In order to do so it first sets out to reduce changeover downtime of the plant from two days to twelve hours, in association with its input suppliers, as well as plant staff. Dotted line F represents the effect on unit costs. Thus it is able to produce 700 units of ten product variants at the same unit cost of 1,000 of one product variant, and at the same cost advantage over firm A as when A is producing 1,000 of *one* product variant.

Further progress in the continuous improvement programme continues to force line F downwards to the position shown in Figure 12.7. Firm B is now able to produce 400 units of twenty product variants at the same unit cost as 1,000 of one product variant. Simultaneously the cost advantage over

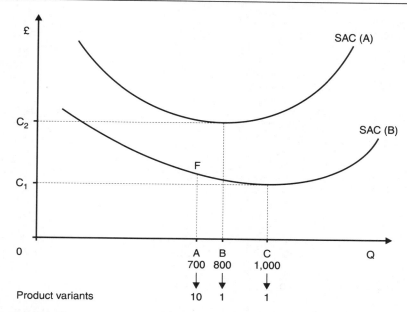

Improvements to change over downtimes enable firm B to produce 700 units of 10 product variants at the *same* unit costs as 1,000 of one product variant. While firm A can only produce 800 of *one* variant at the much higher unit cost of C_2. Firm B has gained a further competitive advantage from flexibility.

Figure 12.6 Continuous improvement firm gains from flexibility: 1

firm A when the latter is producing 400 of one product variant has also increased. The ultimate objective is to force down the SAC curve to the horizontal. *At that stage firm B can produce 1,000 units of up to twenty product variants at the same unit cost as 1,000 of one product variant.*

Thus they are able to differentiate the product in rapid response to changes in customer requirements, without losing the advantage of increasing returns to scale.

'They have achieved the specialist advantage of small batch production with the scale advantage of a high volume flow production line' (Best, 1990: 156, quoted by Cole and Mogab, 1995). The only responses available to firm A are either to restrict itself to a declining niche market, reduce the costs of production by downsizing and compete on price, or invest in several new production lines. Thus the lead won by firm B is increased in the long run as both the range of product variants offered increases, and unit costs are driven down further. Ultimately firm B's market share increases to such an extent that despite high sunk costs, firm A has no choice but to exit the industry.

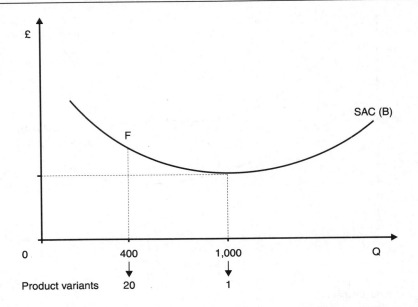

The improvement process continues and firm B is now able to produce *any* combination of product variants from 1 to 20 at the *same* unit cost as 1,000 of *one* variant. The competitive advantage has increased further and continues into the long term. Firm A has *no* satisfactory response and exits the industry.

Figure 12.7 Continuous improvement firm gains from flexibility: 2

A CUSTOMER VALUE APPROACH TO DEMAND

We now need to take a brief look at the demand side of the CIF paradigm. Value in conventional economic theory is measured by utility (satisfaction), and price which is determined by the interaction of supply and demand. A rational consumer seeks to maximize utility from a given income. He or she will purchase more of a good up to the point where utility gained from the last purchases is equal to price. Because the utility derived from a good varies among consumers, the total value achieved by all consumers is greater than market value because the market clearing process establishes a single price. *Consumer surplus* is gained, as shown by the shaded area RPB in Figure 12.8, which is not paid for. (See also Figure 12.9.)

We can therefore say that RPB is a first approximation of **net customer value (NCV)**. This may be defined as: '**Total value realised by the customer from the purchase and use of the good or service LESS that which must be sacrificed to obtain it**' (Cole and Mogab, 1995: 144). This net customer value can be enhanced in two ways, (a) improvement in the

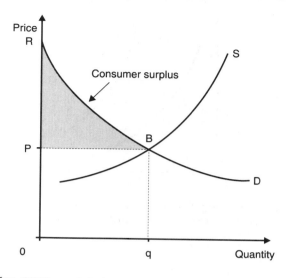

Key: ORBQ = market value
RPB = value received by customers or consumer surplus
ORBQ = Total value

Figure 12.8 A customer value approach to demand

product (b) reduction in opportunity cost, (price). But there are non-price opportunity costs which must be considered, such as convenience, search time, after sales service etc. Thus NCV is less than consumer surplus. The CIF firm seeks competitive advantage by reducing non-price opportunity costs, as well as possibly price. If the perceived value of one product is higher than another – because of reduced non-price opportunity costs – the customer may choose that product even if its price is higher than the other.

The CIF therefore may be able to *both* reduce costs of production, *and* raise price. Or at worst match the competitor's price while still offering higher perceived value. Conventional theory suggests that a firm moves from being a price taker in a fiercely competitive market to being a price maker, first by differentiating the product. In the longer run it will invest to gain economies of scale, and/or create new product variants. The intention is to change the customer's valuation of the product. But in the conventional MP/SM firm this is a discontinuous process which is only possible in the long run.

For the CIF improvement of the product is a short run activity which is an integral part of normal operations and not subject to major investment decisions which in the MP/SM firm may be circumscribed by the need to increase shareholder wealth in the short term. The CIF seeks to maximize long-run market share not short-term profit.

(a)

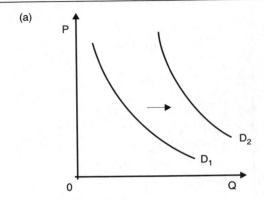

D_1 represents demand for the CIF firms product before the continuous improvement programme. D_2 represents the new demand schedule, with more demanded at any price, and less at risk from substitutes.

(b)

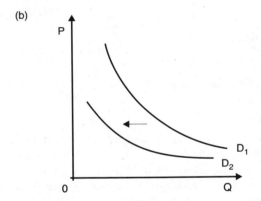

D_1 represents demand for the MP/SM firm's product. D_2 the new demand schedule after the CIF firm adopts continuous improvement. Less is bought at any price, and it is more susceptible to substitution.

Figure 12.9 Continuous improvement and demand

NET CUSTOMER VALUE AND CUSTOMER CHOICE

Instrumental customer value has three aspects, product quality, functional features and delivery/service aspects. Whereas the MP/SM firms in an industry offer the customer a choice of standard, predetermined products, the CIF is focused totally on customer requirements. Thus the whole value-adding process, not just the sales and marketing function, has a marketing aspect. These instrumental aspects of customer value can be objectively compared between products. *The customer is likely to choose the product offering the highest net customer value, that is price plus the opportunity cost value represented by better non-price instrumental factors.* The implications of this proposition for firms are vital.

The lower the non-price characteristics offered, the greater must be the equivalent discount on price for sales to be maintained. *The perceived difference in value constitutes a wedge between the price of the CIF's product and its MP/SM competitor. This wedge grows bigger over time as the continuous improvement programme continues.*

In terms of simple supply and demand theory this has the effect of both shifting the demand curve to the right and tilting it to a more inelastic form. This is illustrated in Figures 12.10 and 12.11. Similarly the demand curve for the MP/SM firm's product will shift left and become more price elastic.

In Figure 12.10 the MP/SM firm, firm A, and the CIF firm, firm B, at the start of the period have identical cost schedules, and products offering similar non-price, instrumental characteristics, both will produce output 0Q, at price 0P. Both will earn supernormal profits, the Pabc shaded area. Once firm B has had established its continuous improvement programme for, say, a year, the demand schedule for firm A's product will have shifted left to AR_1. Its new profit maximizing output will be at $0Q_1$, gaining a lower price $0P_1$. Its supernormal profits will have shrunk to P_1def shaded area.

In Figure 12.11 improvement in product instrumental characteristics has shifted the demand schedule for the CIF to AR_2. Simultaneously the

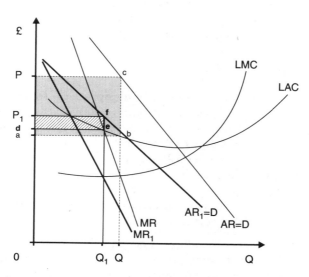

Figure 12.10 Competition between a mass production/scientific management firm and a continuous improvement firm: 1

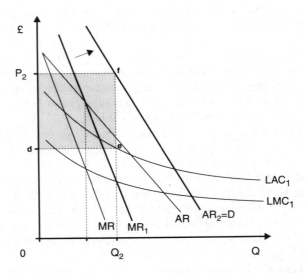

Figure 12.11 Competition between a mass production/scientific management firm and a continuous improvement firm: 2

improvements made to the production process have shifted the LAC down on to a continuous downward trend since no diseconomies of scale are being incurred. As a result the supernormal profit, represented by the shaded area P_2def is bigger than in Figure 12.10, and several times as great as the MP/SM is now earning, represented by shaded area P_1def in Figure 12.10.

CONCLUSION

The ability of the CIF to continuously improve (and reequip) the process over the long term, while simultaneously gaining cost reductions in the short term, enables it to have a permanent and increasing cost advantage over the best of MP/SM firms. Meanwhile the same continuous improvement programme will continuously improve all instrumental characteristics of the product, including instant responsiveness to customer requirements without the loss of economies of scale. This will drive an ever-growing wedge of customer value between the CIF and the MP/SM, to which the latter has no satisfactory response.

- If the CIF chooses to maximize short-term profits, the MP/SM firm can only retain market share by ever deeper price discounting to counter the CIF's increasing perceived product value. The MP/SM must suffer falling profits, possibly losses and even closure.

- If the CIF chooses to maximize market share by offering both improved products, and lower prices, the MP/SM must suffer even greater profit reductions or losses, and eventual closure is certain to follow.

CASE STUDY 14: NICHOLAS SMITH'S (GARAGES) LTD

Nicholas Smith's (Garages) Ltd is an old established family business located near to the bypass round a busy market town which is the main business centre for a large rural hinterland in North Yorkshire. Since 1971 it has been a Renault main dealer. There are four profit centres in the business: forecourt sales of petrol and sundries, car sales (new and used), repair and service workshop, and official Renault parts and spares distribution. Competitors in the town include a main Volkswagen dealer, main Ford dealer and several second-hand car dealers.

The company has a stable and loyal workforce, several of whom have been with them for over ten years. It has a long-standing record locally for good service. Some five years ago a new General Manager, Brett Dawson, was appointed. Young, and an enthusiastic convert to the total quality management philosophy then being adopted by Renault, he was determined to make Nicholas Smith's one of the leading UK Renault dealers.

He began by seeking to develop an even stronger focus on customer service than existed already. Staff in all parts of the business, including the workshop, were encouraged to build on the natural courtesy and friendliness of the personnel. After approximately two years the second part of the General Manager's strategy was undertaken. This was to systemize quality systems in all parts of the business by using the help of a consultant to seek accreditation under BS 5750 and ISO 90000 national and European quality standards respectively. After six months this was successfully achieved. Nicholas Smith's was now one of very few garage businesses in the UK to qualify on those recognized standards.

Garages in general are held in low esteem by customers because they are perceived to be less than honest, and offer a low level of attention to customer needs and poor value for money. Nicholas Smith's was now able to use BS 5750 as a powerful marketing tool as the standard becomes more widely recognized by the public. In addition satisfied customers provided powerful word of mouth marketing.

The third stage of the strategy now commenced. This was to develop a programme of customer surveys of the levels of satisfaction of all regular customers, and customers buying cars, especially new customers. This enabled the General Manager to identify areas where improvement activities could be undertaken. For example it was discovered that the percentage level of very satisfied customers among new customers buying a Renault for the first time was lower than that of regular customers. This was because the survey, one month after the purchase, was too early for the customer to have experienced the quality of response to any problems which might have arisen. Nothing had gone wrong at that stage! The company's response was to set out on paper at the time of sale clear indicators of what the company's service would be – customer promises. In order to further 'delight' the customer who might find a fault developing just after the end of the warranty period, Nicholas Smith's maintained a contingency fund. This was to be used to fully recompense a customer at no cost in such cases.

An important element in the success of this strategy has been high levels of training offered for all grades of staff through Renault (UK) Ltd, or Renault (France). For example the Service Receptionist was enabled to attend several Renault courses, success in which has now enabled her to enrol for a higher level Management Diploma course.

Thought was given to the possibility of seeking accreditation under the government's Investors in People scheme. A consultant advised them that they would easily qualify, but that they are already doing more than is necessary.

Outcomes

1 Consumer service indices – scores all in 95 per cent plus range.
2 Winner of Renault (UK) Master Club Dealer Award in 1994 and 1995.
3 Market penetration by Renault cars – UK 7.29 per cent by Jan 1997.
4 Market penetration by Nicholas Smith's 20.18 per cent in main marketing area.
5 An MBA student remarked that he was 'gobsmacked' by the level of service he received as a passing customer on the forecourt.

Activity 12.1

1 Using standard supply and demand diagrams, demonstrate the impact of this continuous improvement strategy on the market for cars and related services in the district served by Nicholas Smith's (Garages) Ltd.
2 Using conventional theory of the firm models demonstrate the competitive advantage gained by Nicholas Smith's in their market place.
3 What will be the probable impact on pricing policy at Nicholas Smith's (Garages) Ltd of this continuous effort to increase customer satisfaction?
4 What is likely to be the response of the Ford and Volkswagen dealers in the district? What are their chances of competing successfully?

Chapter 13

The regulation of market power

INTRODUCTION

It has been recognized for many years that firms may be able to achieve a degree of market power which is potentially harmful to consumers. The state has therefore, in most industrial economies, put in place regulations designed to prevent abuse of market power. In this chapter we propose to discuss the ways in which markets may be said to fail, and the theoretical and practical senses in which this may be so. We go on to discuss the difficulties involved in establishing a framework for regulation and intervention before summarizing the legislation used in the UK and Europe to monitor and regulate market power.

The concept of Pareto optimality (see Chapter 4) where perfectly clearing markets for goods and factors of production ensure that no one can be made better off in theory making someone else worse off, depends on the existence of perfect competition in all markets. As we have seen (Chapter 8) the assumptions on which this market is based are unrealistic. Even if it were achievable on a temporary basis, it could not persist. This is because there is a conflict between the preference of consumers for clear choice and low prices with the desire of the successful entrepreneur to achieve an orderly and predictable market by erecting barriers to entry by others into the market. These barriers are likely to be sought by product differentiation, economies of scale, control of technology, and the use of advertising and promotion. Nevertheless the forces of competition in a dynamic economy are likely to move the economy closer to Pareto optimality, thus diminishing the tension between private and social efficiency which inevitably stems from the firm's desire for market power.

Markets can be said to fail in two senses. First, if markets are prevented from clearing (see Chapter 4), price will be greater than marginal cost. Firms will earn supernormal profit in product markets, while scarce factors of production will earn economic rent. As a result marginal social benefit will be less than marginal social cost and Pareto optimality cannot be reached. Second, externalities will occur (pollution etc.) which again causes MSB to be less than MSC.

Moving a market back towards more competitive conditions may bring society closer to Pareto optimality, but not necessarily. Competition in markets cannot deal with externalities. Moreover Pareto optimality is not the only goal of society, and may not be consistent with the achievement of other goals such as greater equity of income and wealth distribution, or the provision of public goods (such as defence and law and order) which markets cannot provide, or merit goods (desirable services such as health care, pensions or education) which markets can only partially provide.

Market failure may be said to occur:

- where few firms dominate one market
- where externalities occur
- in the provision of public and merit goods
- in ensuring equity of outcomes
- due to time lags in the clearing of markets in an economy where constant dynamic disequilibrium occurs in conditions of supply and demand
- where Pareto equilibrium in a market economy may not be consistent with some macroeconomic goals such as price stability.

Since we are concerned in this book with the economics of business, we must restrict our comments to the problems arising where firms achieve a high level of market power in their specific markets. We will consider first the question of first best and second best solutions, which governments might adapt.

First best solutions

If we take Pareto optimality through markets to be the best solution, what conditions are necessary for the government to achieve it? Government must be able to identify what it believes to be the social welfare optimum. If it thinks it can do so it must be able (a) to adjust a competitive economy, to achieve this optimum, by *planning*, and (b) to redistribute factor ownership to achieve the desired distribution of income (or accept the given factor distribution and redistribute income via taxation). Since (a) is not possible, and the redistribution of income via taxation would produce price distortions, the first best solution must be abandoned.

Second best solutions

We are driven by the above logic to abandon Pareto optimality. We are forced to either accept the given pattern of factor ownership as equitable, or that the state should on principle ignore matters of income distribution. The criteria of *efficiency* in the market system becomes the only guide to policy. That is to say policy should seek to ensure as near as possible that the economy operates at some point on the production possibility frontier

(PPF). There is, however, no question of choosing one particular point on the PPF as being the equitable outcome to be aimed at. Another way of putting this is to say that policy should aim to maximize volume rather than distribution of production.

On this basis the approach to issues of market power is likely to be piecemeal and operated at a microlevel (case by case). As Hay and Morris (1991: 570) comment, '*any **total** solution to the problem of policy towards the private sector must be discounted*' (emphasis added). The objective must be to identify socially undesirable behaviour and outcomes in private sector markets in the light of welfare criteria. This will involve focus on welfare gains and losses arising from particular changes in markets on the basis of the concept of consumer/producer surplus.

THEORETICAL JUSTIFICATION FOR INTERVENTION

The aim of policy must be to *identify socially undesirable behaviour and outcomes in private sector markets in the light of welfare criteria, based on theory and evidence*. Theoretical analysis of monopolistic and oligopolistic behaviour tells us that a *trade off* between gains and losses occurs. Only empirical investigation can establish the magnitude of such gains and losses to determine whether the net loss is great enough to justify action, given the cost of implementing a specific policy.

Such a policy would be applied in where price substantially exceeds marginal cost. This definition would cover oligopolistic markets which are arguably the most common case. In highly concentrated markets, collusion on price between firms is likely to be *tacit*, whereas in less concentrated and more unstable markets, collusion can only be achieved by formal agreement (a cartel), which is easily identified and usually illegal. A high degree of collusion (even if tacit) will increase price–cost margins, producing supernormal profits. These can be seen as reducing welfare, since (a) a deadweight loss of welfare occurs due to output being below most efficient levels, and (b) because some consumer surplus (see Chapter 2) is appropriated by the firm and its shareholders as supernormal profit.

However it can be argued that there will occur social benefits to be offset against this welfare loss. This possibility is demonstrated in Figure 13.1.

Despite this possible trade off, from a policy point of view it is presumed that collusion will *always* cause a welfare loss. This may be true for two reasons: (1) consumers may be offered an inadequate range of choice of product variants, (2) inefficiency may occur due to the lack of incentive from competitive pressures to use resources efficiently *within* the firm.

The usual argument that monopoly/oligopoly structures are likely to reduce a welfare loss is reinforced by a second argument based on *entry barriers*. It is usually presumed that these are always harmful to consumers. But carried to its extreme, the complete removal of barriers to entry would

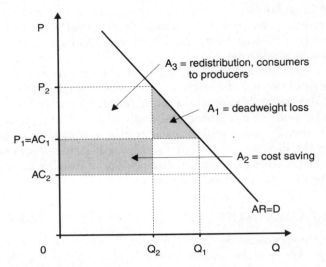

Initially the industry is competitive at $P_1 = AC_1$, producing output Q_1
Economies of scale produce fall in costs to AC_2
The industry is monopolized by one large firm
Price rises to P_2
THE TRADE OFF is cost saving A_2 against deadweight loss of welfare (consumer surplus) A_1
Here the NET EFFECT OF GAINS FROM SCALE IS POSITIVE – $A_2 - A_1 = 70$
It can be argued that quite large price increases are acceptable to achieve gains from scale.

Figure 13.1 Welfare benefits and costs in monopoly or oligopoly

bring the industry into monopolistic competition conditions (see Chapter 6) which would result profits being down to normal levels. This would remove the possibility of supernormal profits being retained to finance R&D to improve variety and quality of products offered, and the production process itself. Thus, easing conditions of entry would push up output but at the expense of higher costs of production (due to loss of scale economies), and lower product quality. The industry may reach the point where there are *too many* firms for it to be allocatively efficient.

This potential dichotomy has led to two opposing schools of thought:

1 Perry concludes that the optimum number of firms in an industry is usually *less* than that which is consistent with free entry conditions. There is therefore *no* presumption that it is better to encourage entry.
2 Baumol argues that entry *always* gives favourable welfare outcomes. This is known as the theory of contestable markets.

However, Baumol's theory of contestable markets is based on a set of assumptions which in practical terms is impossible. Entry is assumed to be free of cost, a new entrant can establish itself before incumbent firms respond to its lower entry price, and in fact they do not respond. Exit is also assumed to be cost-free. In such a market it would be only possible to earn normal profits – monopolistic competition would be the industry structure. This is clearly not so in many markets. The most common market structure is oligopoly, profit margins are correlated with degree of concentration. Barriers to entry (and exit) do exist, while to a degree all such markets are contestable, entry is slow and small scale. Moreover entry on a large scale (as in the plasterboard case) will *always* produce a response by incumbent firms.

GENERAL CONCLUSIONS

At this stage we must ask the question whether conventional theories of the firm offer any general guidelines for policy makers.

- The difficulty of defining discrete markets make conventional concentration measures an unreliable indicator of possible welfare loss. This is because for the purpose of defining a market the product must be assumed to be homogenous. Product differentiation confuses the issue, and is usually present.
- The theory of contestable markets offers no short cut to policy makers. A policy which successfully removes all barriers to entry and exit is impractical and implausible. Further, it would not necessarily increase net social welfare.
- However, the threat of entry may reduce the danger of welfare loss through excessive concentration. Thus a policy which creates more possibility of entry by exposing and penalizing welfare reducing conduct in oligopolistic markets may be helpful.
- Welfare losses through excessive concentration may be less than is supposed because of the cost-reducing effects of economies of scale, and the possibility that supernormal profits may be used to improve both product and process through research and development.
- We must conclude that, in practice, policy to deal with welfare loss through monopoly power or excessive concentration must permit cases to be dealt with on an *ad hoc* pragmatic basis. This is how UK policy appears to work in practice, as can be seen from the cases included in this book.

UK LEGISLATION AND GENERAL WELFARE LOSS

In terms of UK legislation, welfare loss is counted in the very general terms of a criteria of public interest as follows:

- reasonable price levels
- variety of choice of product variants
- relative freedom from entry barriers

- profit levels which are not excessive
- vertical integration not so excessive as to disadvantage consumers, and potential entrants to the industry.

If these conditions are breached in a particular market, then a general loss of welfare may be said to occur due to *allocative inefficiency*. But is it possible to quantify this welfare loss? One possibility is to calculate the deviation of profit rates in an industry from the average of all industry sectors. Calculate as pounds worth of excess profits as a proportion of sales. This and other approaches tend to exaggerate welfare loss. A contrasting alternative approach is to regard monopoly profits as a *reward* for successful innovation, which will eventually be eroded by the entry over time of 'me too' products – as in the case of the coffee industry. If this approach is accepted then the *threat* of entry is very effective in preventing the exploitation of monopoly positions.

The threat of entry may be in many cases now greater than in earlier generations as markets become global. In the plasterboard case BPB failed to recognize the potential threat from foreign companies, or joint ventures between UK and foreign companies. The result was a dramatic deconcentration of the market, leading to more choice of product and product variants, and lower prices – a gain in welfare. But this gain was offset by a loss of welfare due to overcapacity and higher unit costs. What was a stable monopoly market with a homogenous product, now seems to be moving towards a structure much more like the coffee industry, with more players and many more improved product variants. Increase threat of entry may also reduce the possibility of welfare loss through Lieberstein's x inefficiency. This occurs where a firm with great market power has no incentive to maximize its use of resources internally, so failing to operate on its own production possibility frontier. It is possible that losses of welfare of this kind may exceed general allocative welfare losses. As Sir John Hicks remarked, the main advantage of being a monopoly is 'a quiet life'.

We can now conclude our general argument with the following statement (Hay and Morris, 1991): *'concentration measures will never be an adequate indicator of welfare, and; no short cut is available to policy makers.'*

ASPECTS OF MARKET CONDUCT IN OLIGOPOLY

UK legislation sets up a system for referral of cases of market conduct which might be seen as being against the public interest, to the Monopolies and Mergers Commission (MMC), which possesses certain powers to act. The detail of the process is summarized in the Technical appendix near the end of this chapter. At this stage we wish to consider certain practices which might lead to a referral from the economist's perspective. The intention is to set out general principles which might be used to evaluate the decisions made by the MMC in relation to cases included in his book. These principles may also enable us to see why the behaviour of some firms described in other cases included here did not lead to a referral.

Predatory pricing

This is said to occur when a firm responds to a competitive threat in one of its markets by sharply cutting its prices. The intention is to drive out a new entrant in order to preserve monopoly power and profits. This price cut is predatory when it is so deep as to incur temporary losses in that market, which may be offset by higher prices in other markets which are not threatened. This adverse effect on potential entry is said to be detrimental to welfare. Any short-term gain from the new entrant's presence may be offset by longer-term loss of welfare due to the existence of excess capacity (operating at less than MES), and possible subsequent excessive prices and increased concentration through exit by the entrant.

The difficulty for the MMC is the identification of predatory pricing. For example did the above sequence of events occur in the plasterboard case? Was the price-cutting strategy of News International, which was not referred, a case of predatory pricing? Are the major tour operators indulging in predatory pricing to prevent new entrants from becoming established?

Predatory pricing can only be made a credible threat if once actioned, it deters entrants by establishing a reputation for ruthless behaviour. Once a new entrant is in the market it makes more sense to collude. If this is so, how do we explain the behaviour of News International?

Product differentiation

The economist would argue in this case that consumers enjoy a welfare gain from the increasing number of products in the market (as in the coffee case and, latterly, in the plasterboard and railway cases). This stems from an increase in consumer surplus resulting from being able to purchase products with a specification nearer to their individual preferences. They have more choice.

Firms are motivated only by that part of consumer surplus gain which they can appropriate as profit. In the absence of price discrimination this will be less than the whole gain of surplus, and would lead to too *little product diversity*. However the firm might not take into consideration profit lost on existing brands. There would be an incentive to produce *too many* brands. The logic of this argument would be that some collusion between firms to *limit* product proliferation would *increase* welfare. Is this possibly so in the plasterboard market?

Advertising

Advertising has two aspects, the provision for consumers of the *information* which they need in order to make an informed choice in a market, and *persuasion* of consumers to choose a particular firm's product or brand.

Advertising and information

In a growing market economy consumers need a constant flow of information about products and prices. Thus it cannot be argued that all advertising is waste. But can we be sure that the market will generate some correct level of information? The price to the consumer of advertising is zero (the consumer does not have to pay directly for information), but the cost to society is positive (resources used for advertising are not available for some other use). Thus in effect advertising is sold as a *joint product* with the goods, which sell at a higher price as a result. It is difficult to estimate the loss of welfare involved, since the information provided by the advertising has some value to the consumer, while the increased volume of sales resulting from the advertising may reduce unit costs through economies of scale and, so, eventually prices.

Furthermore since advertising causes consumers to be more aware of product variants available from a number of firms, the demand for all product variants will be more price *elastic* (consumers are more aware of possible substitutes), which should cause the price of all variants to be lower than would be the case without advertising.

Since it is difficult to create a market for information for consumers, we perhaps must accept that, from the point of view of the consumer, advertising of an informative kind is useful. (I suppose the nearest thing to a market for product information is the *Which* magazine but since this only reaches a minority of consumers it can be disregarded.)

Activity 13.1

To what extent do you think these arguments justify the amount of advertising expenditure in (a) the coffee industry (b) the detergent/ washing powder industry?

Persuasive advertising

The purpose of much advertising in many consumer goods industries from coffee to cars goes far beyond the provision of useful information. It is intended primarily to persuade consumers to switch from one supplier to another. If successful it will have the effect of changing consumer taste, thus causing the firms demand curve to shift to the right, while that of competitors shifts left, as in Figure 13.2.

But the industry demand curve is not affected since the *same* volume of sales is now distributed differently between firms A and B (see Figure 13.3). Thus *no* welfare gain occurs. It may be argued that such advertising is therefore socially wasteful expenditure, except in so far as the advertising also contains informative matter.

Successful advertising campaigns by a number of coffee producers may cause consumers to use more coffee than before, probably at the expense of a

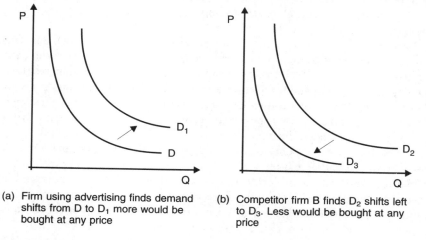

(a) Firm using advertising finds demand shifts from D to D₁ more would be bought at any price

(b) Competitor firm B finds D₂ shifts left to D₃. Less would be bought at any price

Figure 13.2 The effect of changing customer taste on firms' demand curves

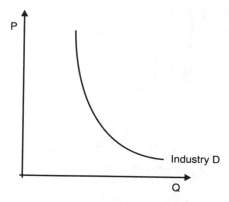

Figure 13.3 Industry demand curve remains unchanged

substitute, such as tea. In this case the combined effort of the advertising campaign may be to shift the *industry* demand curve to the right, as in Figure 13.4.

Successful advertising campaigns by all firms in the industry shifts the industry demand curve to the right. More will be bought at any price.

Is it possible to argue that any welfare gains result from persuasive advertising campaigns (such as the Gold Blend couple, or Renault cars, Nicole and Papa campaign)? If such campaigns are intended to *defend* and *retain* market share (rather than increasing it), then if carried out by several oligopoly firms in a market, they are likely to cancel each other out. Thus no general welfare gains can be identified, but in so far as *uncertainty* is reduced, welfare gains might arise. This is because the firms will have the confidence to invest in research and development to improve the product, and by improving the production process, reduce unit costs and possibly price.

Further if the industry has stabilized, with say five firms, all operating within the range of outputs which represents minimum efficient scale, then no loss of welfare results from the existence of excess capacity. The result of the destabilization of the plasterboard market by the simultaneous entry of Kaarf and RPL was to produce a situation where excess capacity existed, causing a loss of welfare (inappropriate resource allocation). Any gains from the reduction of uncertainty are, however, likely to be lost if cumulatively excessive amounts are spent on advertising – as in the detergent market, and possibly in the coffee market.

Beyond ethical considerations as to what constitutes unsuitable advertising matter and methods, there can be no presumption on which public policy might be based. There are simply no effective alternative ways of providing information, plus the stimulus to buy. The coffee case provides

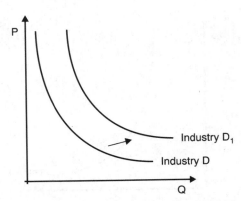

Figure 13.4 The effect of a successful industry advertising campaign on the demand curve

a good example of the Monopolies and Mergers Commission making a pragmatic judgement that advertising was not excessive and not damaging to the public interest.

Activity 13.2

Consider the market for detergents and soap powder. Do you think in this case (which is a duopoly, Unilever and Proctor and Gamble being the dominant players) that advertising is excessive and against the public interest?

Vertical integration

We have seen (in Chapter 10) that firms can grow (a) organically by expansion, (b) by merging with or taking over competing firms, or (c) by taking control of firms up or down the chain of production and distribution. Any of these three strategies may enable a firm to achieve a level of market dominance which may be against the public interest. This is especially so if barriers to entry develop, or are created. It is less obvious why vertical integration should pose a particular danger to the public interest.

In itself vertical integration may cause as many problems for the firm as it brings advantages. If the objective is to drive out of business non-integrated firms (as in the plasterboard case), then policy-makers should be concerned; since it is likely to produce a market dominated by one firm (plasterboard up to 1986) or a few very big firms (brewing up to 1991), where prices are higher, output lower and choice less than in a non-integrated market. If vertical integration is combined with other barriers to entry (such as high MES and huge entry costs, plus high cost of imported supplies as in the plasterboard case), then the danger may be acute. The gains for the vertically integrated firm may include security of supply of inputs at low cost (plasterboard) and guaranteed distribution outlets (as in the case of breweries and tied pubs). In such cases the consumer is deprived of alternative sources of supply, and choice of product. There may however be a compensating welfare gain if the dominant firm is able to exploit economies of scale and generate capacity utilization in large plant at MES, (plasterboard case).

Activity 13.3

What evidence of 'welfare gain' exists as a result of the MMC decision in 1989 (see the HMSO report, 'The Supply of Beer: A report on the supply of beer for retail sale in the UK', Cmd. Paper 651) which broke up the vertical integration of breweries and tied pubs? Was there any offsetting loss of welfare?

THE ROLE OF GOVERNMENT

We saw that the first best solution of Pareto optimality is unobtainable, therefore a second best solution must be sought. This is likely to involve intervention by government in the operation of the market. Any such solution must be pragmatic, recognizing the probability of distortions resulting elsewhere in the market. This approach to policy must be based on 'rules of reason', concentrating on specific cases. The context in which markets are manipulated is one where market-based solutions are generally preferred to the alternative of state provision. Even natural monopolies such as water have now been privatized.

The tools available for government intervention in markets may be summarized as follows:

- Price intervention, e.g. agricultural prices
- Taxation, e.g. windfall tax on excess monopoly profits or land infill tax to correct an externality
- Subsidies, e.g. hill land compensatory allowance for hill farmers – to preserve countryside or subsidies to rail franchisees to provide rural rail services
- Legal regulation, e.g. price reductions forced on privatized utilities to cause them to reduce x inefficiency
- Legally enforced self-regulation, e.g. Securities and Investments Board, to prevent misselling of private pensions etc.
- Investigation, e.g. by Office of Fair Trading and Monopolies and Mergers Commission to prevent abuse of market power.
- Legal standards, e.g. laws such as the Trade Descriptions Act to prevent unethical exploitation of consumers.
- Company law, e.g. to regulate general business behaviour.

In this chapter we are concerned with the regulation of the behaviour of firms in oligopolistic or monopolistic markets through the work of the Office of Fair Trading and the Monopolies and Mergers Commission. The work of the regulatory bodies established to oversee privatized utilities is not considered here for reasons of space. The development of the UK and European law and utilizations designed to regulate the structure, conduct and performance of industries which are believed to be exploiting consumers is set out in summary form in the Technical Appendix to this chapter.

The aims of this regulatory system are as follows:

- to seek out cases for investigation
- to investigate on the basis of laid down criteria
- to act to enforce any judgement made, within the parameters laid down by statute.

The advantage of this approach is that specific cases are treated on their merits. The disadvantage is that the process is costly, which means that only a limited number of cases can be dealt with. Further, the legislation lacks enforcement, and follow-up powers.

COMPETITION POLICY IN THE UK AND THE EUROPEAN UNION

In the UK legislation there is the 'rule of reason', on a pragmatic case by case basis. European Union (EU) law is based on 'prohibition with exceptions'. The focus is on conduct, in the sense of abuse of market power rather than its existence. (Note that in the UK privatization has led to greater concern to influence structure, rather than just conduct in those cases.) The forms of conduct thought to need investigation and possible action usually stem from (a) the degree of concentration, and (b) the existence of barriers to entry.

Market dominance

This is the main concern of competition policy. It may take the form of single firm dominance (monopoly), joint dominance based on collusion or joint dominance without collusion. The questions which must be asked are

- Does the firm enjoy dominance?
- Does the firm abuse its dominance?
- What remedies (or penalties) are available?

Problems are faced by policy makers in *defining markets*, given that market share is the usual measure of dominance (e.g. coffee case). How do we define a possible substitute?
  Abuse of market power might be evident from

- excessive profits
- unfair trading practices (e.g. plasterboard)
- tying in practices (e.g. ice-cream, breweries)
- predatory pricing (e.g. plasterboard).

All these are considered under UK legislation. But the initial market share test is now 25 per cent of market. This enables MMC to investigate **complex monopolies** (i.e. oligopolies such as the ice-cream industry).

Collusion

We have seen that game theory suggests that cooperation between oligopolists may increase welfare compared to a competitive market. Nevertheless UK legislation is strongly anti-cartel. Signs of **parallel pricing** (where prices increase/decrease simultaneously) may lead to investigation. Some resale price maintenance agreements were permitted until recently, e.g. pharmaceuticals (to encourage research) and books (to maintain specialist bookshops), but *only* the former still exists. Formal agreements on price are otherwise illegal.

Vertical supply agreements

Examples such as the case of breweries and tied houses illustrate the difficulty of this area. There may be a welfare gain from the break up of this arrangement, but not necessarily. The increased opportunities for small brewers to obtain access to outlets through guest beer arrangements may represent a welfare gain for consumers, but the development of concentrations of theme pubs in the hands of specialist companies, may cause a new distortion and a welfare loss.

Mergers

Mergers and acquisitions which are designed to acquire market dominance are suspect. Even though dominance itself may not be bad, the means by which it is gained matters. Thus the Sara Lee merger was seen as potentially damaging for consumers, while the growth of Nestlé dominance in the coffee market by product innovation was seen as benign.

UK MONOPOLY AND MERGER LEGISLATION

Mergers and acquisitions may increase concentration in specific market sectors, creating the possibility of abuse of market power. Unitary monopolies or collusion between oligopolists may bring higher prices, less choice and poorer quality, all of which disadvantage consumers and cause deadweight loss of welfare to society. Since 1948 legislation has been used in an attempt to limit such abuses. It has been supplemented by European Union legislation on the same theme but with a different approach.

UK governments have recognized that in some circumstances monopoly power may bring advantages. Accordingly legislation adopts a tentative, case-by-case approach, treating each case on its merits. This legislation is summarized in the Technical appendix to this chapter.

TECHNICAL APPENDIX: THE DEVELOPMENT OF COMPETITION POLICY IN THE UK

1948: Monopolies and Restrictive Practices (Inquiry and Control) Act

- Set up Monopolies Commission.
- Board of Trade (now DTI) to instruct Commission to report where one firm (or colluding group of firms) could restrict competition through control of 33 per cent of the market or more.
- Its enquiries revealed the extent of monopoly in the UK.
- But the Commission was given only advisory powers, and its reports were ignored.

1956: Restrictive Trades Practices Act

- Separated investigation of unitary monopolies from restrictive practices carried out by groups of firms (information agreements on prices etc. *not* included till 1968).
- Restrictive practices to be registered with the Registrar of Restrictive Practices Court (five judges, ten lay persons; status of a High Court).
- Such practices were deemed to be against the public interest unless they could pass through at least one of seven 'gateways'.
- The seven Gateways were:
  1 That it protects the public against injury.
  2 That it confers specific benefits on customers.
  3 That it prevents local unemployment.
  4 That it counters existing restrictions on competition.
  5 That it maintains exports.
  6 That it supports other acceptable restrictions.
  7 That it assists negotiation of fair trading terms for suppliers and buyers.
  An eighth was added in 1968:
  8 That it neither restricts nor deters competition.
- Having passed through one or more gateways, the onus was still on the firm to show that overall benefits exceeded costs – a test which led to the prohibition of many restrictive practices.
- 1956–94 over 10,000 practices registered, but few have come to court, mostly being voluntarily ended in view of the probability of an unfavourable decision by the court.
- 1973 legislation extended to cover services as well as goods (implemented in 1976).

1965: Monopolies and Mergers Act

- Provided for investigation of mergers or acquisitions which might produce or strengthen a monopoly, or where the take-over of assets in excess of £5 million was involved.
- Cases found to be against the public interest by the Monopolies and Mergers Commission, could be prohibited.
- Slowed down rate of concentration, but not by much.
- Less than 3 per cent have been referred and less than 1 per cent prevented.

1973: Fair Trading Act

- Unitary monopoly definition reduced from 33 per cent to 25 per cent of market.
- Two companies which are connected possibly as parent/subsidiary, with 25 per cent market share may be investigated.
- Two companies indulging in tacit collusion, price leadership or in other ways restricting competition may now be investigated.
- Mergers may be investigated where new firm would control 25 per cent or more of the market, or where gross assets exceed £70 million.
- 1973 Act changed method of referral, by creating an Office of Fair Trading which initiates a preliminary investigation on the basis of which the Secretary of State for Trade and Industry is advised as to whether the case should be referred to the (renamed) Monopolies and Mergers Commission for a decision as to whether the merger is against the public interest.
- Only less than 3 per cent of voluntary mergers plus those where the victim company was unsuccessful in its defence are recommended by the Director General of Fair Trading (DGFT) for referral to the Monopolies and Mergers Commission.
- Recommendations of the DGFT are quite often overruled by the Secretary of State, whether it be to refer or not refer.
- Referral has led to abandonment of 33 per cent or so of proposed mergers.
- Yet when the MMC reports, there is no certainty that its recommendations will be implemented.
- If a ruling by the MMC is that a merger is against the public interest, but by less than a two-thirds majority, the Secretary of State cannot forbid the merger. Even if the monopoly is more than two-thirds, the Secretary of State may refuse to implement the recommendation.
- If MMC recommend approval of the merger, the Secretary of State can overrule the recommendation.

1976: Restrictive Practice Act

- Consolidates earlier legislation.
- Director General of Fair Trading now to be responsible for bringing cases to Court.
- But no penalties for not registering a restrictive practice.
- Powers of Office of Fair Trading to investigate suspected secret agreements are too limited.
- The Act is therefore inadequate in dealing with Cartel arrangements.

1980: Competition Act

- More sceptical about benefits of mergers, especially conglomerate ones.
- Since 1984 references to MMC have been based on guidelines laid down by the then Secretary of State, Norman Tebitt, which suggest that references be made not just on market share criteria, but on the grounds of possible loss of competition resulting from the proposed merger. Thus the proposed Lloyds–Midland Bank merger was referred on grounds of loss of competition, but not the Midland–Hong Kong and Shanghai Bank merger.

1989: Companies Act

- Introduced a pre-notification procedure, by which firms planning a merger must submit notice to the Office of Fair Trading together with a completed questionnaire. This information provides the basis for DGFT's recommendation in straightforward cases.
- Clearance of the proposed merger is automatic if no referral is made within twenty days of receipt of notice.
- If referral is recommended the Secretary of State is not obliged to do so. He or she may ask the companies to sell off some assets to decrease any excessive power which may result from the merger.

European Union Merger Policy

- Commission can intervene to control or prevent monopoly through several Articles of the Treaty of Rome.
- Article 85 prohibits agreements between firms which restrict competition and affect trade between member states. (This therefore applies to many UK firms.)
- Article 86 prohibits firms or groups of firms from exploiting consumers.
- Articles 92–94 prohibit subsidies from Governments to firms which threaten or distort competition.

- Since 1989 more precise criteria have been established on which referral to the European Commission might be made. These are 1) combined world turnover of 5 billion ECU or more (total assets in the case of banks and insurance companies), 2) at least two of the companies involved in a merger must have European Union-wide turnover of at least 250 billion ECU each, and 3) where both parties to a merger are located in one member state they will be subject to national not EU controls.
- Where references are made to the European Commission they are vetted against a concept of 'a dominant position' and 'impeding effective competition'.
- If a merger is prevented by the Commission it cannot be overruled by a national body such as the MMC except on the grounds that (a) it is a matter of public security, (b) involves the media, or (c) if competition in local markets is threatened.
- The high thresholds for investigation seem likely to limit the number of referrals to the Commission to no more that perhaps 40–50 cases per year.

CASE STUDY 15: THE SUPPLY OF RECORDED MUSIC

Summary

1.1 The UK record industry is large and internationally important. Retail sales in the UK amount to over £1 billion per annum and UK employment associated with the industry exceeds 48,000. The industry earns considerable income from licensing its recordings overseas. UK sales represent 7 per cent of the world market, but it is estimated that a larger proportion of world sales (about 18 per cent) are recordings involving UK artists.

1.2 Our inquiry has looked at both the record companies and the retailers of recorded music in the UK. On the record companies side five multinational companies, known as 'the majors', account for about 70 per cent of the market. These companies are EMI, PolyGram, Sony, Warner and BMG. We find that a complex monopoly situation exists in their favour by reason of their pricing practices, arrangements on parallel imports and terms of contract with artists. The remainder of the market is made up of some 600 other companies known as independents, many of which are small and specialize in particular genres of music, e.g. dance or jazz. Many of these companies engage in similar practices to the majors but lack the majors' market presence both in the UK and internationally. Across the UK industry the great bulk of sales are of popular records, with classical music accounting for only 9 per cent of sales.

1.3 On the retail side W H Smith, through its own shops and through its subsidiary Our Price, supplies 26.6 per cent by value of the market. Since this amounts to more than 25 per cent, this group of companies has a scale monopoly. Other significant retailers are Woolworths (15 per cent), HMV (13.5 per cent), Virgin Retail (4.2 per cent), Boots (3 per cent) and Tower Records (2 per cent). There are also some 1,100 independent specialist record shops and a growing number of 'non-traditional' outlets such as petrol stations and supermarkets. In addition, mail order and record clubs account for some 12 per cent of the market.

1.4 Copyright is central to the operations of the record industry, both in the UK and internationally. It allows record companies to invest money and enterprise in creating commercial recordings which can be exploited in both the home and overseas markets knowing that they have legal protection against unauthorized reproduction. Copyright is also important in ensuring that the talents of successful artists and songwriters are rewarded.

1.5 The MMC inquiry was prompted by concern about the prices of compact discs (CDs), and particularly the fact that prices appeared to be significantly higher in the UK than in the USA. Much of the apparent difference relates to different tax arrangements. Sales taxes in the USA are considerably lower than the UK's 17.5 per cent rate of VAT. Moreover, record prices are displayed without sales tax in the USA, whereas shelf prices in the UK include VAT.

1.6 We commissioned our own survey of comparative UK/US prices and found that the real price differentials were considerably lower than is often supposed. The survey showed that, when tax is excluded, the prices of full-price popular CDs are on average 7 to 9 per cent higher in the UK than in the USA at an exchange rate of $1.50 to the pound. The differential for full-price classical CDs is greater at about 25 per cent. However, some 55 per cent of classical CDs sold in the UK are in the mid-price or budget categories and there are strong indications that the price differentials covering the complete range of full-price, mid-price and budget CDs are on average lower than the differentials for full-price CDs.

1.7 These price comparisons are based on an exchange rate of $1.50 to the pound, which was the average for the second half of 1993. Variations in exchange rates will lead to changes in the measured US/UK price differentials. We sought to check whether record price differentials were out of line with those existing in other low- to medium-priced manufactured goods associated with leisure activities. We found that they were not. This suggests that the price differentials for CDs are not the result of circumstances specific to the record industry.

1.8 Apart from the influence of particular exchange rate levels it was argued that the much larger size of the US market (resulting in longer manufacturing runs and the ability to recover the high initial cost of a recording over a greater number of sales) and the generally lower US retailing costs (relating particularly to lower premises costs and higher labour productivity) lead to price levels being generally lower in the USA. It has not been possible to quantify the effect of these factors but we believe the arguments have force and apply both to CDs and to a wider range of manufactured products.

1.9 We also compared record prices with those in a number of other industrialized countries and found that UK prices are generally lower. Thus it appears that the UK is not experiencing systematically higher prices for recorded music.

1.10 It was suggested to us that the differential with the USA could be eliminated if the record companies' ability to control parallel imports were removed. We do not believe this would be the case. Such a move would in any event be contrary to the EC Rental Directive and could be damaging because of the increased risk of piracy and the general weakening of copyright protection, which is territorially based.

1.11 We found that the major record companies compete vigorously amongst themselves and with the independent sector. New entrants are a pronounced feature of the industry. The major record companies' strength in the market-place is balanced by powerful retailing groups. The major companies are not therefore able to exercise market power to the disadvantage of consumers and we conclude that prices are set at competitive levels in the UK market. The major record companies are not making excessive profits.

1.12 Record retailing is also a competitive market. There is no evidence that the scale monopoly of W H Smith enables it to exploit its position. Its profits on record retailing are not excessive.

1.13 The record industry is a high-risk business. The great majority of recordings do not sell enough copies to recoup their initial investment. Record prices must therefore be set so that the earnings on successful records will cover losses on the failures. It would not be sensible for the record companies to price CDs, cassettes and vinyl records strictly in relation to manufacturing costs, which make up only a small proportion of the total costs. Instead record companies have developed pricing structures for different recordings and different formats which reflect consumers' perceptions of quality and value and hence willingness to pay. Given the strong competition in the market we believe this pricing policy is justified.

1.14 During our inquiry a number of issues were raised in connection with the contracts between artists and record companies. We found that the record companies compete actively in securing the services of new and established artists. Terms of contract have generally moved in the artists' favour over the last 20 years. Artists are normally professionally advised in their commercial negotiations with the record companies about contract terms, both at the time of the initial contract negotiations and at subsequent renegotiations. Ownership and control of copyright for a significant period is essential to a record company that has made a large initial investment in recordings and in an artist's career. We see no case for any change in the contractual or copyright framework governing the relationship between artist and record company. The proper forum for the resolution of particular disputes between artists and record companies is the court.

1.15 We had some concern about the record companies' practice of giving free singles to retailers as a means of promoting new releases. However, on balance we think no change is required in connection with this practice because it forms part of the competitive process and benefits the independent retailers, who do not receive discounts and other promotional support to the same extent as large retailers.

1.16 Finally, we also felt some concern that consumers might be misled by the practice of some major retailers in displaying charts which show the retailers' predictions of future sales rather than actual sales as recorded in the national charts. Where retailers do this we consider that they should make clear the basis on which the charts have been compiled.

1.17 Although we have found two monopoly situations to exist, we have not found that they operate against the public interest.

(MMC, 1994a)

Questions

1 How would an economist describe (a) a complex monopoly situation (record producers) (b) a scale monopoly (record retailing) using the theories set out in this book?
2 Does the structure of this market justify price discrimination in this industry?
3 Does the structure of this market suggest that barriers to entry are sufficiently low to prevent the welfare loss normally associated with monopoly and oligopoly?
4 Do you agree that 'price differentials for CDs are not the result of circumstances specific to the record industry'?
5 Do you agree with the conclusion that the two monopolies identified do *not* operate against the public interest?

Chapter 14

The presentation case study

INTRODUCTION

In line with our philosophy of creating independent, confident, lifelong learners, for whom economics is an important part of the tool-kit required for strategic business decision-making, we have used a presentation case study as an integral part of our course. Our approach is set out below.

Objectives

1 To enable students to develop oral and visual presentation skills.
2 To enable them to gain experience in the application of economic principles to the analysis of business behaviour.

Methods

1 Each syndicate of four or five students within the tutorial groups is issued with one of the two presentation cases in this chapter.
2 The material issued to each student in the syndicate comprises the 'summary' and 'conclusion' sections of a recent MMC report (we used one report on a monopoly situation, and one on a merger), a note on how to unpick the case and a set of questions to be investigated.
3 The syndicates are expected to do further research:
   a) by reading the finding and evidence sections of the report from a library copy
   b) a literature search for further information to bring the story up to date.
4 Each syndicate is to present its findings along the lines set out below at the final tutorial of the course.

The presentation

1 It is expected that *all* students in the syndicates will play a part in the presentation, and its preparation.

2 Overhead projector slides are to be used to present 'bullet points'.
3 The role model for the research process is to be the coffee industry and plasterboard industry chapters in *Business and microeconomics* (Pass and Lowes, 1994, (the set textbook for the course).
4 The presentation is to deal with issues of *structure, conduct* and *performance* in the markets studied.
5 Questions and issues which needed to be addressed are set out as indicated on the ice cream and Sara Lee/Reckitt & Coleman cases.
6 A list of concepts which might be used, as set out below, are issued.

General issues to be addressed

1 What are the *Key structural features of the market?*
2 How is the *conduct* of the firms influenced by the structure of the market and the forces operating within it?
3 What is your *evaluation of the performance of the firms* in the market in terms of the following?
   a) *Economic efficiency.*
      - price competition
      - choice
      - industry capacity
      - profitability
      - product/service innovation
      - international competitiveness
   b) The public interest
4 Did they agree with the *MMC recommendation?*
5 Have *subsequent events* proved the MMC view to be right or wrong?

Key concepts to be used

- Scale monopoly
- complex monopoly
- duopoly/oligopoly
- industry overcapacity
- market share
- entry barriers
- entry costs
- brand differentiation
- collusion
- return on investment
- profitability
- price differentials
- high risk business

- copyright
- exchange rates
- concentration
- niche markets
- full line forcing
- exclusive dealing
- outlet exclusivity
- reference product
- product branding
- economies of scale and scope
- miminum efficient scale: capacity utilization
- non-price competition
- market segmentation
- patents
- merger/take-over/ management buy out

Some practical problems

1 Where a large cohort of students is involved (as in our case, 250), access to the original MMC report in a library, and other relevant materials may be difficult.
2 Some syndicates may have too high a proportion of non-contributors.
3 If each syndicate has only ten minutes in which to present, they may find timing difficult. Should the tutor cut off in mid-flow a student who is taking up too much time to the exclusion of his or her colleagues? Stress the importance of rehearsing the presentation in advance. Point out that the tutor can manage the overall timing of the syndicate presentation, and will cut the students short if they overshoot, *but* that the tutor must leave the management of the time available for each syndicate to them. If the last contributor is edged out, he or she may well be very upset and will blame the tutor if they have not been acquainted very clearly with the rules well in advance.
4 The students will invest a great deal of time and effort into the presentation and its preparation, and they are likely to want it to figure in the assessment of their course. Be wary of allowing this since it is very difficult to award individual grades within a group effort and injustice is likely to be done, or be believed to have been done. If it is to be used for assessment as coursework then it must, in our view, be based on each individual student writing up his or her contribution to the syndicate's presentation, in some detail. To encourage thorough preparation, and to enable us to reward effort a compulsory question on the cases used is included in the end of course examination.

We used the structure conduct performance model as the focus for our presentation case because we were trying to create an integrated course where lectures, textbook and tutorials were linked by a common theme. It would still be possible to use a presentation case in a more loosely constructed course to advantage.

PRESENTATION CASE 1: ICE CREAM MONOPOLY

Method

Extract from the case material information presented under these headings:

1 *Key definitions of terms*
2 Information concerning the *structure* of the industry
3 Information concerning the *conduct* of firms in the industry
4 Information concerning the *performance* of the industry
5 Key *conclusions* arrived at by the MMC.

QUESTIONS

1 How might we define *public interest*?
2 How might actions be a monopolist which we deem to be against the public interest, be demonstrated by use of the models developed in the *theory of the firm*?
3 What does the MMC mean by (a) *scale monopoly*; (b) *complex monopoly*?
4 How does *freezer exclusivity* reinforce a monopoly situation? Can you think of similar examples of monopoly reinforcing behaviour in other industry sectors?
5 Given the strength of monopoly power of BEW and Nestlés in the impulse ice cream industry, how did you think 1,000 small suppliers survive?
6 How does the nature of *impulse* ice cream as product cause *vertical integration* to be the chief means of creating and reinforcing monopoly?
7 If freezer exclusivity is a serious *barrier to entry*, why did Lyons Maid lose markets share, and Mars achieve market entry?
8 Why is freezer exclusivity less of a barrier now than it was in 1979?
9 On what grounds did the MC decide that freezer exclusivity does not 'operate against the public interest' (despite concluding that BEW, Nestlé and Mars do constitute a *complex monopoly*?
10 How did changes in the *structure* of the market influence *conduct* of firms in the industry, and their *performance* since 1979?

1 SUMMARY

1.1 On 7 May 1993 we were asked to investigate and report on whether a monopoly situation exists in relation to the supply in the UK, otherwise than by retail sale, of ice cream intended for immediate consumption ('impulse' ice cream). If so, the reference (see Appendix 1.1) requires us to report on whether any action or omission on the part of those in whose favour the monopoly situation exists, in respect of the supply to retailers or refrigerated cabinets on terms which prevent the retailer from using the cabinet to stock ice cream from other suppliers ('freezer exclusivity'), operates or may be expected to operate against the public interest.

1.2 We found that a scale monopoly situation exists in favour of Birds Eye Wall's Ltd (BEW), a subsidiary of Unilever PLC (Unilever), which accounts for around two-thirds of the wrapped impulse market and over half of the total impulse market as defined in our terms of reference. We also found that a complex monopoly situation exists in favour of BEW, Nestlé UK Ltd (Nestlé) and Mars UK Ltd (Mars), which between them accounted in 1992 for 88 per cent of sales of wrapped impulse products and a lesser but still very large share of the market for all reference products. The first two companies proclaim and, to the best of their ability, enforce exclusivity. The last does not do so, but we deemed its requirement that its full range be stocked to have a similar practical effect, and Mars acknowledged that this was the case. There are numerous other manufacturers – perhaps as many as 1,000 if the very smallest were included – but having considered their market shares we decided not to include them in the complex monopoly group.

1.3 Ice cream sales in the UK in 1992 were worth about £785 million at retail prices, £275 million of which (35 per cent) comprised reference products. These were mostly wrapped impulse products, the market for which is characterized by a high level of branding, and of associated advertising expenditure. Unlike other impulse products such as confectionery, impulse ice cream needs refrigerated storage and transport and a freezer cabinet at the point of sale, not merely as a display device but as an essential piece of equipment which has limited capacity and without which the product cannot be stocked at all. Effective distribution is a key aspect of competition, particularly because demand is not only seasonal but subject to extreme short-term fluctuations as the weather changes. BEW and Nestlé, which acquired Lyons Maid at the end of 1992, argued that by supplying cabinets 'free' (ie not separately charged for), on an exclusive basis, they had extended the market, and consumers' opportunity to purchase, to many small outlets that would not otherwise have stocked ice cream, and would cease to do so if exclusivity were prohibited. Importance was attached also, by both companies, to the assurance exclusivity gave of economic drop sizes, effective display and quality control.

1.4 The market has changed significantly since a previous MMC report in 1979. In the 1970s, Wall's and Lyons Maid shared between them all but a small part of the market. Thereafter the market share of Lyons Maid significantly declined notwithstanding its insistence on freezer exclusivity whilst that of Wall's (now BEW) increased. Mars entered the market in 1989 with a new product relying on quality and an established confectionery reputation. In four years, Mars ice cream achieved representation in about 50 per cent of outlets and a market share of about 16 per cent in wrapped impulse products (at least 20 per cent in the chocolate bar sector). It has sought to have exclusivity banned, on the grounds set out in Chapter 5, not only in the UK but also elsewhere in Europe. Mars, like Treats Ice Cream Ltd (Treats), the next largest supplier, drew attention to the effects on the market of the degree of vertical integration achieved by BEW as a result of freezer exclusivity operating in conjunction with its distribution system through concessionaires.

1.5 We concluded from the information available to us, including a specially-commissioned market research survey of independent retailers, that exclusivity appeared to pose less of a restriction on supply now than it had done at the time of the 1979 MMC report, when the practice was found, on balance, not to operate against the public interest. Retailers have several options available to them including:

- to install an exclusive freezer, on an agreement terminable at short notice;
- to acquire their own freezer in which case they can generally purchase ice cream at lower prices in the form of extra bonus; and
- to add a second freezer where space permits: this is the case in as much as 80 per cent of outlets.

Recent developments in the market reflect retailers' exercise of their choice between these options.

1.6 BEW and Nestlé made ice cream widely available through their provision of freezers, and continue to do so. There is no restriction on other suppliers doing the same, and investment in developing the market should not be deterred. There is no evidence of excessive profits being made and recent trends in the market suggest that competition has been effective, irrespective of any effects of exclusivity. While the need to offer freezers represents a cost of entry, similar to other costs such as advertising, we did not feel that it constituted a barrier to entry in the specific circumstances (including the differential terms available to those not taking a manufacturer's exclusive freezer) that we found to obtain in this market.

1.7 In many shops – at least half the total – consumers now have a choice of more than one manufacturer's product and most consumers can also choose between different retail outlets: we are indeed not convinced from the information we have seen, including our own survey of retailers, that consumer choice would be significantly improved were exclusivity to be ended. In so far as some prices have increased this appeared to be principally due to consumer preferences for higher-quality products.

1.8 A number of the other public interest issues raised with us related to distribution questions which we found not to fall within our terms of reference. During the course of the inquiry, however, BEW agreed to change the wording in its terms of trade to make it clear that retailers with a BEW-owned freezer who wished to source supplies other than from BEW's concessionaires would not be prevented from doing so. We conducted a thorough analysis of the differential terms available from BEW and Nestlé (not from Mars) to retailers with company freezers as compared with others to see whether retailers' choice was distorted as a result. We concluded that this was not so to any significant extent except in low turnover outlets which account for only a small proportion of sales, and some of which might otherwise not sell ice cream at all.

1.9 We therefore concluded that in the UK market as it is currently developing no action or omission on the part of BEW, Nestlé or Mars in respect of freezer exclusivity operates or may be expected to operate against the public interest.

9 CONCLUSIONS

The reference and the monopoly situations

9.1 Under the reference dated 7 May 1993, made under sections 47(1), 49(2), 49(3) and 50(1) of the Fair Trading Act 1973 ('the Act') – see Appendix 1.1, we are required to investigate and report on whether a monopoly situation exists in relation to the supply in the United Kingdom otherwise than by retail sale of ice cream intended for immediate consumption; and, if so, by virtue of which provision of sections 6 to 8 of the Act that monopoly situation is to be taken to exist; and in favour of what person or persons that monopoly situation exists. We are also required to examine whether any action or omission on the part of that person or those persons in respect of the supply to retailers of refrigerated cabinets on terms which prevent the retailer from using the cabinet to stock for sale ice cream supplied by other suppliers – a practice commonly referred to as 'freezer exclusivity' – operates or may be expected to operate against the public interest.

9.2 'Ice cream' is defined in the terms of reference to include water ices, ice lollies, frozen yoghurt and ice cream to which substances such as fruit and chocolate have been added, but does not include soft mix ice cream. Ice cream intended for immediate consumption is generally referred to as 'impulse' ice cream; this term is sometimes used to include soft mix ice cream as well as the reference products although, as explained in paragraph 9.7, we have regarded 'impulse' ice cream for the purposes of this report as synonymous with the reference products. As shown in Table 3.1, Birds Eye Wall's Ltd (BEW) – a subsidiary of Unilever PLC – accounted for about two-thirds of sales by value of wrapped impulse products in the UK in 1992; its share of the total reference products (wrapped impulse products plus scoop ice cream but excluding soft mix) was somewhat less, but nonetheless above 50 per cent. We have, therefore, concluded that a monopoly situation exists in the supply of impulse ice cream by virtue of section 6(1)(a) of the Act (a 'scale monopoly' situation). We further conclude that the monopoly situation we have identified exists in favour of BEW.

9.3 We also considered whether a complex monopoly situation exists as defined in section 6(1)(c) of the Act, ie whether at least one-quarter of the goods specified in the terms of reference are supplied by two or more persons who voluntarily or not, or by agreement or not, so conduct their respective affairs as in any way to prevent, restrict or distort competition in connection with the production or supply of those goods. As was apparent in Table 3.1, the three largest suppliers of wrapped impulse ice cream are BEW, Nestlé UK Ltd (Nestlé – how the owner of Lyons Maid) and Mars UK Ltd (Mars), together accounting in 1992 for about 88 per cent of sales of wrapped impulse ice cream and slightly less of the reference products as a whole. Both BEW and Nestlé supply exclusive cabinets; Mars supplies cabinets on terms which require the stocking of a full range of Mars products and which, although not explicitly preventing other suppliers' products being stocked, have a similar effect given the size of most of Mars' cabinets. In our view, therefore, BEW, Nestlé and Mars are members of a group which supplies at least one-quarter of the reference products in the UK, and which conduct their affairs so as to restrict competition in the supply of impulse ice cream, in that they supply to retailers refrigerated cabinets on terms which prevent the retailer from using the cabinet to stock for sale ice cream available from other suppliers. We conclude that a complex monopoly situation exists by virtue of section 6(1)(c) of the Act, and that this complex monopoly situation exists in favour of BEW, Nestlé and Mars. Neither this conclusion nor that relating to the scale monopoly in itself implies the existence of any facts which operate or may be expected to operate against the public interest.

Market shares

3.33 Nielsen Audit data is the source of data used by all three leading companies to provide a basis for estimating market shares. It is based on a sample of CTNs, independent grocers and petrol station forecourts during the summer season. In addition to the Nielsen Retail Audit, BEW uses a Consumer Monitor which consists of daily interviews asking respondents what impulse ice cream they have purchased in the previous two days. On the basis of these two external sources of data and its own sales BEW produces an estimate of the size of the impulse market and market shares.

3.34 Mars told us that in addition to the Nielsen data it uses information collected for the Confectionary Market Audit by the National Market Research Agency (NMRA). The NMRA audit is wider than that of Nielsen covering off-licences, cinemas theatres and beach kiosks. Mars claims that outlets in what it calls the leisure sector account for about 40 per cent of sales of impulse ice cream. Mars has no data on scoop and soft mix sales having no products in that part of the market.

3.35 Table 3.1, based on Nielsen data, shows how, following the entry by Mars, the market share of BEW in the wrapped impulse market measured by value fell between 1989 and 1990. In 1991 BEW's market share fell again before a strong recovery in 1992 which is partly explained by the difficulties encountered by Lyons Maid during its brief ownership by Clarke Foods. Table 3.1 also shows how Lyons Maid saw its market share shrink from nearly one-quarter to one-tenth within the four years after 1988.

Table 3.1 Market shares in the wrapped impulse market

					per cent by value	
	1988	*1989*	*1990*	*1991*	*1992*	*1993**
BEW	67	68	62	59	67	67
Lyons Maid	23	23	21	18	10	11
Mars	0	†	11	12	11	14
Others	10	8	6	11	12	8
Total	100	100	100	100	100	100

Source: BEW based on Nielsen Audit data.

9.4 As is clear from Chapters 3 and 7, there are a large number of other suppliers of impulse ice cream – perhaps as many as 1,000 – in the UK. We received information from about 50 such suppliers, about a quarter of whom acknowledged that they supplied cabinets on an exclusive basis. Taking into account, however, the much smaller market share of such other suppliers, we decided that it was inappropriate to include them as members of the complex monopoly group. It may be noted that, in a number of cases, the terms on which freezers are supplied rest on informal understandings rather than on written contracts and that even where exclusivity is formally claimed, both the intention and the capacity to enforce it are widely variable. Some manufacturers think it worth supplying a cabinet if it results in a reasonable level of sales of their products, and do not exert themselves to expel intruders so long as those sales do not fall below what they regard as a tolerable level.

9.5 We have therefore to examine whether any action or omission in respect of freezer exclusivity on the part of BEW as a scale monopolist or on the part of BEW, Nestlé or Mars as members of a complex monopoly group operates or may be expected to operate against the public interest.

The market for impulse ice cream

9.6 The size of the total UK ice cream market in 1992 has been estimated at some £785 million at retail prices including VAT. Sales of the reference products are estimated at some £275 million, and soft mix accounts for a further £55 million. Of the reference products, sales of wrapped impulse are estimated at some £233 million, and sale of scoop ice cream at some £42 million. Other than the reference products and soft mix, ice cream is sold in multi-packs – supermarket sales of products otherwise classified as impulse but sold for subsequent consumption – and in the form of other take-home products, such as ice cream sold in blocks, to be served in individual portions at home.

9.7 As discussed in paragraphs 3.3 to 3.6, the distinction between 'impulse' and 'take-home' ice cream is not rigid, although the nature of the purchase is somewhat different as are the outlets at which they are generally sold, and the products serve somewhat different needs: hence also the considerably higher price for impulse than for take-home products. Similarly, there is a degree of overlap in some circumstances between soft mix and impulse products as defined in the terms of reference, although many of the outlets selling wrapped impulse products do not sell soft mix, which requires a separate machine to be staffed at the point of sale. We acknowledge that scoop ice cream (included in the reference products) also differs in some aspects from wrapped impulse products, often being sold in different outlets, or from different cabinets, but this does not significantly affect our analysis. We therefore regard impulse ice cream, as defined in the terms of reference, as a sensible market in the context of the current investigation. It also distinguishes those ice cream products, sold from freezers, in which the issue of freezer exclusivity has arisen.

9.8 Wrapped impulse products have themselves been subdivided into a number of categories appealing to different sectors of the market: for example, chocolate bars aimed somewhat more at adult consumers, filled cones, refreshment (including water ices) and lines presented specially for children.

9.9 A further distinctive feature of the impulse sector is that it continues to be served by leading branded products, the development of own brands being barely evident in the case of wrapped impulse products. (Supermarket groups have developed their own brands of multi-packs but these are not part of the impulse market.) The importance of branded products is reflected in the substantial advertising expenditure particularly of some new entrants to the market, in one case of over 20 per cent of turnover.

The MMC's 1979 report

9.10 The MMC reported on ice cream and water ices in 1979.[1] It found a number of practices to be against the public interest, including:

(a) A requirement as a condition of supplying reference goods to a retail outlet that the reference goods of other suppliers should not be stocked – 'outlet exclusivity'. The MMC recommended that this practice should end, which took effect as part of a number of undertakings given by the main suppliers of ice cream to the Secretary of State (see Appendix 3.1).
(b) Provision of a refrigerated cabinet on terms which prevent the customer (in general the retailer) from using it to stock reference goods of other suppliers when the supplier providing the cabinet cannot meet the customer's requirements. The MMC recommended express provisions permitting the customer to stock and sell reference goods of other suppliers when the supplier himself cannot meet the customer's requirements. This provision is now incorporated in contracts of the main companies for supply of refrigerated cabinets. Otherwise the MMC acknowledged that provision of exclusive cabinets excluded other suppliers from a retail outlet too small to be expected to sell from more than one cabinet. The MMC did not, however, find freezer exclusivity *per se* to be against the public interest. Their report noted the

1 *Ice Cream and Water Ices: a Report on the Supply in the United Kingdom of Ice Cream and Water Ices*, Cmnd 7632, August 1979.

argument that 'if cabinets were no longer provided the number of outlets, particularly those of smaller retailers, selling reference goods might fall significantly. This would reduce the scope for competition in the retail market, the opportunities for entry to the market or for increased sales on the part of the smaller suppliers, and limit consumer choice'. The MMC did, however, express the hope that the two main suppliers at that time – BEW and Glacier Foods Ltd (Glacier), predominantly owned by Lyons Ice Cream Holdings Ltd – would in the longer term make it easier for customers to buy their own cabinets.

(c) Various practices by Glacier, eg the requirement that wholesalers of Glacier products should not sell the reference goods of other suppliers; that customers buying soft ice cream mix from Glacier should also take Glacier's supplies of hard ice cream; that Glacier's franchisees should only stock or sell specified brands. The MMC recommended that these requirements should cease, as was done.

(d) The period of BEW's and Glacier's agreements, which the MMC recommended should be of no more than 12 months' duration, and arrangements for payment of retrospective bonuses: these practices were subsequently amended, in the sense the MMC proposed, though with some changes to the detailed recommendations.

9.11 During the present inquiry, we did, however, become aware of a number of cases in which landlords (including some local authorities) sought tenders for sale of impulse ice cream on an exclusive basis. The extent and effect of such 'elective exclusivity' is not directly relevant to our inquiry, given our restricted terms of reference. We also found evidence of a number of agreements between BEW and retailers which, at the request of the retailers, were longer than the one-year period stipulated in the undertakings following our earlier report. These were regarded by BEW as within the spirit if not the letter of the undertakings, but again were not of direct relevance to the issue of freezer exclusivity *per se*.

Recent market developments

9.12 There have been a number of significant changes in the structure of the market since our previous report. BEW estimates that in 1979 BEW and Lyons Maid each had about 45 per cent of the impulse market. BEW's share of the wrapped impulse market has subsequently increased to about two-thirds, that of the Lyons Maid brands has slumped to only about 10 per cent. The decline of Lyons Maid is discussed in more detail in Chapter 3: the business went through two changes of ownership before the main brands were recently acquired by Nestlé and many in the industry regard it as having failed to invest adequately and compete effectively in the 1980s.

9.13 There have also been a number of new competitors in the market, notably Mars. Mars estimated its share of the wrapped impulse market in 1992 at about 16 per cent: but it suggested that in the summer of 1993 it had a higher share, some 20 per cent, in that sector of the market – chocolate bars – where it has mainly chosen to compete, with a share of some 30 per cent of chocolate bars outside the leisure sector where it has found distribution to be particularly difficult. Mars' entry to the market was based on established confectionary brands, and supported by significant advertising expenditure. Mars told us, however, that when it first entered the market with one product, it had assumed it would be able to secure distribution from existing cabinets in retail outlets: when it found that this was often impossible, it provided its own cabinets to secure retail distribution. Other recent entrants include Treats Ice Cream Ltd (Treats) (formerly owned by BEW, now an independent company following a management buy-out), Häagen-Dazs UK Ltd (Häagen-Dazs) (a subsidiary of Grand Metropolitan PLC) and Schöller Ice Cream Ltd (the subsidiary of a major supplier of ice cream elsewhere in the EC).

9.14 A number of parties referred to Mars' entry to the market as providing an additional stimulus to product innovation. Mars' products, based on well-known confectionary brand names, incorporated a higher quality both of ice cream and chocolate. Its entry appears to have stimulated a demand for 'chocolate-bar' products, particularly among adults, of a quality and price higher than previously prevailed in the market: following Mars' entry, the quality and price of a number of existing BEW brands were also increased (see Table 3.9). BEW, on the other hand, argued that it had itself introduced a succession of new products irrespective of competition from Mars.

Profitability

9.15 As shown in Chapter 2, there is no evidence of excess profitability on sales of impulse ice cream. BEW's return on net assets – which averaged about 15 per cent over the last four years – is somewhat below that for the economy generally over that period.[1] The financial performance of some other main suppliers is significantly poorer than that of BEW, although we received no indication that they would have to consider withdrawing from the market.

---

1 MMC analysis of Extel Micro-EXSTAT database of some 600 manufacturing company accounts gives return on capital employed (trading assets) of 20.4 per cent in 1989, 18.9 per cent in 1990, 14.9 per cent in 1991 and 13.0 per cent in 1992 – an average of 16.8 per cent. The average for all companies in the database, including non-manufacturing, was some 16.3 per cent over the four years.

Distribution

9.16 As discussed in Chapter 3, ice cream must be kept at a low temperature at all stages of production and distribution, from the factory to the point of retail sale. To supply the retail market, manufacturers need their own distribution network, including cold stores and refrigerated vehicles, or access to a distributor with such facilities.

9.17 Almost all parties from whom we heard agreed that distribution is a key aspect of competition given the nature of the product, with demand highly sensitive to weather and rapid delivery required to cope with unpredictable peaks of demand given the typical retailer's limited facility for holding stocks. It was suggested to us that specialist distributors were better able to respond to such demand. It was also agreed that there were important economies of scale in distribution due, for example, to the high costs of temperature-controlled storage and transportation, and the low unit value of the products: one estimate was that a 10 per cent increase in quantity delivered could reduce unit distribution costs – which account in some cases for over 20 per cent of total cost – by as much as 10 per cent in the long term.

9.18 BEW currently distributes almost two-thirds of its impulse products through 38 exclusive concessionaires. These concessionaires cover the entire UK except the area within the M25, accounting for about 11 per cent of BEW's sales, where BEW distributes its products direct from its own cold storage depot. Its remaining sales are distributed through Wall's Whippy franchises, through general wholesalers (although it refuses to supply regional or local wholesalers), and to a few accounts which have negotiated direct delivery.

9.19 BEW's current distribution arrangements have evolved from the in-house distribution system used at the time of our previous report, its concessionaires often acting as marketing agents for BEW, as well as distributors. It told us that it would keep its current arrangements under review, taking into account the relative performance of its concessionaires and its in-house distribution system used within the M25 area.

9.20 A number of other suppliers claimed that BEW's exclusive concessionaire system put it at a significant advantage: given, for example, economies of scale, any competing distribution system would be unable to provide as good a service to retailers, and would incur higher unit costs. BEW's current arrangements would appear to have some similarities to those of Glacier, on which we commented in our previous report, but it is only open to us to consider these arrangements in so far as they relate to the issue of freezer exclusivity. We return to this point in paragraph 9.56.

Freezer exclusivity

9.21 The retail sale of impulse ice cream requires a freezer cabinet to ensure the quality of the product. The supply of freezer cabinets to retailers has been one means of promoting retail sales of impulse ice cream.

9.22 BEW and Nestlé currently supply freezers 'free' (ie not separately charged for) on loan on condition that they are not used to stock competing products unless their products are temporarily unavailable. Nestlé, however, distributes certain Mars products which do not directly compete with its own range and which can be stocked in Nestlé cabinets. Mars initially sold freezers to retailers, but with an equivalent value of Mars ice cream supplied free: more recently, it has supplied freezers free-on-loan subject only to the requirement to stock the full Mars range.

9.23 Of other suppliers, Treats sells freezers with vouchers permitting the cost of the freezer to be recovered by purchase of its products. Häagen-Dazs suppliers freezers on exclusive terms and with fittings designed for Häagen-Dazs products. About a quarter of other manufacturers from which we heard acknowledged that they insisted on exclusivity, but some others requested it, or aimed to secure a good representation of their products in the cabinet, or stipulated a minimum percentage of space to be used for stocking their products. One supplier offered retailers the choice of a 'free' cabinet on an exclusive basis, or a 'hired' one on a non-exclusive basis. Those suppliers of impulse ice cream who did not supply freezers generally felt themselves to be at a disadvantage. We are also aware of wholesalers who supply or facilitate the supply of freezers to retailers sometimes on condition that they provide the stock, which may come from several manufacturers.

9.24 At the time of our previous report, comprehensive evidence was not available on the extent to which ice cream was sold from exclusive cabinets. Information in the report suggested, however, that some 15 to 20 per cent of retailers then had their own freezers, the remainder being subject to both freezer and, in many cases, outlet exclusivity. We received varying evidence on the extent of freezer exclusivity during the current inquiry (see paragraphs 3.64, 4.59 and 6.21 and Appendix 3.2).

9.25 BEW estimated, as summarized in paragraph 3.64, that there are some 90,000 general trade outlets (excluding, for example, multiple grocery outlets) selling wrapped impulse ice cream, some 63,000 of which stock BEW ice cream. It also estimated that about one-third of outlets – some 32,000 – have one or more BEW freezers but no other cabinets; while some 30,000 outlets – also about one-third of the total – currently have their own cabinets: similar to the proportions from a much larger survey of 46,000 outlets conducted for Nestlé.

9.26 We ourselves commissioned a survey of some 1,500 retail outlets – see Appendix 3.2. The survey did not give a fully representative sample of retail outlets, excluding multiple confectionery/tobacconist/newsagent outlets (CTNs) from whom we received evidence direct (most of whom have cabinets provided by more than one ice cream supplier, and sell more than one supplier's products in many of their outlets) and leisure outlets, where Mars has had more difficulty competing: it did, however, supplement other evidence as to the extent of freezer exclusivity and provided a sample of the views of independent retailers.

9.27 BEW remains in our survey the most widely available brand, being stocked in some 80 per cent of outlets compared with nearly 50 per cent for Mars. These were similar to the figures in the Nestlé survey, and one survey carried out for BEW (although BEW subsequently argued that Mars' availability was understated and could be as much as 73 per cent of outlets, weighted by turnover). All the surveys we saw showed that about one-quarter of outlets sold Nestlé brands.

9.28 About 36 per cent of respondents to our survey had only one front freezer for exclusive use and no other, but a similar proportion of respondents did not have a manufacturer-owned freezer at all. (Much the same picture emerges from the Nestlé survey.) About one-quarter of outlets had more than one freezer: the Nestlé survey gave a somewhat lower figure. The Nestlé survey and our own also showed that at least one-half of outlets sold more than one manufacturer's products.

9.29 On the figures available to us, therefore, freezer exclusivity appears to pose less of a restriction in supply of impulse ice cream than at the time of our previous report. This itself is to a large extent explained by the investment made by Mars in installing second freezers in retail outlets, and the decision of retailers themselves to install a second manufacturer's freezer, or their own.

9.30 A number of parties from whom we heard argued that many retail outlets did not have 'space' for a second freezer. The availability of space cannot be regarded as purely a physical constraint, but as shorthand for the perceived opportunity cost compared to other uses of any sales area. About 34 per cent of respondents to one BEW survey had a single freezer and stated that they would not have space to install a second, or two smaller freezers. On the other hand, BEW estimated that only some 12 per cent of its sales were to outlets with BEW exclusive freezers and unable to install a second freezer. About one-quarter of respondents to our survey had only an exclusive freezer and said that lack of space was the reason for not getting a second freezer; but the figure is reduced to less than one-fifth after allowing for those who said that they would consider installing two smaller freezers instead of the present larger one. The survey results also showed that these are predominantly smaller or medium-sized outlets, accounting for a somewhat lower proportion of sales.

9.31 The variety of information we have seen shows the extent of choice available to retailers as to the products to be stocked, and the means to be used for stocking them. Retail outlets with space for only one freezer and unwilling to substitute two smaller freezers for the existing freezer – no more than one-third of outlets on the information we have seen and possibly a lot fewer – have the option to install one exclusive freezer supplied by a manufacturer, or to install their own freezer free of any restriction: an increasing proportion of outlets do so in order also to stock other frozen products. Even if they should choose a manufacturer's freezer, they are initially obliged to maintain that freezer in place for no more than a year, and subsequently are able to switch at much shorter notice. Other retail outlets – the majority on the figures we have seen – can also consider installing a second manufacturer's freezer, or their own freezer additional to one supplied by a manufacturer. We were told of one market research study indicating that a second freezer would increase sales: some other research showed that a larger 'industry freezer' free of restrictions would produce better sales than two smaller freezers although subsequent experience casts doubt on this. Retailers themselves are clearly in a position to make their own judgment, as some of the multiple CTN chains, experimenting in the use of industry freezers, are attempting to do.

Charges for use of exclusive freezers

9.32 Unlike practice in some other EC countries (the Republic of Ireland, for example) both BEW and Nestlé generally charge, in their standard terms, lower prices for supply of ice cream (by means of a higher retrospective bonus) for retailers without exclusive freezers. As shown in Table 2.7, BEW has no bonuses for outlets with gross sales value (GSV) of purchases from BEW of below £800, above that amount there is a differential bonus of 6 per cent for outlets with gross sales value of between £800 and £1,070, declining to 2 per cent for outlets with GSV above £4,610. (Multiples, large buyers etc will generally negotiate terms; BEW told us that there was no inducement to take BEW rather than industry freezers, as evidenced by the number of such customers that had chosen to buy their own, and we see no reason why multiples or similar buyers should not be able to obtain better terms if they install their own freezer reflecting the cost saving to BEW). Nestlé's bonus system is applied only to retailers with purchases of at least £1,000 in a year: the differential bonus varies between 5 per cent on the first £795 of turnover at trade list price and 2.5 per cent on turnover in excess of £4,916. Mars, on the other hand, does not distinguish in its charges between retailers with and without its cabinets.

9.33 BEW acknowledged that there was no systematic basis to its differential bonuses, but argued that the differential in terms broadly covered the cost to BEW of supplying freezers. On the figures supplied to us by BEW (see Table 2.8), it is clear that the lower bonuses on sales of impulse ice cream (in effect, the higher prices) to retailers with exclusive cabinets in many cases fall short of the cost to BEW of supplying exclusive cabinets, but the shortfall is significant mainly at lower GSVs where no bonus of any kind is paid. The annual cost to BEW of supplying a 1-metre freezer (the most common size), for example, is estimated at about £61. The higher charges (in the form of lower bonus) to retailers with an exclusive 1 metre freezer vary from zero at sales of £750, to £60, broadly equivalent to the cabinet cost, at £1,000 annual sales. For a 1.5 metre cabinet (the second most common size) the annual cost to BEW of about £69 compares with higher charges for use of an exclusive cabinet varying between £43.75 (below cost) on £1,250 sales and £100 (above cost) on £2,500 sales. There is a similar relationship between Nestlé's differential charges and its freezer costs. We have also noted that the amount of BEW's and Nestlé's charges for the use of a freezer can only be estimated at the time the cabinet is installed, since they reflect the difference between the two scales of retrospective bonuses (if any), depending on the level of sales actually achieved which is not known until the end of the year. The charges will therefore be affected both by the sliding scale nature of the bonus system, being based on the percentage of GSV, and by the variation in terms according to the size band in which sales to a retailer fall. We return to these points in paragraph 9.60.

9.34 BEW's calculations also showed a more significant net benefit to a retailer of having an exclusive cabinet rather than purchasing his own (paragraph 2.38), but in our view this comparison is less relevant. It reflects BEW's belief that it can acquire freezers at lower cost than retailers themselves due to its greater bargaining power. We see no reason why the benefits of BEW's bargaining power should not be passed on to its users in this way, although we are doubtful that retailers would necessarily have to acquire freezers on terms as unfavourable as BEW suggests. Retailers already have a wide degree of choice in acquiring freezers: they can, for example, purchase from impulse ice cream suppliers who offer freezers with an equivalent value of 'free product'. We are also not aware of any distortion in the market sufficient to prevent the development of further competition in supply of freezers, on terms as favourable as those available to BEW. Retailers' overall turnover may also benefit if they sell a greater product range, which is not allowed for in BEW's calculations.

The public interest

9.35 Concern about freezer exclusivity relates primarily to its imposition by BEW as the scale monopolist, although we have also considered the imposition of freezer exclusivity by BEW, Nestlé and Mars as members of the complex monopoly group identified in paragraph 9.3. Freezer exclusivity has moreover to be considered as it is at present applied and in the current circumstances of the impulse ice cream market in the UK. We are aware of an appeal by Mars to the Irish Supreme Court against a recent ruling of the Irish High Court upholding exclusivity and of other related proceedings by the European Commission (see Appendix 5.1): while we recognize that the eventual ruling of the European Commission may have implications for member states generally, including the UK, we have to consider the issue of exclusivity on its merits and solely in the circumstances of the UK market and in the context of domestic legislation.

9.36 As is apparent in Chapters 4 to 8, we received a wide range of views on the effects of freezer exclusivity. A majority of suppliers from whom we heard argued that the practice was against the public interest, inhibiting competition and entry, and adversely affecting consumer choice, innovation and price.

9.37 As well as BEW, Nestlé argued strongly in favour of freezer exclusivity, the retention of which it regarded as necessary if Lyons Maid was to recover market share and compete on equal terms with BEW given BEW's other competitive advantages, in particular in distribution. Nestlé further argued that the removal of freezer exclusivity would enhance BEW's market share, a point accepted in part by BEW. Smaller suppliers on balance argued against exclusivity even when they themselves practise it partly in response to BEW, although some were not opposed and one suggested that, following the example of some multiple CTNs, freezer exclusivity might be abandoned over time anyway, as retailers increasingly chose to install their own cabinets.

9.38 There was a range of views from retailers, our own survey showing at the most a very slight balance against the practice, although some individual retailers from whom we heard were clearly irritated with the methods used to enforce exclusivity. Our survey did, however, show widespread satisfaction with BEW's delivery and maintenance arrangements, as with that of other suppliers. Noticeable also, however, from our retailers survey was the limited extent to which retailers told us that they were asked for products they did not stock. We received very little evidence direct from consumers, although the Consumers' Association argued against the practice.

9.39 In our previous report we referred to the argument that freezer exclusivity increased the number of outlets offering ice cream: similar arguments were put forward during the current inquiry. To sell ice cream, a retailer needs a freezer cabinet, and a supplier of ice cream must persuade the retailer both to make space for the cabinet and to find some means of financing its capital and maintenance costs. If the retailer is unable or unwilling to finance the cabinet himself, the supplier may provide the retailer with a cabinet, but if he does so the supplier will expect to achieve a return on his capital investment. Ice cream suppliers have done this by demanding that only their products will be sold from their cabinet, so that they are guaranteed sales from the cabinets they supply: in this way, it was argued, by supplying free-on-loan exclusive freezers, the two main suppliers, BEW and Lyons Maid, have developed the market for impulse ice cream, to the benefit of retailers and consumers.

9.40 It was suggested that without freezer exclusivity suppliers could not be expected to provide freezers on their current terms. Since charges for use of freezer cabinets were based on turnover, loss of sales from a cabinet would lead to an under-recovery of freezer costs, while competitors would have free access to cabinets, and be in a position to secure retail distribution without contributing to freezer costs. The present differential charges, based on sales, would need to increase; or cabinets would have to be rented or sold to retailers at a price more closely related to cost: as shown also in paragraph 9.33, this could result in a significant increase in charges for retailers with a lower volume of sales.

9.41 It was again argued that this would result in a reduction in the number of outlets selling ice cream, but we received conflicting evidence on the point. Only 3 per cent of retailers responding to the MMC survey said that, if current arrangements changed, they would expect to stop selling impulse ice cream, suggesting that the market may now be at the stage where abandonment of freezer exclusivity would have only a limited impact on availability of impulse ice cream. A survey by BEW suggested that between 12 and 20 per cent of retailers would stop stocking impulse ice cream, although the higher figures may reflect a rather high estimate in the question put to retailers of the costs associated with buying or renting a freezer. Even if the results of our survey were correct on this point, BEW's investment in developing the market should not, in our view, be put at risk, nor should any future such investment by BEW or other suppliers be deterred, unless there were clear evidence that freezer exclusivity now operated against the public interest.

9.42 In considering effects adverse to the public interest, we initially identified eight issues which we put to BEW, Mars and Nestlé:

(a) Whether consumers would benefit from:
   (i) greater choice;
   (ii) keener price competition,
   if retailers were free to stock competing products in what would often be the one freezer cabinet for which there was room on their premises.

(b) Whether the present arrangements prevent other manufacturers from entering the impulse ice cream market or raise the cost of entry or adversely affect the profitability of BEW's competitors, thereby further damaging competition.

(c) Whether there has been an adverse effect on competition at the wholesale level.

(d) Whether freezer exclusivity is not in some circumstances tantamount to outlet exclusivity.

(e) Whether freezer exclusivity may diminish incentives to innovation (eg in introduction of new products) and greater efficiency.

(f) Whether the terms on which ice cream is supplied to retailers with/without exclusive cabinets distort retailers' choice between using exclusive freezers or acquiring their own freezers.

(g) Whether aspects of the distribution system may be regarded as reinforcing the effects of freezer exclusivity and are likely to require attention if any remedies are to be effective. These aspects are (i) refusal by BEW to supply, in the case of regional wholesalers, and (ii) exclusive supply – the obligation on retailers with BEW's cabinets to buy only from a concessionaire, and on concessionaires not to handle competitors' products.

(h) Whether freezer exclusivity itself has the adverse effect of allowing the maintenance of exclusive distribution arrangements, which may be both uneconomic, and detrimental to competition.

Effect on competition

9.43 Recent developments in the market, to which we referred in paragraphs 9.12 to 9.14, themselves suggest that competition has been effective, irrespective of freezer exclusivity. Poor performance by Lyons Maid – in particular the failure to develop its brands and difficulties in both production and distribution – resulted in a dramatic reduction in its market share notwithstanding its insistence on freezer exclusivity. BEW, on the other hand, has maintained and increased its market share not only due to any advantages that may arise from its installed base of exclusive freezers, but by developing its brands and competing effectively on price, product range and the efficiency of its delivery arrangements to replace Lyons Maid in a large number of outlets. Conversely, BEW can only retain its existing position if it continues to compete effectively. Hence, the experience respectively of Lyons Maid and BEW demonstrates in our view that, notwithstanding the advantages of freezer exclusivity, market share has to be won or sustained by effective competition in other ways, particularly given recent entry to the market.

9.44 The main new entrant – Mars – has built up a share of the overall market of over 10 per cent, but a significantly higher share – some 20 to 30 per cent – of that sector of the market (chocolate bars) where it has chosen to concentrate, and its products are available in about one-half or more of retail outlets. Lyons Maid itself now offers the prospect of much improved competition under the new ownership of Nestlé, which it believes it can only sustain if freezer exclusivity is maintained. Other entrants to the market have established a significant presence.

9.45 Although some impulse ice cream prices have increased faster than inflation (see Table 3.9), this would appear to reflect, given the wide choice of products available, a consumer preference for high-quality, higher-priced product. The evidence of at most modest profitability, to which we referred in paragraph 9.15, would not suggest that prices are above competitive levels, a point to which we return in paragraph 9.55.

9.46 Given recent market developments, freezer exclusivity can be regarded as adversely affecting competition (the issue in paragraph 9.42(a)(ii)) only in a narrow sense. A retailer with an exclusive cabinet can clearly not stock competing products in that cabinet, hence in one-half or less of outlets there is no competition to supply the consumer at the point of sale. As we have noted, however, there are many options open to the retailer. In the majority of outlets, he can choose to install a second manufacturer's cabinet, or his own freezer. Even in smaller outlets, there is active competition to supply the single freezer, and retailers have the choice of installing their own freezer.

9.47 In this context, we also considered the argument that freezer exclusivity may be regarded as tantamount to outlet exclusivity (the issue in paragraph 9.42(d)). As we indicate above, the proportion of outlets with one exclusive cabinet, and without the space to install a second freezer or the inclination to install two smaller freezers in place of the manufacturer's freezer, appears to be limited to at most a third of all outlets and possibly a lot fewer. Even in these outlets, retailers can choose to install their own cabinets, free of any exclusivity. Any resulting outlet exclusivity is, therefore, a matter of informed choice on the part of the retailer – 'elective' rather than dictated by BEW or any other suppliers.

9.48 We considered, on the other hand, whether recent developments may present too optimistic a view of the market and whether freezer exclusivity could not inhibit competition in the longer term by raising entry costs (the issue in paragraph 9.42(b)). The extent of competition currently owes much to Mars' own efforts to install freezers, at considerable expense, as well as to its marketing and product innovation. Its success in establishing its current market share shows that freezer exclusivity is less a barrier to entry than a cost of entry, no different in its effects to other costs such as advertising. Mars is still incurring [*] losses, but there is no evidence that it is reconsidering its presence in the market, and it is too soon in our view to suggest that its financial position shows any fundamental weakness as a result of freezer exclusivity.

9.49 A number of smaller manufacturers have also, through supplying exclusive freezers, been able to establish strong regional or local positions or concentrated on certain sectors of the market, such as cinemas: the supply of exclusive freezers – although in part a defensive move – is one means of competing against heavily advertised national brands. Other manufacturers have been able to establish a limited presence in the market without supplying exclusive freezers. It is indeed unclear to us whether the wider use by retailers of non-exclusive freezers would necessarily benefit the smaller, regional manufacturers. Fewer than 10 per cent of retailers responding to our survey said that they would increase the range of products stocked were freezer exclusivity to be ended. A number of multiple CTNs to whom we spoke who have installed their own freezers stock products of only the three main suppliers. Smaller manufacturers could still be disadvantaged, therefore, by the brand strength and distribution arrangements of the major suppliers.

9.50 We considered the further argument that freezer exclusivity required a supplier to provide a full range of products, the more so if he was to replace an existing supplier's sole cabinet in any retail outlet. Mars' success partly results from its current agreement for Nestlé to distribute certain of its products, and for these products to be stocked in Nestlé's cabinets. Given the strength of the Mars brands, such an arrangement, either with Nestlé or with an alternative supplier, would seem in both parties' interests. We would be surprised if competitors to BEW proved unable to put together combinations of product ranges and freezer offers that would compete effectively with BEW.

9.51 We also noted Nestlé's argument that, without exclusive cabinets, it could not achieve the drop sizes necessary for efficient delivery of its

---

* Detail omitted. See note on page iv.

products: hence, it may not be economic in terms of frequency and drop size to supply retailers' own freezers, unless all distributors were free to supply a wider product range. We acknowledge that, with current arrangements, freezer exclusivity may enable some of the main suppliers to maintain the drop sizes necessary to secure economies in distribution of impulse ice cream (to which we referred in paragraph 9.17) and that, in the short term, any weakening of freezer exclusivity could increase distribution costs. We would not, however, be surprised if, as some parties suggested to us, the industry continued to evolve in response to the initiatives of suppliers, and the demands of retailers and their customers to stock wider ranges of products, so reducing the extent both of freezer exclusivity and of exclusivity in distribution arrangements, and improving distribution economies; freezer exclusivity would not, in our view, prevent this happening.

Effect on consumer choice

9.52 We considered the argument, of some suppliers and the Consumers' Association, that consumer choice requires the stocking of different manufacturers' products in the same freezer, or at least the same retail outlet: and that freezer exclusivity inhibits such choice (the issue in paragraph 9.42(*a*)(i)). Despite freezer exclusivity, there is, as mentioned in paragraph 9.27, wide availability of the main brands, particularly BEW brands and to a somewhat lesser extent those of Mars. Of the main brands, availability of Nestlé brands is the most limited, but Nestlé appears determined to improve this, as long as freezer exclusivity is maintained. Other suppliers have established their products in a more limited range of outlets – specializing, for example, in health food, or video rental shops. There is therefore a wide choice of different suppliers' products available in different outlets.

9.53 Mars quoted evidence to us that, if a customer's preferred product is not stocked in a shop, most consumers will choose from the products that are available: very few will go to another shop. On the figures we have seen there is a choice of more than one manufacturer's product in at least one-half of outlets. Customers of shops with only one exclusive cabinet clearly have only the one manufacturer's products from which to select: but in our view this represents a restriction of choice also only in a very limited sense. Consumers normally still have the option of using other retail outlets, of which there will often be several nearby (generally with the main brand stocked clearly advertised in the street): that consumers may well not do so suggests that they themselves may not perceive any significant limitation on choice.

9.54 In addition, as paragraph 9.31 has explained, there are a number of alternatives open to the retailer; in reaching his decision, the retailer will himself take customer preferences into account. We are, moreover, not convinced that the uniform adoption of retailers' own cabinets would itself significantly improve choice for consumers: the range of products stocked is likely to be limited by space constraints, and retailers may still prefer mainly to stock one manufacturer's products given, for example, ease of supply and invoicing arrangements. We noted in paragraph 9.49 the limited proportion of retailers who said that they would increase the range of products stocked were freezer exclusivity to be ended.

Assessment

9.55 In our view, therefore, there is insufficient evidence to demonstrate that the imposition by BEW, Nestlé or Mars of freezer exclusivity as applied in the UK market as it is currently developing inhibits competition or consumer choice. Moreover, there is no evidence that it is adversely affecting the level of prices paid by retailers or consumers, as is also indicated by the limited profitability in the UK market. Similarly, given recent market developments, we find it difficult to argue that freezer exclusivity diminishes incentives to innovation or efficiency (the issue in paragraph 9.42(e)), or otherwise adversely affects consumers or the public interest. We received no evidence that BEW was in any sense inefficient: its distribution arrangements in particular, indeed, were regarded as highly efficient, hence the desire of some of its competitors that BEW concessionaires should be allowed to distribute their products. In our view, therefore, the imposition of freezer exclusivity in the UK market as it is currently developing does not operate against the public interest. This conclusion applies equally to freezer exclusivity considered as a practice of BEW as the scale monopolist, and more widely to freezer exclusivity considered as a practice of BEW, Nestlé and Mars as members of a complex monopoly group.

Effects on wholesaling and distribution

9.56 As we mentioned in paragraph 9.20, it is clear that a number of BEW's competitors were concerned about BEW's exclusive concessionaire system and its restrictions on supply to certain wholesalers. Similar concerns were expressed by the wholesalers themselves. It is not open to us to consider whether BEW's current distribution arrangements may have anti-competitive effects, other than in the context of freezer exclusivity (the issues identified in paragraph 9.42(c), (g) and (h)). There is no doubt, however, that the concessionaire system is a highly efficient method of distribution for BEW, and has contributed to BEW's strong competitive position. It is a development of BEW's own previous in-house distribution system, to which BEW would be free to revert although at some cost, and against which some of BEW's competitors acknowledged they would have fewer grounds to object.

9.57 Some suppliers argued that without freezer exclusivity, guaranteeing sales in outlets with exclusive freezers, the exclusive concessionaire system could not be maintained. We are not convinced by this, particularly given the concern expressed to us that, even if freezer exclusivity were abandoned, the strength of BEW's exclusive concessionaire arrangements was such that BEW's predominant market share would not be put at risk.

9.58 Many in the industry said that retailers with BEW exclusive cabinets were required to obtain supplies solely from its concessionaires. BEW firmly denied this and told us that it had taken steps to ensure that no pressure was being brought to bear on retailers not to purchase products other than from concessionaires, although its system for paying retrospective bonuses on purchases invoiced through concessionaires does understandably provide an incentive to use the concessionaire system. Given that denial, BEW's distribution arrangements must, in our view, be regarded as an issue separate from that of freezer exclusivity and on which we cannot in this inquiry comment further: we are similarly inhibited from commenting on the restrictions imposed by BEW on the products that can be stocked by its franchisees. Given also our overall finding on freezer exclusivity, the recommendations put to us by other suppliers – notably Mars (see paragraph 5.38) – relating both to exclusive cabinets and exclusive distribution arrangements do not therefore arise.

9.59 We did, however, suggest to BEW that its standard conditions of trade (as shown in Appendix 2.4) for use of its cabinets misled retailers, and could be regarded as contributing to a widespread misapprehension, in requiring that 'the customer will use the refrigeration only for the purpose of storing products supplied by the company or its distributors', unless the company or its distributors are unable to deliver. BEW told us that the term 'distributors' was not intended to be confined only to concessionaires, but included other wholesalers it supplied: although concessionaires could offer better service and better terms, it accepted that it should not block other legitimate channels of trade. It, therefore, agreed to remove the above reference to distributors from its conditions (see paragraph 4.54). In the circumstances, therefore, we have not concluded that BEW's standard conditions for use of exclusive freezers operate against the public interest.

BEW's terms

9.60 In examining the effects of freezer exclusivity, we put considerable emphasis on the options available to retailers. We considered whether the terms on which exclusive freezers are supplied, particularly by BEW given its large market share as the scale monopolist, could distort retailers' choice between using exclusive freezers, and acquiring their own (the issue in paragraph 9.42(*f*)).

9.61 One concern was that these terms are insufficiently transparent. BEW told us that, not only are its terms clearly stated in its retail price list, but they have also received prominent publicity in the trade press. We would be surprised, therefore, if retailers were unaware of the higher prices they pay for impulse ice cream if the manufacturer supplies the freezer.

9.62 In reaching our conclusion that freezer exclusivity does not operate against the public interest, we were significantly influenced by the current terms on which freezers are supplied, including the limitation of the duration of contracts to no more than one year, and the differential charges particularly of BEW for supply of impulse ice cream to retailers with and without exclusive freezers. We are satisfied that these charges cover the bulk of the costs associated with supplying freezers but we considered nevertheless whether the failure particularly of BEW to reflect freezer costs fully in the prices charged for each freezer could adversely affect competition.

9.63 The shortfall between BEW's costs and charges can, however, only be regarded as significant at relatively low levels of GSV – particularly purchases by the retailer of £800 a year and below: above that amount, the shortfall rarely amounts to more than 1 or 2 per cent of GSV. On BEW's figures, sales to retail outlets with BEW cabinets and a level of turnover below £800 amount to less than 5 per cent of the total value of BEW sales of impulse ice cream – hence BEW's failure to cover freezer costs affects only a relatively small proportion of its sales.

9.64 It follows that to reflect costs in charges would imply a significant increase in charges for retailers with relatively limited sales: it would require either an annual charge (of about £61 to reflect the cost of a 1 metre freezer, for example), irrespective of the volume of turnover, or – perhaps more difficult to implement – a downward extension of the differential in the current turnover-related charge between users with and without exclusive freezers. The increase in charges for a small retailer with an exclusive freezer could be as much as some 7.5 per cent or more of GSVs, a significant element of the retailer's margin. The sector of the market that would be affected is that which is most likely to reconsider stocking ice cream. The effect of BEW's current policy may, therefore, be to promote overall sales of ice cream rather than to increase its market share at its competitors' expense. This is a strategy BEW should be free to pursue should it so choose: it may indeed be profitable for it to do so, as well as beneficial to consumers, on the basis of BEW's incremental costs.

9.65 There is insufficient evidence in our view, therefore, that BEW's charging policy operates against the public interest. We have no concern about the differential charges made by Nestlé for use of cabinets or Mars' charges for supply of ice cream which do not distinguish between retailers with and without exclusive freezers, given the more limited market share of both companies and their need to compete effectively with BEW and other suppliers.

Conclusions

9.66 We have found insufficient evidence to demonstrate that freezer exclusivity as applied in the UK market as it is currently developing inhibits competition or choice, or adversely affects prices, innovation or efficiency or other aspects of the public interest; nor have we found any aspect of the conditions on which exclusive freezers are supplied or the charges for the use of exclusive freezers to have any effects adverse to the public interest. We have therefore concluded first that the following actions on the part of BEW as a scale monopolist do not operate and may not be expected to operate against the public interest:

(a) the imposition of terms for supply of refrigerated cabinets which prevent the retailer from using the cabinet to stock for sale ice cream supplied by other suppliers (paragraph 9.55);
(b) the conditions imposed by BEW for use of exclusive cabinets (paragraph 9.59); and
(c) BEW's charges for use of exclusive cabinets (paragraph 9.65).

We have concluded secondly that the following actions of BEW, Nestlé and Mars as members of a complex monopoly group do not operate and may not be expected to operate against the public interest:

(a) the imposition of terms for supply of refrigerated cabinets which prevent the retailer from using the cabinet to stock for sale ice cream supplied by other suppliers (paragraph 9.55); and
(b) the charges made for use of exclusive cabinets (paragraph 9.65).

H H LIESNER (*Chairman*)
A FORSTER
A P L MINFORD
L PRIESTLEY
  A J NIEDUSZYNSKI (*Secretary*)
14 January 1994

(MMC, 1994b)

PRESENTATION CASE 2: RECKITT & COLMAN/SARA LEE PROPOSED MERGER

Method

Extract from the case material information presented under these headings:

1 *Key definitions of terms*
2 Information concerning the *structure* of the industry
3 Information concerning the *conduct* of firms in the shoe care industry
4 Information concerning the *performance* of firms in the industry
5 Key *conclusions* arrived at by the MMC.

Questions

1 How might we define *public interest* in this case?
2 What is meant by the *market share test*?
3 What were the key features of the *structure* of this market which were the driving force behind this proposed merger?
4 Why does the MMC refer to it as *complex market*?
5 If no formal *barriers to entry* exist, why did the MMC see the merger as being likely to affect *competition* in the *self selection* sector of the market?
6 Can the *theory of the market* explain why *demand is largely insensitive to price* and the proposed merger likely to cause a *substantial increase in price* before Sara Lee's high market share is put at risk?
7 On what basis did the MMC decide that the proposed merger was likely to be against the *public interest*?
8 Why did one member dissent from this conclusion?
9 On what grounds do *you* agree/disagree with the MMC conclusions and recommendations?
10 How have changes in the retail sector affected the *structure*, *conduct* and *performance* of the shoe care industry?

1 SUMMARY

1.1 On 4 October 1991 a subsidiary of the Sara Lee Corporation (Sara Lee) acquired part of the shoe care business of Reckitt & Colman plc (Reckitt & Colman), including the Cherry Blossom and Meltonian brands. Sara Lee already possessed the Kiwi brand, among others. On 13 March 1992 we were asked to investigate the completed merger (see Appendix 1.1).

1.2 Shoe polish products are a small but complex market, worth about £13.5 million a year at manufacturers' prices or double that figure at retail prices. Demand is static or declining. As a result of the merger Sara Lee's market share increased from 24 to 53 per cent. The next largest supplier, Punch Sales Ltd (Punch), a subsidiary of an Irish company, has 26 per cent; and there are a few other suppliers, each with a share of under 6 per cent. The market comprises a number of different products: pastes, liquids, creams, sponges and others; and is divided into two sectors: the *special trades*, comprising shoe retailers, shoe repairers and the wholesalers who serve them, and *self-selection*, in which the well-known supermarket chains are prominent. About 57 per cent of sales are through the special trades and about 43 per cent through the self-selection sector.

1.3 In the special trades, where retail prices are higher, Sara Lee was relatively weak before the merger and competition was chiefly between Reckitt & Colman and Punch. Following the merger, Sara Lee's share of this sector is 37 per cent. Punch has 38 per cent, another supplier 10 per cent and each of five others 5 per cent or less. In this sector of the market there is effective competition among the existing suppliers, and entry is relatively easy.

1.4 In the self-selection sector, Sara Lee's share has risen as a result of the merger from 44 to 74 per cent. The only other suppliers are Punch, Carr & Day & Martin Ltd (CDM) and S C Johnson & Co Ltd (S C Johnson), each with under 10 per cent.

1.5 The main issue in the inquiry is the effect of the merger on competition in the self-selection sector of the market. There are no formal barriers to entry, but an important practical barrier is the strength of the long-established and widely familiar brand names, especially Kiwi and Cherry Blossom. Having considered the prospects of expansion by the existing suppliers, and of entry to the United Kingdom market by continental European producers, we conclude that the only realistic possibility of competition is from own-label sales, at present confined (among the leading grocery supermarkets) to J Sainsbury plc (Sainsbury). Shoe polish products are low-value items, infrequently purchased, and demand is largely insensitive to price. Sales volumes are low. In these circumstances, and given the strength of the Kiwi and Cherry Blossom brands, there is limited countervailing power on the part of the supermarkets, nor do they have much incentive to constrain price increases by introducing own-label products or otherwise. On the evidence which we have received there is scope, following the merger and the loss of competition between the two dominant brands in this sector, for a substantial increase in prices before Sara Lee's high market share is put at risk.

1.6 We do not believe that the benefits of the merger, including the benefit to employment at Honley, outweigh the expected adverse effects of loss of competition and higher prices. We conclude, therefore, that the merger may be expected to operate against the public interest. We recommend by way of remedy that Sara Lee should be required to divest itself of the Cherry Blossom brand.

1.7 One member of the group, Professor A P L Minford, dissents from our conclusions. While accepting that Sara Lee's share in the self-selection sector of the market is high, he sees no detriment to competition because there are many alternative suppliers and the supermarket buyers have strong bargaining power. Moreover the remedy proposed might, he believes, disrupt operations and threaten the future of the Honley plant. Professor Minford has set out his views in a note of dissent following Chapter 6.

6 CONCLUSIONS

The merger situation

6.1 Under the reference (Appendix 1.1) dated 13 March 1992 (made under sections 64, 68 and 69(2) of the Fair Trading Act 1973 – the Act), we are required to investigate and report whether a merger situation qualifying for investigation has been created in that enterprises carried on by or under the control of Reckitt & Colman plc (Reckitt & Colman), incorporated in the United Kingdom, have within the six months preceding the date of the reference ceased to be distinct from enterprises carried on by or under the control of Sara Lee Corporation (Sara Lee). For this purpose, the terms of reference refer to the test specified in paragraph (a) of section 64(1) of the Act, the market share test, in respect of the supply in the United Kingdom of applied shoe care products. If the market share test is satisfied, the reference requires us to exclude the alternative assets test prescribed by section 64(1)(b) of the Act.

6.2 As stated in paragraph 2.36, Sara Lee Household & Personal Care UK Ltd (SL/HPC UK), a subsidiary of Sara Lee, acquired the United Kingdom shoe care business of Reckitt & Colman on 4 October 1991. Enterprises carried on by or under the control of Reckitt & Colman have therefore ceased to be distinct from enterprises carried on by or under the control of Sara Lee within the six months preceding the date of the reference to us.

6.3 As regard the market share test, we are required by section 64(1)(a) and (2) of the Act to be satisfied that, as a result of the enterprises having ceased to be distinct, at least one-quarter of the supply of applied shoe care products in the United Kingdom is by the same person (or persons by whom the enterprises are carried on) – or, if this was already the case, that the supply of these products by that person (or those persons) is enhanced. Applied shoe care products are defined in the terms of reference as 'polishes intended for use on any type of footwear in such form as paste, wax, cream, liquid, gel, or impregnated sponge or cloth'. As shown in paragraph 3.49 and Table 3.12, prior to the acquisition of the shoe care business of Reckitt & Colman, Sara Lee, through its subsidiary SL/HPC UK, accounted for 31 per cent of supply of applied shoe care products as defined in the terms of the reference. The Reckitt & Colman share was 28 per cent, and so as a result of the acquisition Sara Lee's share has increased to some 59 per cent.

6.4 We conclude that the market share test has been satisfied in respect of applied shoe care products in the United Kingdom, and that a merger situation qualifying for investigation has been created. We have therefore to consider whether the creation of that merger situation operates or may be expected to operate against the public interest. The merger having only recently been completed, its effects are not yet fully apparent, and we have concentrated on whether it 'may be expected' to operate against the public interest.

The companies

Sara Lee

6.5 Sara Lee is a multinational United States corporation with headquarters in Chicago, and operations in over 30 countries around the world. It employs more than 110,000 staff, and has a world-wide turnover (see Table 2.1) of some $12.4 billion. Its businesses comprise the manufacturing, marketing and distribution of high-quality branded consumer products; its stated aim is 'to enjoy leading positions in each of the product and geographical markets in which it operates'.

6.6 Prior to the merger Sara Lee's main brands in the United Kingdom shoe care market were Kiwi and Tuxan. Its shoe care interests in the United Kingdom began in 1984 when it acquired Nicholas Kiwi, an Australian public company. Nicholas Kiwi was itself formed out of a merger in 1981 of two long-established Australian companies, namely Nicholas International Ltd and the Kiwi Polish Company Pty Ltd. Sara Lee's United Kingdom shoe care businesses, in which we are most interested, form part of the activities of SL/HPC UK. (Prior to a corporate reorganisation which took place in 1991 in connection with the group's sale of its pharmaceutical interests to the Hoffman-La Roche group, the relevant business in the United Kingdom was carried on by a different subsidiary, Nicholas Laboratories Ltd.) For management purposes, SL/HPC UK reports to Sara

Lee/DE NV (SL/DE) in Utrecht, the management company for most of Sara Lee's European operations including its shoe care business based in France; SL/DE is wholly owned by Sara Lee. Sales of shoe care products in the United Kingdom were some £3.4 million in the year to June 1991.

Reckitt & Colman

6.7 Reckitt & Colman is a United Kingdom-based international group also engaged in the manufacture and marketing of consumer goods. Its products are sold in over 120 countries: total sales in 1991 were some £2 billion. Reckitt & Colman Products Ltd and Reckitt & Colman (Overseas) Ltd were the companies in the Reckitt & Colman group which dealt in shoe care products in the United Kingdom; gross sales of the United Kingdom shoe care operation were some £6.6 million in 1990.

The merger

6.8 On 4 October 1991, SL/HPC UK acquired the Reckitt & Colman United Kingdom shoe care business, including its export business from the United Kingdom (the relevant Australian and New Zealand trade marks being assigned to Sara Lee's Australian subsidiary, Kiwi Brands Pty Ltd). Reckitt & Colman's USA shoe care businesses were at the same time acquired by Kiwi Brands Inc, another Sara Lee subsidiary. The brands acquired by SL/HPC UK were Cherry Blossom, Meltonian, Properts, Wrens and Magix; Reckitt & Colman retained, however, the Nugget brand (not recently sold in the United Kingdom), and its shoe care businesses in many countries of Asia, Africa and Latin America and some European countries, notably Spain. The sale contract includes a non-competition clause, lasting for three years, after which Reckitt & Colman would be free to re-enter the United Kingdom market. The total consideration for the United Kingdom and the USA transactions was some £[*] million. [*] of this amount was apportioned in the United Kingdom transaction, representing almost entirely trade marks and goodwill.

6.9 Certain stock was acquired, and a limited range of manufacturing equipment, in particular a liquid (angle neck) filling line, a jar line for creams, a dye line, and mixing tanks and other processing equipment for liquid and cream polishes. This equipment was transferred to Sara Lee's plant at Honley in Yorkshire, but one of the main products sold under the Cherry Blossom brand – paste polish – is now manufactured on Sara Lee's existing equipment together with the Kiwi paste polish. Reckitt & Colman continued to manufacture polishes under contract to Sara Lee for six

---

* Details omitted.

months following the merger at its unit in Hull; this unit has subsequently been closed, and the remaining equipment sold or disposed of throughout the Reckitt & Colman group.

Reasons for the merger

6.10 As is apparent in Table 2.17, the Reckitt & Colman shoe care operations made a loss both in 1990, and in 1991 up to the time of its acquisition by Sara Lee. Reckitt & Colman told us that it had established its Shoe Care Division as recently as 1990, as a means of improving the profitability of its Household Division, in which shoe care was formerly included. Part of the purpose of this move was to simplify the Household Division, by removing the more complicated shoe care business, but the aim was also to improve the performance of the shoe care business, particularly in the special trades (discussed in paragraph 6.17). The reorganisation had helped Reckitt & Colman to halt a decline in its market share of shoe care products in the United Kingdom over the previous five years; however, the contribution from shoe care proved to be substantially lower than anticipated, and the cost of operating a separate division, developing the Meltonian brand range and expanding market share turned out to be significantly higher than expected.

6.11 Reckitt & Colman accordingly considered a number of options to improve the profitability of the Shoe Care Division, one being the use of contract packers, which would have entailed a restructuring cost of £1.5 million. At around this time, Sara Lee approached Reckitt & Colman, initially to acquire only the Meltonian brand. Without this brand, however, the remaining Reckitt & Colman shoe care business would not have been viable. Reckitt & Colman therefore offered to sell all its United Kingdom and United States shoe care business and its brands, not only because of the poor performance of the business, but also because of its expectation of the lack of growth potential in the shoe care market, the complexity of the business (with some 600 product lines, resulting in lower sales per line than in any other of its businesses), and its substantial dependence on specialist distribution channels, ie shoe shops and shoe repair shops. Reckitt & Colman said that it preferred to focus its selling resources on those outlets through which virtually all its other products were sold, namely grocery outlets and chemists.

6.12 Sara Lee told us that it regarded shoe care as a core activity for the group world-wide, but before the acquisition it had lacked penetration through the specialist distribution channels in a number of important markets, notably the United Kingdom. For this reason, it had initially expressed an interest in acquiring the Meltonian brand, in response to which Reckitt & Colman had offered the whole of the United States and United

Kingdom operations. The acquisition enabled Sara Lee to acquire a complete shoe care product range by adding a full complement of specialist applied shoe care products; Reckitt & Colman's know-how in supplying the special trades (see paragraph 6.17); and established distribution channels into the special trades sector. It would, Sara Lee told us, have been possible to have established a stronger presence in the special trades without an acquisition, but this could have taken up to three years to do. At the same time, the acquisition enabled Sara Lee to achieve the volumes necessary to justify continuing commitment to a declining market, and to increase production capacity at its Honley plant, which before the merger it had intended to close.

6.13 Sara Lee told us that, following the merger, it intended to maintain its Kiwi brands, as well as the brands acquired from Reckitt & Colman. There would, however, be some product rationalisation with the use of the same formulation for Cherry Blossom and Kiwi products where produced on the same filling line at Honley. Kiwi and Cherry Blossom paste polishes, for example, would be made to the Kiwi formulation; and the two liquid wax polishes – Kiwi Elite and Cherry Blossom Readywax – to the Readywax formulation.

The market for shoe polish products

6.14 Our terms of reference define applied shoe care products with particular reference to polishes. Polish is used by consumers to enhance or otherwise restore the appearance of shoes, to provide a degree of waterproofing, and hence to extend the life of shoes. Various other chemical products also serve this purpose – in particular whiteners for white shoes, and aerosols for cleaning suede shoes and waterproofing – and we have included these products when considering the relevant market. The product definition we have adopted is also that used by Nielsen Market Research in its analysis of polish sales in the grocery sector, and comprises pastes, liquids, creams, whiteners, sponges and aerosols. Some 26 per cent of these sales are accounted for by pastes, 24 per cent by creams, 23 per cent by aerosols, and 13 per cent by liquids (although we note Sara Lee's comment that the allocation between these categories may be arbitrary for some products).

6.15 The total value of shoe polish products on this definition in the United Kingdom in 1991 was about £13 to £13.5 million at manufacturers' prices, and about £26 million to £27 million at retail prices. It is a small but complex market. As well as consisting of a number of different products, as already discussed, there is also a wide range of colours, as well as different types and sizes of container.

6.16 Demand for shoe polish products has been static or declining, one reason being a switch from formal shoes to trainers, another being reduced interest on the part of consumers in the appearance of their shoes. Overall demand is relatively insensitive to price, and because the products are an infrequent purchase, and the items are comparatively low-priced, consumers tend not to shop around or be sensitive to differences in price between retail outlets. These are considerable: we have noted within two small areas of London variations in retail prices of a standard tin of black polish from 40p (an own-label polish) to 99p (a branded polish), depending on the brand and type of outlet. Retail margins are also high – about 50 to 60 per cent of the selling price, reflecting in part the low turnover of the product: suggested retail prices are extensively followed or exceeded, other than by multiple grocers.

The supply of shoe polish products

6.17 All parties to whom we spoke agreed that it was useful to distinguish market sectors by means of distribution (see paragraph 3.22). Some 43 per cent of sales by value (a higher share by volume) are through the 'self-selection' outlets, the majority of these being the multiple grocery retailers, the main supermarket chains such as Sainsbury, Tesco and Safeway. Distribution through these channels is often by the retailer's own distribution system, and the range of products stocked is relatively limited. The remaining 57 per cent of sales by value are through the 'special trades', namely shoe shops and shoe repair shops. They stock a far wider range not only of shoe polish products, but also other shoe care products such as insoles, laces, and shoe horns. In the case of shoe shops, shoe polish products are often not displayed, but sold on the recommendation of the sales assistant, at the time shoes are purchased: the range of colours sold will therefore match the current colours of shoes sold. We were told that shoe repair shops were also seeking more actively to encourage their customers to buy shoe polish and other shoe care products. Consumers are, of course, free to purchase from either sector – self-selection or special trades – but as mentioned in paragraph 6.16 they are largely insensitive to the differences in prices between retail outlets: prices tend to be substantially higher in shoe retail and shoe repair shops compared with the self-selection sector, reflecting, we were told, the greater element of customer service and wider range of products provided.

6.18 Because the market is small, individual retail outlets tend to stock only one or two brands (rarely more) of any particular product. Competition between suppliers, therefore, tends to take the form of competition to secure retail shelf space by offering favourable terms, including selective discounts, and efficient distribution, rather than competition for the consumer at the point of sale between a range of brands on the basis of retail price, quality or brand name.

The suppliers

6.19 We are aware of ten suppliers of shoe polish products in the United Kingdom; their estimated share of self-selection outlets, the special trades sector, and the market as a whole are as follows [see Table 6.1].

6.20 Before the merger some 45 per cent of Reckitt & Colman sales were to the self-selection outlets and 55 per cent to the special trades, sales to the special trades being mainly of the Meltonian brand, and sales to self-selection outlets being mainly Cherry Blossom. Sara Lee sales, on the other hand, were concentrated mainly on the self-selection sector. Following the merger Sara Lee supplies about 74 per cent of sales of shoe polish products to self-selection outlets, 37 per cent of sales to the special trades and 53 per cent of total sales.

6.21 We are aware of only three other firms supplying self-selection outlets: Punch Sales Ltd (Punch), S C Johnson & Co Ltd (S C Johnson) (which sells only one product, a sponge applicator), and Carr & Day &

Table 6.1 Share of sales of shoe polish products in the United Kingdom in 1991

	Self-selection outlets	Special trades	per cent Total
Reckitt & Colman	30	27	29
of which Meltonian brand	7	20	14
of which Cherry Blossom brand	22	2	10
Sara Lee	44	9	24
Sara Lee total following merger	74	37	53
Punch	9	38	26
Dunkelman	—	10	6
S C Johnson	7	—	3
Carr & Day & Martin	9	1	4
Dougmar	—	5	3
Salamander (Woly)	—	4	2
Salzenbrodt (Collonil)	—	5	3
Mars Oil	—	1	1
Total	100	100	100
Value of sales (£m at producer prices)	5.7	7.5	13.2

Source: MMC study.
Note: Figures may not sum due to rounding.

Martin Ltd (CDM). Before the merger, Punch was the largest supplier to the special trades, with some 38 per cent of sales; and it accounts for about one-quarter of the market as a whole. The remaining five firms of which we are aware – Dougmar Ltd, Dunkelman & Son Ltd, Salamander AG (a German company, which supplies the Woly brand), Salzenbrodt GmbH & Co KG (also German, which supplies the Collonil brand) and The Mars Oil Company Ltd (which has a very small share of the market) – supply only the special trades.

6.22 Market shares also vary by product. As shown in Table 3.12, Sara Lee is estimated after the merger to account for about 80 per cent of the supply of pastes (the largest product category), between 60 and 70 per cent of liquids and whiteners, and about 50 per cent of sponges.

Prospects for entry into the market

6.23 Market share has to be considered in the context of the prospects for new entry into the market or expansion by existing competitors. We have found no evidence of 'formal' or regulatory barriers to entry – for example trade barriers, product standards, or patents.

6.24 As regards manufacturing costs, the process is straightforward and equipment easy to acquire, although new entrants could be at some disadvantage in competing with Sara Lee, a relatively high proportion of Sara Lee's capital costs being 'sunk costs'. The minimum cost of establishing facilities has been variously estimated at £150,000 to £200,000 (Punch), £350,000 to £380,000 (Sara Lee), £350,000 (CDM). These are not particularly high figures, even for such a limited market, and it was suggested to us that the cost would be lower still if second-hand equipment was to be used. Higher figures of up to £3 million capital investment have, however, been quoted for a new supplier of a full range of shoe polish products.

6.25 Various possible economies of scale have been mentioned to us. Reckitt & Colman doubted whether there was much scope for these in production terms but thought (as did Punch and others), that they might apply to the purchase of metal tins and particularly printed metal lids. A new entrant could, however, overcome some of the diseconomies of low production by use of contract packers.

6.26 Some companies referred to economies of scale in distribution. Punch, for example, said that a turnover of £3 million per year was necessary to cover costs of selling, warehousing and dispatch, although this in part reflects the emphasis it has put on providing national distribution and a particularly high standard of service. An alternative is to use wholesalers. A further possible economy of scope arose from the requirement of some retailers in the special trades for a full range of applied and other shoe care products, although others preferred to select individual products from different suppliers.

6.27 These factors do not appear to us individually or cumulatively to be major barriers to new entry, or to expansion by existing smaller competitors. Potential entrants might, however, regard as intrinsically unattractive a small, stable or declining market, with long-established, financially strong suppliers, particularly as these are in a position to offer selective discounts against competitors which are not transparent in the market.

Sources of entry

6.28 Among the potential entrants mentioned to us by Sara Lee were existing European suppliers of shoe polish products, and suppliers of similar household or cleaning products. We saw no evidence of any potential interest by producers of other household goods in supplying shoe polish products. One adhesives firm in the United Kingdom told us that the merger could itself deter it from trying to enter the shoe polish market.

6.29 We have discussed the European market for shoe polish in paragraphs 3.51 to 3.54. Sara Lee is itself believed to be the leading supplier of shoe care products in Europe as a whole with about 22 per cent of the European market. We are, however, aware of other European suppliers which may be in a position to supply the United Kingdom.

6.30 Transport costs appear modest. These were, for example, estimated as 5 per cent of producer sales value for products manufactured in the United Kingdom, 7 to 8 per cent for products from elsewhere in Europe, and 12.5 per cent for products from outside Europe.

6.31 Punch, whose products are manufactured in Ireland, has achieved a substantial share of the United Kingdom market and has competed successfully with domestic manufacturers, in part by developing a particularly effective distribution system. Continental European suppliers, however, have not to date been successful in the United Kingdom. Werner & Mertz (one of the largest suppliers in Germany and Austria, with a significant market share in France and Netherlands) attempted to break into the market in the 1980s but subsequently withdrew. Similarly Henkel KGAA had limited success in the United Kingdom with the Pilofix brand. The Woly and Collonil brands are supplied to the United Kingdom market, but only in the more expensive shoe shops; they have minimal market shares and their presence in the market does not exert any downward pressure on the general level of prices.

6.32 The limited market share currently accounted for by the continental European suppliers may reflect the effectiveness of competition between the United Kingdom producers (and also Punch), and the resulting level of prices in the United Kingdom. We therefore asked a number of companies about the scope for competition from continental European manufacturers should prices increase. A large wholesaler told us of a recent increase in interest from European suppliers, one of which had previously quoted prices some 5 per cent above the United Kingdom level, which could therefore be competitive were United Kingdom prices to rise. On the other hand, the largest shoe retailer (British Shoe Corporation) and a major shoe repairer (Timpson Shoe Repairs Ltd) told us that they would be reluctant to source outside the United Kingdom, since service could be subject to greater uncertainty. One European company, indeed, currently supplying the United Kingdom on a small scale, itself expressed concern about the merger and about Sara Lee's market power elsewhere in Europe.

6.33 As mentioned in paragraph 6.23, there are no formal barriers to trade within Europe. Manufacturing costs (notably labour costs) may be slightly higher on the Continent, and there would be some additional transport costs, but these are not a major impediment to trade. There might, on the other hand, be some difficulty in meeting the service requirements of some of the larger customers, and a need to establish warehousing and distribution facilities in the United Kingdom, particularly if the suppliers were attempting to service the supermarkets and shoe repair outlets which require and demand rapid service delivery in order to minimise their own product stockholding. The success of Punch, however, has shown that such problems can be overcome by a determined new entrant, at least in the special trades sector.

Brands

6.34 The barrier to new entry into the market, or to expansion by existing suppliers which was most frequently mentioned to us by the parties from whom we heard, is the strength of the long-established brands – in particular Kiwi and Cherry Blossom in the self-selection sector, and Meltonian in the special trades sector. The importance of brands varies by sector.

6.35 Kiwi and Cherry Blossom seem not to be of great significance among shoe retailers, where own-label products or other brands, in particular Punch, are successfully sold on the recommendation of sales assistants. Among shoe repairers, on the other hand, one company believed that some sales – but not very many – would be lost if established brand names were not available; it was reluctant to pit an unknown brand against the established brand names. A major wholesaler to the shoe repair business (although not against the merger) also suggested that repairers could not do without established brands, the most successful of which he regarded as Punch, Meltonian and Dasco.

6.36 In our view, the strength of the established brands is not a major barrier to entry to the special trades, particularly in the case of shoe shops. New products need to be promoted mainly to the buyers or owners of these outlets, with competition on the basis of price and service: products can be promoted to the consumer by the sales assistant. Sara Lee estimated a cost of £20,000 to £30,000 to promote trade awareness in this sector.

6.37 The importance of the Kiwi and Cherry Blossom brands lies mainly in the self-selection sector. Some of the evidence we received referred to 'considerable brand recognition, but little brand loyalty' (a phrase used by both Sara Lee and Punch). On the other hand Punch, now the main competitor to Sara Lee, said that it was very difficult to attack the established brands particularly for paste (the largest single product category in which it still has a very limited market share of less than 2 per cent); hence it had developed alternatives to pastes. Similarly CDM said that brand names were the most significant factor in maintaining customers. One of the supermarket groups also referred to what is in effect a dual brand loyalty: consumers would buy whichever of Kiwi or Cherry Blossom was available. In view of the extensive testimony as to the strength of brand loyalty in the self-selection sector, we are unconvinced by Sara Lee's evidence (including the market research study referred to us by Sara Lee purporting to show that customers are relatively indifferent to brands.

6.38 In a small market, the cost of consumer advertising to promote a new brand would be prohibitive. In our view, the only realistic entry on any scale in the self-selection sector of the market would be through sale of own-label products, to which we now turn.

Own-label

6.39 Own-label represents a potential means of entry for a manufacturer wishing to avoid the cost of promoting awareness of a new brand, and for a retailer to provide a means of competition to a well-established brand. Own-label is well developed, at a price premium, in shoe shops, where consumers appear willing to give weight to the recommendation of sales assistants, but not in shoe repair shops; and it is also relatively limited compared with other grocery items in multiple grocery retailers.

6.40 Multiple retailers' own-label polishes are currently confined to Sainsbury, Superdrug, and one other soon to be discontinued. Sainsbury's own label accounts for over 50 per cent of its polish sales and is sold at a retail price some 15 to 20 per cent less than the branded polishes, with a lower price to the manufacturer than on branded products. The retailer mentioned in paragraph 5.89, however, told us that own-label did not successfully compete against branded products, despite a 20 per cent lower retail price – hence its decision to discontinue them. We cannot infer from the limited development of multiple retailers' own-label to date how great a price differential would be necessary were own-label to be promoted more widely. The price differential required to promote an unknown brand in the self-selection sector would be likely to be greater than that required to promote own-label.

6.41 Other multiple retailers told us that they did not stock own-label polishes, because of the small level of turnover of these products. Among the other specific factors mentioned to us were the number of separate products involved; the cost of establishing own-label (because, for example, of the need to specify and monitor the product), for a limited benefit; the minimum production runs; and the need for large stockholdings.

6.42 We considered the argument that the limited development of own-label to date may in part reflect effective competition between brands, but that it could nonetheless represent a source of potential competition were prices to rise. We asked all the multiple retailers whether an increase in price to them would cause them to introduce own-label shoe polish products: their replies are included in Chapter 5. Several told us that the low level of turnover in these products would still probably preclude them from introducing own-label. Others said that they could consider introducing own-label if prices increased: in one instance, a 12 per cent increase in prices would be necessary before this would happen. Some suggested that they could attempt to introduce other branded products if prices increased by 6 to 10 per cent. Several, however, indicated that they would have to pass on any increase in prices. One multiple retailer currently stocking own-label products suggested that its prices would follow any increases in prices of branded shoe polish products, with little risk to its levels of sales.

6.43 On the evidence we have seen, we believe that there could be a substantial increase in price to the multiple retailers, possibly of 10 per cent or more, before they sought to introduce own label products, or other alternative suppliers. Shoe polish products are low-value items, infrequently purchased, and demand is largely insensitive to price. The products are unlikely to figure in retailers' promotional campaigns. In this context, there is relatively little incentive for supermarkets to resist price increases, nor is it easy for them to do so given the strength of the Sara Lee brands.

6.44 For manufacturers, therefore, while entry into multiple retailers' own-label may be one means of overcoming the brand loyalty barrier, it also has disadvantages. Supermarkets would be reluctant to take these products, unless offered at significantly lower prices, which would limit the profitability of such new entry. Punch told us that it preferred to sell its own branded products, and did not have a policy of deliberately seeking to supply own-label in grocery outlets. On the other hand has been particularly successful in own-label sales.

The effects of the merger

6.45 Sara Lee argued that the merger would not have any adverse effects, on the grounds, *inter alia*, that:

(a) there was little overlap in the special trades sector before the merger; and
(b) the supermarkets, on the other hand, had countervailing power as they were able to develop own-label products or buy branded products from other companies including overseas sources.

6.46 It was generally agreed among the parties from whom we heard that there had been strong competition in the market between Sara Lee and Reckitt & Colman before the merger, particularly over the past two years, with retailers able to seek competing bids from the two suppliers. The financial performance of Reckitt & Colman's Shoe Care Division had clearly been unsatisfactory, but it had been considering alternative means of staying in the business, possibly by using contract packers, which would have entailed a restructuring cost of some £1.5 million. Another option it was considering was to dispose of some only of its brands. In our view, therefore, there is insufficient evidence to suggest that the level of competition prevailing before the merger could not have been sustained.

The effect on competition in the special trades sector

6.47 As is shown in Table 6.1, the effect of the merger is to increase Sara Lee's direct share of the market in the special trades from some 9 to 37 per cent mainly from the acquisition of the Meltonian brands. A French subsidiary of Sara Less also supplies polish to one of the other suppliers in this sector of the market, but that firm expressed no concerns about the merger, and would be free to source elsewhere.

6.48 Punch is an established competitor in the special trades sector, with a market share similar to that of Sara Lee following the merger. It offers effective competition, particularly in sales to shoe retail shops, and there are six other companies with a more limited presence in the market. Furthermore, entry into this sector is relatively easy; the strength of the established brands is a less important barrier: other products, including own-label, can be successfully promoted by sales assistants at higher prices than in the self-selection sector of the market. Shoe retailers and shoe repairers (and wholesalers supplying these outlets) were fairly evenly divided between those who felt the merger had reduced competition and those unconcerned about its effects. We conclude that there is little cause for concern about the effect of the merger on competition in the special trades sector.

The effect on competition in the self-selection sector

6.49 The self-selection sector of the market accounts for 43 per cent of sales by value, and is the sector where retail prices are lowest. Table 6.1 shows that the effect of the merger is much more pronounced in this sector, where Sara Lee's market share is now some 74 per cent. Table 6.2 demonstrates that the impact is greatest in pastes, liquids, whiteners and aerosols. Generally, the increase in Sara Lee's market share arises from the acquisition of the Cherry Blossom brand, but in the more limited product area of whiteners it reflects the sales of Meltonian products (see also paragraph 3.37).

6.50 As mentioned in paragraph 6.45, Sara Lee argued that the supermarkets in particular had countervailing power, and could sell other branded polishes supplied from other United Kingdom or overseas sources,

Table 6.2 Market shares of self-selection sector in 1991

	Pastes	Liquids	Creams	Whiteners	Sponges	Aerosols	Per cent Total
Reckitt & Colman	29	17	23	58	38	30	30
Sara Lee	55	59	44	27	14	53	44
Total following merger	84	76	67	85	52	84	74
Other	16	24	33	15	48	16	26
− of which Punch	−	15	28	10	12	16	9
− of which S C Johnson	−	−	−	−	36	−	7
− of which CDM	16	9	5	5	−	−	9
Value of sales (manufacturers' prices, £m)	2.5	0.7	0.8	0.3	1.2	0.3	5.7

Source: MMC study.
Note: Figures may not sum due to rounding.

or sell own-label products acquired from such suppliers. Most of the retailers in the self-selection sector from whom we heard, however, suggested that the merger would have adverse effects on competition, referring to their strong negotiating position prior to the merger and their previous ability to play Reckitt & Colman off against Sara Lee, a negotiating position now much reduced.

6.51   The effect of the merger on competition in the self-selection sector of the market is the main issue in our inquiry. In evaluating this effect, it is necessary to weigh the loss of competition between the two most successful brands, Kiwi and Cherry Blossom, against the prospect of effective competition developing from companies that have not effectively competed to date in the sector.

6.52   As discussed in paragraphs 6.23 to 6.27, there are no formal barriers to trade, or to entry to the market; we also feel that economies of scale are unlikely to be sufficient to deter new entry, or expansion by existing smaller competitors. We believe, however, that the strength of the long-established brands in the market is an important practical barrier, reducing the prospect of entry of new branded goods into the self-selection sector from other United Kingdom suppliers, or from overseas: the cost of promoting a new brand is likely to prove prohibitive in such a small market and one which is static or declining. We do not therefore accept the argument that entry into this sector of the market is so easy that prices can be regarded as determined primarily by potential domestic or international competition, and that we should be unconcerned about the loss of actual competition between the two most successful brands.

6.53   In our view, the only realistic possibility of competition in the self-selection sector is from own-label sales, currently confined to only three of the multiple retailers, one of which is to discontinue such sales, and one other of which is currently supplied by Sara Lee. However, as we discussed in paragraphs 6.41 to 6.43, shoe polish products are an unattractive area for the development of supermarket own-label sales, mainly because of the low volume of sales. They are low-value items, the demand for which is largely insensitive to price, and in our view there is little incentive for the supermarkets to resist price increases, nor would it be easy to do so given the strength of the Sara Lee brands.

6.54   It follows therefore that we do not believe that the supermarkets have effective countervailing power; nor do we believe that reliance can be placed on the emergence or potential emergence of new brands or new own-label products to maintain competition in this sector of the market.

6.55 Before the merger, strong competition between the Sara Lee and Reckitt & Colman brands served to constrain the level of prices in the self-selection sector of the market. Following the merger, and the loss of competition between the two dominant brands in this sector, we believe there is scope for a substantial price increase, possibly of 10 per cent or more (see also paragraph 6.43), without putting at risk Sara Lee's market share.

6.56 We believe therefore that the merger may be expected to have effects adverse to the public interest. These are that there is a significant reduction in competition in the supply of shoe polish products to the self-selection sector of the market; Sara Lee has the opportunity, of which it may be expected to take advantage, to introduce substantial increases in prices to retailers without constraining forces being brought into play; and such increases are likely to be passed on to consumers.

Other issues

6.57 A number of other concerns were raised with us. First, it was suggested that the merger would result in a loss of choice from rationalisation of products, some Kiwi and Cherry Blossom products now being identical. We do not regard this suggested detriment as significant, it being generally agreed that there was little quality difference between the products before the merger.

6.58 Secondly, there was concern that Sara Lee would be in a position, by temporary reductions in price, to cause smaller competitors to withdraw from the market, whereupon it would raise prices again; a similar concern was that Sara Lee would reduce prices in retaliation against new entrants to the market. There is no evidence that Sara Lee has initiated such practices to date. There may be an opportunity to engage in selective price reductions against competitors, by use of discounts and retrospective overriders. Most suppliers, however, were confident that they could stay in the market; and retailers themselves may not wish to lose their alternative sources of supply. We have insufficient grounds for supposing that Sara Lee would engage in any such anti-competitive practices, although it is possible that the fear of retaliation by Sara Lee could itself deter new entry to the market.

6.59 Thirdly, concern was expressed that Sara Lee might seek to extend its range of other shoe care products sold to specialist outlets by 'full-line forcing' of such products or use of solus agreements or retrospective discounts to the same effect, with adverse effects on other suppliers. Some shoe retailers and repairers have themselves seen advantage in acquiring a full range of shoe care products from one supplier, and Sara Lee's general policy of widening its product range is not unreasonable. Punch and some of the smaller suppliers appear to do the same. Sara Lee had inherited various 'solus' agreements from Reckitt & Colman, but denied that it had a policy of entering into such agreements, although one supplier of accessories complained that this was happening already. We have insufficient reason, however, to conclude that the merger has placed Sara Lee in such a dominant position in the supply of shoe care products to specialist outlets that it could act in this way.

Benefits of the merger

6.60 We considered whether there were any benefits from the merger that could offset the adverse effects identified in paragraph 6.56. The main benefit brought to our attention was related to the future of Sara Lee's plant at Honley (although the merger also had the immediate effect of a reduction in employment at Reckitt & Colman's plant in Hull). Sara Lee's Board minutes and other internal papers show that a decision in principle was taken by the company in October 1989 to consolidate all its shoe care manufacturing in Europe on one site in Rouen. Any move with respect to Honley was, however, delayed for two or three years, following which production costs and other matters were to be again reviewed. After the merger the decision in principle taken earlier was shelved. We recognise that the merger has undoubtedly removed the uncertainty as to the Honley plant for the immediate future. Sara Lee told us that the decision to maintain production at Honley would be reviewed should it be required to divest any of the brands or assets acquired, and the greater the extent of any divestment the higher the probability that production would be moved to Rouen. There is, however, no certainty that Sara Lee would not in any event reconsider at some future time its decision concerning the maintenance of production at Honley.

6.61 We believe that the benefits described in paragraph 6.60 are insufficient to outweigh the adverse effects of the merger described in paragraph 6.56.

Conclusion

6.62 We have therefore concluded that the merger situation we identified in paragraph 6.4 may be expected to operate against the public interest by reason of the particular effects adverse to the public interest identified in paragraph 6.56.

Recommendation

6.63 We are therefore required to consider what action, if any, should be taken for the purpose of remedying or preventing these adverse effects.

These arise only in the self-selection sector of the market. They result mainly from the acquisition by Sara Lee of the Cherry Blossom brand which is sold principally to the self-selection sector (see paragraphs 6.20 and 6.49), and an appropriate remedy is therefore divestment of that brand.

6.64 This remedy will not directly address the reduction in competition in respect of whiteners, which results from the acquisition by Sara Lee of the Meltonian brand (see paragraph 6.49). Whiteners, however, make up such a small part of the market (about 5 per cent) that it would in our view be disproportionate to recommend divestment of the Meltonian brand by way of remedy. We have in mind, too, that sale of the Cherry Blossom brand would incidentally enable the purchaser to offer competition for Sara Lee in whiteners under a well-established brand name. In these circumstances we make no separate recommendation with regard to whiteners.

6.65 We have considered whether divestment of the Cherry Blossom brand would be a disproportionate remedy, in the light of Sara Lee's submission to us that it would give rise to another review of the future of the Honley plant. The Honley plant would still benefit from the production of the other brands acquired: on the other hand, Sara Lee argued that its profitability would be worse than before the merger, since production of other products had been transferred out of Honley, to make room for the additional shoe polish products acquired, and it would not be worthwhile to relocate them back to Honley. The outcome of any review of the future of the plant must be speculative and, to judge from the papers we have seen relating to the earlier review (in 1989), may depend on the balance of a wide range of factors, many of which are unrelated to the direct or indirect consequences of the merger. In all the circumstances we do not regard the remedy as disproportionate.

6.66 Among other possible remedies which we have considered is price control, which Sara Lee told us it would be prepared to accept. Such a remedy, however, would not directly address the loss of competition resulting from the merger and is in our view a poor second best.

6.67 We therefore recommend that Sara Lee should be required to divest itself of the Cherry Blossom brand and associated trade marks and, pending divestment, to keep the brand and trade marks in good standing by, for example, maintaining production of the branded products, their quality and their prices at present levels. Prior to reaching our conclusions and making this recommendation, we have given full consideration to the arguments put forward in the note of dissent which follows.

P H DEAN (*Chairman*)
R O DAVIES
J EVANS
R YOUNG
APL MINFORD, being a member of the Group, dissents from the conclusions for the reasons set out in the note of dissent included in this report.
S N BURBRIDGE (*Secretary*)
17 June 1992

Note of dissent by Professor A P L Minford

1. While I accept that Sara Lee's share of the 'self-selection' (ie mainly supermarket) trade is high, at around 70 per cent, after the merger, I can see no competitive detriment from this situation. First, there are many alternative suppliers, both domestically and on the European continent. Secondly, the supermarket buyers have strong bargaining power, and are fully capable of searching out these alternatives and presenting them to the consumer as thoroughly competitive products.

2. I can also see two sources of potential damage to the public interest from the remedy proposed in the majority report (divestment of the Cherry Blossom brand by Sara Lee). First, there is the possibility that Sara Lee's operations will be disrupted in the short term by the upheaval of divesting these fully-integrated products. This disruption could be prejudicial to the quality of service the consumer receives.

3. Secondly, the future of the Honley plant, never perhaps fully assured, may well be brought into active question by the loss of nearly half its throughput on the paste polish line currently producing both Kiwi and Cherry Blossom. The loss of output and employment in Yorkshire, an area of high unemployment, would clearly be a serious damage to the public interest; while small in absolute terms, it is large relative to any (claimed) competition gains in this small market.

4. In the rest of this short note I develop these arguments in more detail.

5. This market is a normal traded good one, in which there is competition, actual and potential, between domestic and imported brands. Apart from Cherry Blossom and Kiwi, the actual brands are own-label, notably Sainsbury's, and less well-known ones such as Punch, CDM and Dasco, while potential entrants are new own-label, Nugget (after the three years' prohibition on Reckitt & Colman), and a fair number of continental brands (notably those of Salamander, Werner & Mertz, and Salzenbrodt). One must also not forget the large potential capacity from chemical producers and

'contract packers' (see paragraphs 3.66 and 3.67). There are no import barriers apart from transport costs which are agreed to be very low: importing as such is clearly not a problem since one of the major suppliers in the wider market is Punch, an Irish firm. Sara Lee itself is a major European producer, but does not have undue market power, with around 22 per cent of the total EC market for shoe care products (Werner & Mertz has about 20 per cent – see Table 3.15). Within the United Kingdom Sara Lee has only 30 per cent of the shoe care market (see Table 3.14). Its 70 per cent share in the narrow category of self-selection shoe polish is in a sector where there is considerable countervailing power from supermarket chains, with choice from a large array of alternative suppliers at home and abroad.

6. There is a standard model in international trade theory for a market like this. The diagram overleaf illustrates [see Figure 14.1]. Prices are set over the medium term by the going international rate. This price level gives an efficient EC producer a reasonable return on capital. The size of the domestic industry is set by the efficiency of local producers. If they can compete with the best in Europe then they may drive imports out altogether and the United Kingdom will become an exporter. If not they will contract until the available capacity is competitive at the going price.

7. The existence of brands introduces a short-run ability by producers to set price because most consumers will stay loyal to the brand – 'imperfect competition'. However, freedom of entry will drive the brand price to the competitive level in the longer run; and in the short run too the knowledge of this will restrain brand price-setting in order to deter entry by new brands. This must be distinguished from 'predation' or extreme cuts (actual

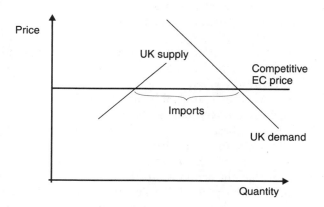

Figure 14.1 Typical traded goods market within Europe

or threatened) in price aimed to deter entry. In a traded good market such as this one such strategies would be a foolish waste of money: the equilibrium will be immune to it, as there are too many potential entrants.

8. It is argued in the majority report that the two big United Kingdom paste brands, Kiwi and Cherry Blossom, are so strong in the self-selection sector of the United Kingdom market that imports in particular would be effectively deterred from entering. The evidence for such extreme brand strength is weak. There merely appears to be a fairly standard price premium (of 15 to 20 per cent) for these brands over weak or 'own' brands. An entrant with a weak brand has not invested as heavily as the brand leader and so carries less financing cost (than, for example, Sara Lee which has paid heavily for its leading brands). There is of course nothing in brands *per se* that confers illegitimate market power; the question is whether there are actual and potential alternatives.

9. The report also argues that the low price elasticity of this product and the small size of its market confer market power on the brand leader. However, the same low price elasticity and small market size applies to many grocery products which are 'necessities'. That has not prevented effective competition, since free entry ensures that competing brands of the same product set a competitive price.

10. In this particular market we have limited information about the likely competitive price level. From the facts we have seen, a reasonable interpretation is that prices in the United Kingdom have been lower than this (and specifically lower than actual continental prices) for the recent past, partly perhaps because of the severe United Kingdom recession, partly because of long-term overcapacity (both Honley and Hull factories were operating their paste lines at low utilisation). With or without the merger therefore prices would probably have to rise.

11. As for United Kingdom production at the competitive price this will depend on how much efficient capacity we have in the United Kingdom. The Honley operation is in Sara Lee's words 'an efficient little operation': with the merger, it is even conceivable that it could expand production and export to contiguous markets such as Ireland and Scandinavia. Without the merger of Kiwi and Cherry Blossom it is clear that the Honley factory's paste line will be substantially underutilised – there are modest but definite economies of scale in paste manufacture. (Table 3.16 and paragraphs 2.42 and 2.43 indicate that the withdrawal of the Cherry Blossom lines could reduce the operating surplus of Honley by some £0.25 million to £0.5 million, as against Honley's total operating profits which according to my estimates are in the range of £1 million to £1.5 million.) The rationale for the

whole factory, which appears to be critically balanced on the margin of viability, will then quite probably disappear; though distribution (which takes place at Lutterworth) will need to remain in the United Kingdom, manufacturing may be relocated and Honley therefore closed.

A P L MINFORD
17 June 1992

(MMC, 1992)

Glossary

allocative efficiency efficiency in consumption

bounded rationality limited liability to obtain and assess all relevant information

cartel a formal agreement to collude on price

competition the attempt to win and retain buyer demand

competitive strategy the formulation of strategic plans to meet/beat competitors in supplying a particular product market within its business portfolio

complex monopolies oligopolies such as the ice cream industry

contestable market where it is possible for a new entrant to compete on the same cost basis as established firms or if any firm in the market can exit without loss

control loss costs of co-ordination exceed the costs of market transactions

costs expenses incurred in producing and distributing the outputs for sale

costs of waste, scrap and rework 'hidden' costs resulting from inspecting quality into a product at the end of the production process

diseconomies of scale increasing unit costs as output rises resulting from increased efficiency and savings in production, purchasing, marketing and financial processes

earnings residual profits less tax

economies of scale falling unit costs as output rises resulting from increased inefficiency in management and control of production and distribution

efficiency when output is on the product possibility frontier and when no individual can become better off without making someone else worse off

external benefits benefits of consumption or production are experienced by persons other than the consumer or producer

external costs cost is borne by persons other than the consumer or producer

fixed costs costs attributable to plant and key workers, which in the short term cannot be adjusted to changes in output

index number a number which expresses data relative to a given base value

law of demand the quantity of a good demanded (per period of time) will rise as price falls (other things being equal)

law of supply producers of goods will increase quantity of a good supplied at a high price and produce less at a low price (other things being equal)

law of diminishing returns where some factors of production are fixed, beyond some level of input of variable factors, further increases in inputs of variable factors lead to diminishing additions to output

long-run average cost curve describes the change in average cost per unit of output as output increases, assuming that all factors of production are variable

macroeconomics deals with the behaviour of whole economic systems

marginal cost the extra cost of producing one additional unit

marginal revenue the extra income from selling one additional unit

marginal unit the last unit to be consumed or produced

market an exchange mechanism that brings together buyers and sellers of a product, factor of production (land, labour or capital) or financial security

microeconomics deals with the behaviour of individuals, households and firms within a market-place

minimum efficient scale that output at which the long-run average cost curve becomes horizontal, there being no further economies of scale to be obtained

net customer value total value realized by the customer from the purchase and use of the good or service less that which must be sacrificed to obtain it

nominal costs costs measured in current prices, no adjustment being made for changes in the value of money due to inflation

normal profits the earnings which are just sufficient to make it possible to retain in the business the original capital invested, and the proprietor's input of time

opportunity cost the value of the rejected opportunity

parallel pricing where prices increase/decrease simultaneously

Pareto optimal welfare condition a position whereby no individual can become better off without making someone else worse off

price acts as the signal which can contain the information required for the consumer to make the comparisons needed to measure opportunity cost and make rational decisions

production possibility frontier describes in graphical terms the outputs of good A which may be produced given outputs of good B, defining the combinations of A and B which may be produced where resources are fully utilized

profit provides the motive and the signal for owners of factors of production in deciding to what use those factors might be put

real costs costs after allowance is made for changing value of money due to inflation, allowing comparisons over time

revenue amount earned by selling products over a given period

short-run average cost curve describe the change in average cost per unit of output as output increases, where some factors of production are fixed, and some variable with output

supernormal profits residual earnings of the firm after all other costs have been met, including normal profit

technical efficiency efficiency in production

time series graph a graph which shows time periods on the horizontal axis and numbers describing the entity of interest on the vertical axis

transaction costs costs that arise from the need to collect and use information in decision-making

variable costs costs attributed to factors of production (usually materials, power and some labour) which may be applied in variable quantities to a given quantity of unchanging fixed factors (usually plants and key workers), over the immediate future

x inefficiency all the possibilities for inefficient use of resources within a firm, stemming from management failure

Bibliography

Bannock, G. and Daly, H. (1980) *The Promotion of Small Firms: A Seven Country Study*, vols 1 and 2, prepared by Economists Advisory Group for Skill (UK).

Baumol, W. J. (1967) *Business Behavior, Value and Growth*, New York: Harcourt Brace and World.

Begg, D., Fischer, S. and Dornbusch, R. (1991) *Economics*, Maidenhead: McGraw-Hill.

Best, M. (1990) *The New Competition: Institutions of Industrial Restructuring?* Cambridge, MA: Harvard University Press.

Buckley, P. J. and Carter, M. J. (1996) The economics of business process design: motivation, information and coordination within the firm, *International Journal of the Economics of Business* 3(1): 5–24.

Coase, R. (1937) The nature of the firm, *Economica*, 4: 386–405.

Cole, W. E. and Mogab, J. W. (1995) *The Economics of Total Quality Management*, Oxford: Blackwell.

Daly, H. and McCann, A. (1992) How many small firms? *Employment Gazette*, 100/2.

De Jonquieres, G. and M. M. Davos (1995) Murdoch may put up newspaper prices as raw material costs rise, *Financial Times*, 1 February.

Deutsch, M. (1960) The effect of motivational orientation upon trust and suspicion, *Human Relations*, 13.

Drucker, P.F. (1988) The coming of the new organization, *Harvard Business Review*, January–February: 45–53.

Economist (1995) National newspapers: paper thin, *The Economist*, 4 February.

Elliott, H. (1996) Travel firms insist big is better for the customer, *The Times*, 8 November.

Farrell, S., Bale, J. and Durman, P. (1996) Tour firms face monopoly inquiry, *The Times*, 8 November.

Ferguson, P. R., Ferguson, G. J. and Rothschild, R. (1993) *Business Economics*, Basingstoke: Macmillan.

Griffiths, A. and Wall, S. (1997) *Applied Economics*, 7th edn, London: Longman.

Hay, D. A. and Morris, D. J. (1991) *Industrial Economics and Organisation*, 2nd edn, Oxford: Oxford University Press.

Hennart, J. F. (1986) What is internationalisation, Weltwirtschaftliches Archive.

Hirschey, M., Pappas, J. L. and Whigham, D. (1993) *Managerial Economics*, London: Dryden Press.

Keynes, J. M. (1973) *The General Theory of Employment, Interest and Money*, London: Macmillan.

Lex Column (1995) *Financial Times*, 1 February.

MacArthur, B. (1995) Readers the price war, *The Times*, 14 June.

Mackintosh, M., Brown, V., Costello, N., Dawson, S. and Trigg, N. (1996) *Economics and Changing Economies*, London: International Thomson.

Marris, R. (1964) *The Economic Theory of Managerial Capitalism*, London: Macmillan.

Mishan, E. J. (1969) Rent controls, in *21 Popular Economic Fallacies*, London: Penguin.

Monopolies and Mergers Commission (MMC) (1992) *Sara Lee Corporation and Reckitt & Colman plc: A Report on the Acquisition by Sara Lee Corporation of Part of the Shoe Care Business of Reckitt & Colman plc*, Cm 2040, London: HMSO.

Monopolies and Mergers Commission (MMC) (1994a) *The Supply of Recorded Music: A Report on the Supply in the UK of Pre-recorded Compact Discs, Vinyl Discs and Tapes Containing Music*, Cm 2599, London: HMSO.

Monopolies and Mergers Commission (MMC) (1994b) *Ice Cream: A Report on the Supply in the UK of Ice Cream for Immediate Consumption*, Cm 2524, London: HMSO.

Nellis, J. G. and Parker, D. (1992) *Essence of Business Economics*, Englewood Cliffs, NJ: Prentice Hall.

Oakland, J. S. (1993) *Total Quality Management*, Oxford: Butterworth Heinemann.

Parkin, M. (1990) *Economics*, Harlow: Addison Wesley.

Parkin, M. and King, D. (1992) *Economics*, Wokingham: Addison Wesley.

Pass, C. and Lowes, B. (1994) *Business and Macroeconomics*, London: International Thomson Business Press.

Pass, C., Lowes, B. and Davies, L. (1988) *Dictionary of Economics*, London: Collins.

Pass, C., Lowes, B. and Robinson, A. (1995) *Business and Macrioeconomics*, London: International Thomson Business Press.

Peters, T. (1992) *Liberation Management*, London: Macmillan.

Porter, M. E. (1980) *Competitive Strategy: Techniques for Analyzing Industries and Competitors*, New York: Free Press.

Porter, M. E. (1985) *Competitive Advantage: Creating and Sustaining Superior Performance*, New York: Free Press.

Prescott, E. C. and Visscher, M. (1980) Organisational capital, *Journal of Political Economy*, **88**: 446–61.

Skipworth, M. and Victor, P. (1993) Supermarkets and suppliers accused of food price fixing, *Sunday Times*, August.

Sloman, J. (1991) *Economics*, Hemel Hempstead: Harvester Wheatsheaf.

Snoddy, R. (1995) Murdoch adds 5p to price of Times, *Financial Times*, 26 June.

Trybus, M. (1992) paper given at the Forum of the British Deming Association.

Index